ROUTLEDGE LIBRARY EDITIONS:
THE GERMAN ECONOMY

Volume 13

JOINT STOCK BANKING IN GERMANY

JOINT STOCK BANKING IN GERMANY

A Study of the German Creditbanks Before and After the War

P. BARRETT WHALE

Routledge
Taylor & Francis Group

LONDON AND NEW YORK

First published in 1930 by Frank Cass and Company Limited

This edition first published in 2018
by Routledge
2 Park Square, Milton Park, Abingdon, Oxon OX14 4RN

and by Routledge
711 Third Avenue, New York, NY 10017

Routledge is an imprint of the Taylor & Francis Group, an informa business

British Library Cataloguing in Publication Data
A catalogue record for this book is available from the British Library

ISBN: 978-1-138-29360-1 (Set)
ISBN: 978-1-315-18656-6 (Set) (ebk)
ISBN: 978-0-415-78900-4 (Volume 13) (hbk)
ISBN: 978-0-415-78904-2 (Volume 13) (pbk)
ISBN: 978-1-315-22301-8 (Volume 13) (ebk)

Publisher's Note
The publisher has gone to great lengths to ensure the quality of this reprint but points out that some imperfections in the original copies may be apparent.

Disclaimer
The publisher has made every effort to trace copyright holders and would welcome correspondence from those they have been unable to trace.

JOINT STOCK BANKING IN GERMANY

A STUDY OF THE GERMAN CREDITBANKS
BEFORE AND AFTER THE WAR

P. BARRETT WHALE

Published by

FRANK CASS AND COMPANY LIMITED

67 Great Russell Street, London WC1

by arrangement with Macmillan & Co. Ltd.

Published in the U.S.A. by A. M. Kelley,

24 East 22nd Street, New York, U.S.A.

First edition   1930
New impression   1968

Library of Congress Catalog Card No. 67—24753

Printed in Great Britain

ACKNOWLEDGEMENTS

It is a pleasure to acknowledge the cordial assistance which I have received from German economists and bankers during my visits of investigation. My debt is perhaps greatest to Dr. Otto Jeidels, Managing Partner in the Berliner Handelsgesellschaft, to Dr. Melchior Palyi, Economic Adviser to the Deutsche Bank, to Dr. Darmstädter-Helvessen of the Comerz-u. Privatbank, and to Prof. Kurt Singer, Joint Editor of the *Hamburger Wirtschaftsdienst*. But amongst others whose help I gratefully recognise, mention should be made of : Dr. Schacht, until recently President of the Reichsbank; Herr Jakob Gold-schmidt, Managing Partner in the Darmstädter und Nationalbank; Herr Urbig, Managing Partner in the Discontogesellschaft; Regierungsrat Dr. Kleiner, President of the Deutsche Girozentrale; Dr. Landauer, Director of the Reichskreditgesellschaft; Dr. Mohrus of the Dresdner Bank; Dr. Erich Welter, Financial Editor of the *Frankfürter Zeitung*; Herr Bernfeld, Editor of the *Magazin der Wirtschaft*; Dr. Stolper, Editor of the *Deutsche Volkswirt*; Prof. Kalveram, Frankfurt a.M.; Prof. Julius Hirsch, Berlin; Prof. Bonn, Berlin; Dr. Rudolf Dalberg, Berlin; and Dr. Schweer, Prof. Waltz and Dr. Mezger, of the Hamburg Welt-Wirtschafts Archiv. (The records of the latter institution were of the greatest use to me, and should be better known to foreign students.) In Berlin I have also received much valuable help from Mr. H. C. F. Finlayson, formerly Financial Secretary to the British Embassy; from Mr. Shepherd Morgan, of the Office of the Agent General for Reparation Payments; and from Mr. Powys Greenwood, of the Darmstädter und Nationalbank. This help has saved me from many mistakes. I owe it, however, to those of the above who are actively engaged in banking, to say that the information they have given me is mostly general in character, and that they are not responsible for any remarks I may make about the institutions with which they are connected.

I am also glad to take this opportunity of thanking Mr. Dudley Ward, of the British Overseas Bank, for helping me with introductions, and the University of Birmingham for contributing towards the expenses of one of my visits to Germany.

P. B. W.

CONTENTS

APPENDICES

INTRODUCTION

COMMERCIAL banking on the Continent presents certain important differences from the practice of this country. In the main these differences may be defined by saying that the Continental banks are less specialized, and combine with short loan banking other functions, particularly the equipment of undertakings with permanent capital.

The earliest examples of the Continental type of bank may perhaps be found in the Belgian *Société Générale*, established in 1822, and the more famous *Crédit Mobilier* of France, established in 1852; and the latter at any rate served as a model for banks promoted in several other countries in the years immediately following—the *Bank für Handel und Industrie* (Darmstädter Bank) in Germany (1853), the *Oesterreichische Kreditanstalt*, Vienna (1855), and the *Schweizerische Kreditanstalt*, Zurich (1856). But the subsequent course of banking development has been exceptional and uncertain in France, whilst elsewhere it has diverged in significant respects from the programme of the Crédit Mobilier. In the present century the continental type of general credit institution is best represented by the German *Kreditbanken*.

An account of these banks should, therefore, be of interest as a contribution to a chapter in the comparative study of financial institutions: a chapter which has been somewhat neglected owing to the preoccupation of economists with the problems of central banks. From a more definitely practical point of view, it may be hoped that it will be of value to those who are seeking to discover the most efficient methods of financing industry.

The name ' creditbank ' is a label which is applied to the banks with which we shall be concerned, but which might, for all its natural meaning, be applied to any kind of bank.   It has come to be used in preference to the more descriptive titles *Anlagebank* (investment bank) and *Effektenbank* (stock-and-share bank) once employed, because these were recognized to be misleading, and no more appropriate one could be found.   The circumstances which account for the difficulty of finding a suitable name also make it difficult to define the institutions in question.   All that can be done is to say that the creditbanks are joint stock banks carrying on general banking and acquiring their constitution under the general law relating to companies.   (*Aktiengesellschaften* or *Kommanditgesellschaften auf Aktien*.   See Appendix I.)

It is the purpose of the following chapters to expand this definition.   Here some idea may be given of the place of the creditbanks in the German credit system as a whole by a brief reference to the other elements of which the latter was composed before the War.

In addition, then, to the creditbanks there were:

(1) *Note-issuing banks (Notenbanken).*
The right to issue notes was confined to banks recognized by the Bank Act of 1875; and this Act also regulated their business.   After 1905 there were, apart from the central bank, the *Reichsbank*, only four note-issuing banks—the *Bayerische Notenbank*, the *Sächsische Bank*, the *Württembergische Notenbank*, and the *Badische Bank* (the so-called *Privat-Notenbanken*).

(2) *Joint-stock mortgage banks (Hypothekenbanken).*
These are institutions which, on the one hand, lend money on mortgages on real property (chiefly urban land and buildings) and, on the other, raise money by

issuing a special class of obligations or debentures (called *Pfandbriefe*) covered by these mortgages. These banks are registered under, and regulated by, the *Hypothekenbankgesetz* of 1899, which defines the limited scope of their business. Out of respect for vested interests, creditbanks at that time engaged in this branch of business were allowed to continue to combine it with their wider functions, but the number of such 'mixed' institutions was never more than eleven and has steadily diminished. The most important of them before the War were: the *Bayerische Hypotheken- u. Wechselbank*, the *Bayerische Vereinsbank*, and the *Allgemeine Deutsche Creditanstalt*.

(3) *Landschaften*, or associations of landowners, under special law, with the purpose of raising mortgages on their lands, secured by their collective credit. The *Landschaft* holds the mortgage and gives the owner, not money, but *Pfandbriefe* in its own name. The landowner then obtains the money which he requires by selling these *Pfandbriefe*. The payment of interest upon these obligations, and their redemption as prescribed, are guaranteed by the entire resources of all the members.

(4) *Landesbanken, Provinzial-Hilfskassen.*
These are institutions maintained by provincial governments. Their functions are partly to give agricultural mortgage credit, partly to give financial assistance to subordinate local authorities, and partly to act as regional central banks to the savings banks (see below). Because of the similarity of their functions, one may conveniently place in this class certain banks maintained by minor states (e.g. *Braunschweigische Staatsbank, Staatliche Kreditanstalt Oldenburg*).

(5) *Sparkassen or Savings banks.*
As the name implies, these were established with the purpose of promoting saving, particularly amongst

the less well-to-do sections of society. Already before the War there was a tendency for their clientèle to become more middle-class, less working-class, but they retained their original character to the extent that their concern with the investment of money was secondary and derived from the necessity of earning interest upon their deposits. The German savings banks are almost exclusively the creation of municipal authorities, which guarantee their solvency; in each state they are regulated by law or administrative decree. They have a comparatively long history, the first being established at Hamburg in 1778.

(6) *Creditgenossenschaften* or *Co-operative credit societies*.

These societies are composed of independent craftsmen and small traders, if in a town, or of small cultivators, if in the country—of persons, in short, who might find it difficult to satisfy a large commercial bank that they were trustworthy borrowers. They lend only to their members (apart from balances placed with central institutions), but borrow and receive deposits from others. They are governed by the *Genossenschaftgesetze* of 1889 and 1896, under which they must be registered.

(7) *Königliche Seehandlung* (literally *Royal Sea· Trading Coy.*).

This institution was originally founded by Frederick the Great in 1772 as a general trading company. In accordance with its name, it was interested in overseas trade, but it also participated in manufacturing enterprises at home. In the course of time, however, whilst retaining some industrial participations, it became primarily a bank. In this capacity it owed its importance to its position as repository and financial agent of the Prussian Government, the considerable sums often at the disposal of this Government making the Seehandlung a very influential member of the Berlin money market. Its capital is entirely owned by the Prussian Government, but it has enjoyed more or less complete independence of political control.

A second state-owned bank in Berlin was the *Preussische Zentralgenossenschaftskasse.* (*Central Co-operative Bank.*) This was created in 1895 to serve as a central bank for the Prussian co-operative credit societies and as the channel through which the Prussian Government gave these societies a certain amount of financial assistance. It also has relations with co-operative banks outside Prussia.

The essential difference between the creditbanks and the banks of the first two types above is to be found in the fact that the latter were privileged to obtain resources by issuing special kinds of credit documents—bank notes and *Pfandbriefe* respectively—and were regulated by special laws to prevent the abuse of this privilege; whereas the former, procuring their funds from shareholders and depositors, were not directly the subject of legislation. Freedom from regulation permitted the creditbanks to have a more general and elastic programme. This characteristic also distinguished the creditbanks from the other types of credit institutions enumerated, with the exception perhaps of the Seehandlung; but here there is a further difference in that the creditbanks were designed to earn profits for private persons.

Freedom from regulation, an undefined sphere of activity, and the motive of private profit, are all features which the creditbanks shared with yet another class of credit organ—namely, the *private banking firm.* But the differences in legal constitution between joint stock companies and one-man businesses or partnerships have had as important consequences in German banking as in that of England.

The foregoing enumeration of other kinds of banking institution has been restricted, it will be noticed, to those existing before the War. This is in accordance with the general plan of the book which follows. My main purpose being to show the working of a particular type of credit institution, it has been desirable to relate my account to a period in which that type was relatively stable; and, owing to the effects of the War and inflation, the most recent period of any length to permit such stability is that which comprises the years immediately preceding the War. Accordingly the first and rather larger part of the book has been devoted, after a preliminary historical chapter, to a survey of the operations of the creditbanks, in certain main fields and as a whole, during the decade or so before 1914. But clearly it is also desirable to bring the account as far as possible up to date; and so, in a second part, the historical form of exposition has been resumed, in order to trace the changes of the War and post-war years. In this way it is hoped to arrive at a rough definition of the present character of the creditbanks—and even of their probable future character—in terms of divergencies from the pre-war type.

In the second part I have attempted to give a fairly complete account of the creditbanks to the end of 1928. On certain points it has been possible to notice later developments in the text, and some more recent statistics will be found in the appendices.

PART I

THE CREDITBANKS BEFORE THE WAR

CHAPTER I

THE DEVELOPMENT OF THE CREDITBANKS

THE German creditbanks may be said to have originated in the fifties of the last century. Actually the oldest of them, the *A. Schaaffhausen'scher Bankverein* of Cologne, was chartered in 1848; but for the first few years its activities were limited, partly by the general political and economic difficulties of the time, and partly by special difficulties inherited from the private banking firm from which it derived its name. If one year is to be selected as a starting point, perhaps it should be 1853, which saw the foundation of the *Bank für Handel und Industrie* at Darmstadt (hence called the *Darmstädter Bank*). This bank and its programme at once excited public interest as a ' new model ' in German banking. Following this model more or less closely, a number of other banks were formed in 1856. Of these the most important were the *Berliner Handelsgesellschaft* and the *Discontogesellschaft* of Berlin,[1] the *Mitteldeutsche Creditbank* of Meiningen, the *Allgemeine Deutsche Creditanstalt* of Leipzig, the *Vereinsbank* and *Norddeutsche Bank* of Hamburg, and the *Schlesische Bankverein* of Breslau.

[1] The Discontogesellschaft was originally established in 1851, but on a different basis and with different purposes.

The Discontogesellschaft of 1856 and the Berliner Handelsgesellschaft were organized as *Kommanditgesellschaften auf Aktien* because of the difficulty of securing charters as *Aktiengesellschaften*.

The Mitteldeutsche Creditbank enjoyed for a time the right of note issue.

It will be observed that the establishment of these banks (with the exception of the A. Schaaffhausen'scher Bankverein) followed very closely upon that of the French Crédit Mobilier.[1] As in France, so in Germany, the primary aim of the new financial organs was to promote industrial development; and in Germany their creation was a phase of that first stirring of enterprise which culminated in the boom and crisis of 1857. To understand the precise tasks which they set before themselves, it is necessary to refer to the conditions till then prevailing in the German capital market.

Little capital was put into German industry during the first half of the nineteenth century, and many undertakings languished for lack of it. This has led to the acceptance of the view that there was at this time a general shortage of capital in Germany—a cause as well as an effect of general economic backwardness. This view, however, more particularly with respect to Prussia, has been disputed by Brockhage[2] and confronted with an array of facts which, if they do not prove that capital was really abundant, at least remove the impression that its scarcity was the factor immediately limiting economic progress. It is impossible to attempt here even a summary of the material which he brings to light; the most interesting points are: that there were active markets for government securities, which commanded high prices and gave their purchasers low yields; that the obligations of foreign

---

[1] 1852. The question of how far the *Kreditbanken* were copies of the Crédit Mobilier has been the subject of much sterile dispute. It is known that the Pereires, founders of the Crédit Mobilier, took a part in promoting the Darmstädter Bank, and that the 'statutes' of the latter follow closely those of the French institution. But the Schaaffhausen'scher Bankverein, earlier than either of these, had much the same programme ; and in any case the practice of the German banks diverged very early from that of the Crédit Mobilier.

[2] '*Zur Entwicklung des preuss-deutschen Kapitalexports*' — *Schmollers Forschungen,* Heft 148.

governments figured here to a considerable extent; and that this indication of an export of capital from Germany is confirmed by a study of trade statistics. With these and other facts, Brockhage supports the conclusion:

'The condition of Prussian economic life in the twenty-five years after the second treaty of Paris was such that there was continuously more capital available than was put to productive economic use.'[1]

Later he extends this conclusion to the years 1840-50. If, therefore, industry was handicapped by want of capital, it was largely because investment was misdirected. Those who had the necessary funds were for the most part neither willing nor fitted to become progressive entrepreneurs themselves, nor would they trust their money with others who had the required qualities.

If now we accept this explanation as correct, it is readily to be seen that there was a place for some kind of agency which should obtain the confidence of the investing class, and use this confidence to direct their capital towards sound industrial undertakings. On the evidence the existing organs did not meet the need. The small private bankers—the most numerous class— were engaged principally in money changing, supplemented, especially in towns like Frankfurt a. M., by dealings in public securities. No doubt, too, they made advances to their clients out of their own funds, but not on a large scale nor for long periods. The great bankers, of the Rothschild type, were occupied with the financial needs of the more important governments and stood aloof from struggling business concerns. The bankers of intermediate standing, less cosmopolitan than the great firms and inspiring more confidence than the small, might have answered the

---

[1] *Op. cit.* p. 182.

purpose better and probably were of some help; but on the whole they were too conservative and fearful of risking their reputations. Of banks, the only class to be considered is that of the *Notenbanken*; and they were not at this time very numerous, nor—with the exception of the Preussische Bank, established only in 1846 —influential. Such as they were, they were too busy maintaining the volume of their note circulation to concern themselves with the utilization of other people's capital, while their own resources were only suitable for liquid investment.[1]

It was primarily to fill this place that the new credit banks were formed, and accordingly they gave a prominent place in their programme to the promotion of joint stock companies. The original statutes of the Bank für Handel und Industrie, for example, empowered the bank (Article III K.)

'to bring about or participate in the promotion of new companies, the amalgamation or consolidation of different companies, and the transformation of industrial undertakings into joint stock form; also to issue or take over for its own account the shares and debentures of such newly created companies.'[2]

Quotations to the same effect might be made from the statutes (or articles) of the other creditbanks founded at this time, the only exception being the case of the A. Schaaffhausen'scher Bankverein. This exception—attributable to the rather earlier date at which this bank was established—did not correspond with an exception in actual practice.

The promotion of companies meant, of course, equipping them with capital, but those in charge of the new banks were fully alive to the dangers of extensive participation on their own account in the concerns

---

[1] Two note-issuing banks—the *Leipziger Bank* and the *Bayerische Hypotheken- u. Wechselbank*—seem to have been more adventurous than the rest ; later they surrendered their rights of note issue.

[2] Quoted Bosenick : *Die neudeutsche gemischte Bankwirtschaft*, p. 67.

which they brought into existence. To quote again from the original statutes of the Darmstädter Bank, the enumeration of the kinds of transaction in which the bank might engage opens thus:

'The Bank is authorized to carry on all banking transactions. According to its judgment, it will devote its activity and its resources to transactions, such that it can withdraw its money after agreed notice or whenever else this seems desirable or necessary.'[1]

Similarly, the Discontogesellschaft in Article 40 of its (1856) statutes declared:

'The resources of the company shall be so employed, as practically to obviate all danger of its being unable to meet its obligations punctually, even in the conditions of any likely commercial crisis. In particular therefore has the management to guard against locking up for a considerable time sums too large in proportion to the means and business of the company by purchasing or lending on securities.'[2]

How this caution might be reconciled, at least in theory, with the rôle the banks wished to play in the development of industry is well shown by the following quotation from the annual report of the Schaaffhausen'- scher Bankverein for 1852:

'The management has proceeded from the principle that it is the function of a great banking institution not so much to call great new branches of industry into existence through large scale participation on its own account, as to induce the capitalists of the country by the authority of its recommendations, based on thorough investigations, to apply their idle capital to under- takings which, properly planned, corresponding to real needs, and equipped with expert management, offer prospects of reasonable profits.'[3]

Company promotion was the part of the programme of the creditbanks which at the beginning was most

---

[1] Bosenick: *op. cit.* p. 66.   [2] *Ibid.* p. 68.
[3] Huth: *Die Entwicklung der Grossbanken*, p. 11.

prominent, the part, further, in which their ambitions most clearly exceeded those of the older institutions; but it must not be thought that it was more than a part. On the contrary, they intended to combine with their newer and more distinctive tasks the cultivation of all the recognized branches of a banker's business, upon an enlarged scale and with a special view to the encouragement of industry. This may be illustrated by an extract from the first annual report of the Darmstädter Bank. Speaking of the objects of the bank, after mentioning in the first place what was to be done in the way of equipping promising industrial concerns with capital, it proceeds:

' Its (the bank's) organs at home and abroad shall facilitate the export trade and the thousand other relations between German industry and the money market. It has the right and duty to transfer the capital which one industrialist has temporarily to spare to another who is at the same time in need of it, and by this continual interchange to stimulate and increase industrial activity. . . . As in the case of large scale industrial undertakings, so also is it entitled to participate in the projects, creations and financial transactions of governments, and to assist investment in this field. The Bank für Handel und Industrie, in a word, is a banking house raised to a higher power, furnished with vast funds and with various organs assured of an existence as long as that of the company itself.'[1]

There was, however, one self-imposed limitation of their business which it is interesting to notice. Although ready to accept deposits from their customers, they did not think it advisable to endeavour to attract them for the purpose of augmenting their working funds. To quote from the report of the A. Schaaffhausen'scher Bankverein for 1856:

' We do not consider it desirable in the interests of the complete security of our institution to attract increased deposits by offering favourable terms, since we prefer, so far as is compatible

[1] Weber: *Depositenbanken u. Spekulationsbanken*, 2nd edition, pp. 62-3.

with the nature of banking business and the interests of our customers (correspondents) to carry on our business with our own resources.'[1]

The foregoing quotations illustrate the aims and principles of the early creditbanks. Turning now to their practice, it may be said that they all took a hand in the many industrial promotions of the middle fifties. The A. Schaaffhausen'scher Bankverein and the Darmstädter Bank, because they were earlier in the field—the former also because of its location at the financial centre of Rhenish Westphalia—were able to do most; but the others were not slow to take their more limited opportunities. While so far fulfilling their programme, however, they did not succeed, as they had hoped, in confining themselves to the rôle of intermediaries. Lack of support from private investors, a failure to foresee the impending crisis of 1857, and (less certainly) the necessity of buying in shares during that crisis to prevent a catastrophic fall in their price, all seem to have contributed to the result that the reaction found them with large holdings in the companies which they had created. Of these holdings they were unable to relieve themselves for many years, and often then only after they had been heavily written down.

With part of their resources thus immobilized and some losses to discourage them, it is not surprising that they were disinclined to undertake further industrial promotions in the sixties. In any case, circumstances, especially political circumstances, were unfavourable for operations of this kind. It must be said, too, that little or nothing came at that time of the Darmstädter's plans for assisting foreign trade, although experiments were made with 'commandit partnerships' abroad. Their current account connexions, however—that is,

---

[1] Huth : *op. cit.* p. 15.

their relations with customers, now in debit, now in credit,[1] supplemented by public loan transactions, yielded them a sufficient amount of business.

The victory of 1871 and the completion of national unification opened out vast new possibilities for German business enterprise. The perception of these, even before the war was definitely concluded, started a trade boom, which later was given additional stimulus by the payment of the French indemnity and by changes in the currency. At such a time the promotion of many new enterprises is to be expected, and at this time it was aided by the substitution of a very liberal general company law for the older system requiring government sanction for each new company. So numerous in fact were the promotions that the early seventies have come to be known as the ' Gründerjahre ' or promotion years.

Included among the concerns erected at this time was a large number of creditbanks. Many of these, particularly those formed to win speedy gains from the prevailing mania for speculation, were short-lived; but others were lasting and important additions to their class.

First place amongst the latter must be given to the *Deutsche Bank* (Berlin). To be quite accurate we should say that this bank was founded before the war, in the early part of 1870; but, as its name indicates, it belongs essentially to the period of German unity. Still more clearly does it belong to the new epoch in virtue of the objects which it set in the front of its programme. Section 2 of its statutes runs:

' The purpose of the company is to carry on banking transactions of every description, in particular to further and facilitate the trading relations between Germany, the other European countries and the overseas markets.'

---

[1] For further account of term ' Current account ' in German usage, see Chapter II, pp. 37-39.

Not only did the Deutsche Bank grow to be the largest bank in Germany, but it assumed in the years following 1870 the leading, pioneer rôle which had previously been played by the Bank für Handel und Industrie.

The next bank in importance which dates from this period is the *Dresdner Bank*, established with its headquarters at Dresden in 1872. The Deutsche, Dresdner, Darmstädter and Discontogesellschaft, standing at the head of the creditbanks, are often spoken of as the ' 4 D-Banken.' Other important banks originating at this time were:

1870 - {Commerz- u. Discontobank, Hamburg.
Breslauer Discontobank.

1871 - Bergisch-Märkische Bank.

1872 - {Essener Creditanstalt.
Rheinisch-Westfälische Discontogesellschaft.[1]

The Deutsche Bank held aloof, rather as a matter of principle, from industrial promotions during its earlier years, and was in any case fully occupied in

---

[1] An interesting development of the same years was the formation by banks already established in the more important financial centres of subsidiary concerns which, while having their headquarters in the same town as their parent institution, were to open branches in other towns throughout a more or less defined region. In this way the parent banks sought to extend their influence to new places while limiting their own risks to the amount of capital invested in their subsidiary. The leading examples of this development are :

The Provinzial Discontogesellschaft, Berlin, formed by the Discontogesellschaft ;

The Provinzial Wechselbank, Berlin, formed by the Berliner Wechselbank ;

The Provinzial Gewerbebank, Berlin, formed by the Gewerbebank, H. Schuster & Co. ;

The Suddeutsche Provinzialbank, Stuttgart, formed by the Stuttgarter Bank ; and

The Allgemeine Deutsche Filialenkreditanstalt, Leipzig, formed by the Allgemeiner Deutsche Kreditanstalt.

This first attempt to build up a system of branch-banking proved premature, however, and all of these ' provincial ' subsidiaries had disappeared by the end of the decade. But some of their branches continued in existence as provincial banks in the ordinary sense.

For whole development see Wallich : *Die Konzentration im Deutschen Bankwesen.*

equipping itself for the special tasks which it had undertaken. The other creditbanks, however—true to
their original purpose—took an active part in the
flotations of the *Gründerjahre*. In so doing, while
they no doubt contributed in many instances to the
permanent development of Germany, they also laid
themselves open to the reproach of having encouraged
much blind speculation. A true judgment in this
matter would probably have to discriminate between
the more responsible D-banks and other, decidedly
reckless institutions, but in the dismay caused by the
crisis of 1873, few, if any, creditbanks escaped blame.

A consideration of the circumstances of that crisis
need not detain us here. It was the familiar termination of a nineteenth century boom—especially acute
because the boom had been especially exaggerated.
As has been already indicated, many of the newly
formed banks succumbed during the crisis, and several
of the surviving banks, including the Berliner Handelsgesellschaft, were handicapped for some years by the
losses it occasioned. On the other hand, certain of the
more successful banks were able to consolidate their
position by taking over the assets and connexions of
competitors forced into liquidation.[1]

[1] Thus the *Deutsche Bank* took over in liquidation :
  Deutsche Unionbank, Berlin (which had itself liquidated numerous
    other banks).
  Berliner Bankverein,
  Berliner Wechselbank,
  Allgemeine Depositenbank, Berlin,
  Frankfurter Bankverein,
  Elberfelder Diskonto und Wechselbank,
  Niederlausitzer Bank, Kottbus (apparently reorganised).
The *Dresdner Bank* similarly took over the :
  Sächsische Kreditbank ⎫
  Dresdner Handelsbank ⎬ Dresden,
  Sächsischer Bankverein ⎭
  Thüringische Bank, Sondershausen.
The *Wurttembergische Bankverein* of Stuttgart liquidated the Stuttgarter
Bank.

Wallich, *op. cit.* pp. 38 *et seq.*

From the ensuing depression trade emerged only slowly. The aftermath of the crisis had to be endured, and, in addition, the country was hardly ready for the great advances expected of it. In some respects we may compare unified Germany to a new territory—a colony, for example—rich in potential wealth but not able to realize it until some years have been spent in steady preparation and development.[1]   While, then, by the end of the nineteenth century Germany had been transformed from an agricultural to a manufacturing nation, competing successfully with the older manufacturing countries in most of their markets, we find that the greater part of the change came about with apparent suddenness in the last ten or twelve years. Following the depression of the seventies, there was a recovery, which almost promised a period of brisk trade, in 1879; but the hope was disappointed, and progress was slow until the late eighties. The years 1888 and 1889 constituted the first period of real prosperity and trade expansion since the *Gründerjahre*; but there was another check in 1890, when depression again set in for several years. Then in 1895 began a remarkably long boom, which lasted until the beginning of the new century and established Germany as an industrial power.

The course of general trade was reflected in the business of the creditbanks. During the seventies and most of the eighties there was little to be done in the field of company promoting ; and public loan transactions and current account banking became again—as in the sixties—the banks' chief interests.

---

[1] The comparison might be made with the Canadian West at the same time. Of course the nature of the preparation necessary was not the same in the two cases. In the case of Germany we are thinking of such things as the necessity of acquiring up-to-date industrial technique, commercial organization and connexions in foreign markets. We may also mention the laborious work of codifying the laws.

It might be thought that the Deutsche Bank, with its distinctive aims, would have been able to make more progress.   In the early seventies, while other banks were devoting themselves to financing home industry, it gave its attention to opening branches in the German seaports, Bremen and Hamburg, in London, and even in Shanghai and Yokohama.   It also acquired about the same time the *La Plata Bank* in South America and a partnership interest in a New York banking firm.   In these ways it sought to put itself in readiness to assist German foreign trade.   But here, too, reverses were encountered; within a few years it was found necessary to close the two Far Eastern branches and to liquidate both the La Plata Bank and the New York partnership.   These misfortunes—due to fluctuations in the value of foreign currencies and the difficulty of finding able and trustworthy managers for overseas establishments—did not deflect the Deutsche Bank from its purpose; but the necessity of starting afresh upon more cautious lines, together with the slow growth of the exporting industries, retarded advance for some years.

Rather more success rewarded the efforts made during this same period (1874-1888) to attract deposits.   That these were made at all indicates, it will be noticed, a departure from the policy adopted by the early creditbanks.   As in the attempts to foster foreign trade, so here the lead was taken by the Deutsche Bank; indeed the two lines of development were related, since the deposits were to provide cheap funds for the assistance of traders, and mercantile bills were to provide a safe and liquid investment for the deposits.   In order to be able to compete with the *Sparkassen* in obtaining deposits, the banks found it necessary to supplement their chief offices and branches—then few in number and located in the main business centres—by special offices (*Depositenkassen*) in suburban residential districts. The first of these offices was opened by the Deutsche Bank in Berlin so early as 1871. But their establishment and maintenance involved a good deal of expense, which was not likely to justify itself unless full and profitable employment was available for the deposits which might be obtained by their means. It is not altogether surprising, therefore, that after twenty years the Deutsche Bank had no more than twelve of these offices open, while only one other bank—the *Nationalbank für Deutschland*[1] with nine—had any number at the same date (1890). In this respect also we must regard the eighties as years of preparation rather than of achievement.

The end of the eighties brought a change to greater activity for the banks as for other economic organs. With the resumption of brisk industrial expansion, company promotion became again after fifteen years an important branch of banking. Even the Deutsche Bank abandoned the attitude of indifference (if not repudiation) which it had hitherto maintained towards this kind of business, and made itself solely responsible for an industrial flotation—*Deutsch-Oesterreichische Mannesmann Rohrwerke*—for the first time in 1890.[2] In the last half of the nineties it pursued this new course considerably further. The other banks, which had no scruples to overcome, were naturally even more active in this direction in both periods. With many promotions to their credit, chiefly of electrical undertakings, light railways, mining and metallurgical concerns, chemical works and land development companies in Germany, and of railways and petroleum companies abroad, one may speak of a return of the creditbanks to the larger financial transactions in

[1] This bank was established in Berlin in 1881.

[2] Already in 1888 it had helped to transform the *Deutsche-Edison A. G.* into the *A.E.G.*, and in 1889 it had promoted the Anatolian Railway.

the interest of private business. These transactions were now common to all the leading banks; whilst their number and importance varied in later years according to the conditions of trade and of the stock markets, it was the accepted policy of the banks to engage in them whenever the circumstances seemed favourable.

But this was only one of the directions in which the business of the creditbanks began to expand rapidly towards the close of the century. Not less important were the developments in the following branches of banking:

(1) In the *financing of foreign trade* much greater headway was made from this time onwards, partly because of the progress of German industry, and partly because successful overseas banks, affiliated to the creditbanks, were at last established. The *Deutsche Ueberseebank* (later *Deutsche Ueberseeische Bank*), *Brasilianische Bank für Deutschland*, and the *Bank für Chile u. Deutschland*, three banks specializing in South American trade, and also the *Deutsch-Asiatische Bank*, all came into existence in the last twelve years of the century. Early in the twentieth century they were followed by several other foreign and a few colonial banks. In this development, not only the Deutsche Bank, but also the other three D-banks took an active part.

(2) The *bank acceptance*, first introduced in connexion with foreign trade, became popular both in home trade and as a pure finance bill. Thus not only the individual bank, but also the banks as a class found a means of helping their customers at little or no expense to themselves, since bank acceptances came to be bought on a considerable scale by such institutions as Insurance Companies.

(3) The *deposits* entrusted to the banks increased very greatly, as shown in the table opposite. In the

case of the Deutsche Bank, deposits grew from
4·8 million marks in 1871 to 71·8 million in 1894 and
779·5 million in 1908.

BANK DEPOSITS (including current account balances)
1889-1913.[1]

Dec. 31st.				All Banks.	Nine Berlin Banks.
1889	-	-	-	1,392·18	743·67
1890	-	-	-	1,286·24	649·03
1891	-	-	-	1,281·38	633·92
1892	-	-	-	1,282·94	621·16
1893	-	-	-	1,321·50	653·66
1894	-	-	-	1,627·91	902·11
1895	-	-	-	1,769·38	1,016·46
1896	-	-	-	1,868·19	1,019·00
1897	-	-	-	2,069·07	1,143·90
1898	-	-	-	2,510·78	1,481·95
1899	-	-	-	2,837·58	1,612·80
1900	-	-	-	3,128·05	1,726·36
1901	-	-	-	3,014·81	1,699·13
1902	-	-	-	3,380·56	2,001·82
1903				3,709·55	2,214·52
1904	-	-	-	4,355·99	2,642·65
1905	-	-	-	5,298·40	3,212·54
1906	-	-	-	6,304·75	3,739·45
1907	-	-	-	6,625·50	3,669·63
1908	-	-	-	7,256·14	3,699·79
1909	-	-	-	8,112·71	4,173·28
1910	-	-	-	9,123·12	4,881·88
1911	-	-	-	9,413·08	4,969·30
1912	-	-	-	9,360·00	4,919·60
1913	-	-	-	9,641·59	5,148·63

Million Marks.

One result of this increase in deposits was that
although the capital of the banks was repeatedly
raised by large amounts (that of the Deutsche Bank
grew from 15 millions in 1870 to 200 millions in

[1] *Deutsch-Oekonomist* Annual Review ‘*Die deutschen Banken im Jahre
1913*,’ p. 15. The term ‘All banks’ covers all creditbanks having at least
one million marks capital.

1913), it declined as a proportion of the total working funds at their disposal.[1]

(4) The banks came to employ much more money in the *organized money (short loan) market*. The increase in their liabilities in connexion with deposits and acceptances necessitated an increase in the funds devoted to liquid investments. But further it was desirable that a considerable proportion of those liquid funds should be employed (*a*) near the offices from which the whole disposition of the banks' resources was directed; (*b*) in ways which made the careful scrutiny of each transaction unnecessary; and (*c*) in ways which did not involve continuous relations with customers, accompanied by hampering obligations for the banks—so that, in short, the bank could approach each transaction from the standpoint of its own interest solely. Money market loans (including bill-discounting) in the larger financial centres, above all, Berlin, alone satisfied these three conditions.

(5) *Commission business in connexion with the Stock Exchange* increased very greatly in importance especially for the Berlin banks. Contact with the stock market on the one hand, and the large numbers of investors who used their deposit offices on the other hand, gave the big banks splendid opportunities for this kind of business.

[1] Deposits and current account balances as percentage of total working funds (not including acceptance liabilities) :

					All Banks.	Berlin Banks.
1895	-	-	-	-	58·8%	51·0%
1905	-	-	-	-	66·2	69·1
1906	-	-	-	-	67·8	71·2
1907	-	-	-	-	67·7	70·2
1908	-	-	-	-	69·0	87·6
1909	-	-	-	-	70·6	73·2
1910	-	-	-	-	72·2	75·3
1911	-	-	-	-	71·5	74·8
1912	-	-	-	-	84·5	74·9
1913	-	-	-	-	72·0	75·9

It is impossible, of course, to assign precise dates for the origin of any of these developments. They became very noticeable towards the close of the last century, and were continued down to the outbreak of the War.

With regard to the business of the creditbanks as a whole, extended in these several ways, there are two points to be noticed.

Firstly, it became more than ever varied, 'many-sided.' In addition to the business of an English Joint Stock Bank, it included now the functions which we regard as proper to company promoters, issuing houses, underwriters, discounting and accepting houses and stockbrokers.[1] We may further point out that, although there remained differences of degree between the business of one bank and that of another, this mixed character was henceforward common to them all. In the early years of the Deutsche Bank it might have seemed as though the banks were going to divide into two classes, like the French *banques de dépôts* and *banques d'affaires*; but this did not happen. The Deutsche Bank adopted the industrial policy of the other banks, and the other banks the special features of the Deutsche Bank.

Secondly, what we may call the larger financial transactions—the promotion of companies, the taking over of new capital issues and obligations of existing companies, the taking over of public loans—transactions which may individually involve the locking-up of considerable sums of money—now occupied a more subordinate place. This, as we have seen, was not due to any positive decline in business promotions undertaken by the creditbanks. To some extent it

---

[1] Bosenick has, therefore, proposed that the German banks should be called 'gemischte Banken.' This term has not been adopted, but it is in view of the above developments that the old name 'Anlagebanken' has been dropped in favour of the more vague 'Kreditbanken.'

may be ascribed to a falling off in public loan transactions towards the end of the century.   But primarily
it was the result of the more rapid development of the
other branches of banking mentioned above.

Statistical confirmation of this second point is to be
found in a decline in the proportional contribution
made to gross profits by the *Effekten und Konsortialkonten*
(Security and Syndicate Accounts) and a corresponding
increase in the proportional contribution made by
the *Zins und Provisionskonten* (Interest and Charges
Accounts).   The following figures for the nine leading
Berlin banks taken together, averaged for the quinquennial periods 1871-5, 1896-1900, and 1906-1910,
are given by Bosenick [1]; the percentages for 1912 and
1913 are calculated from materials given in the
Deutsch-Oekonomist annual reviews for those years.

	(1) Security and Syndicate Accounts.	(2) Interest and Charges Accounts.
1871-5 - -	25·6%	67·1%
1896-1900 -	18·4	72·9
1906-1910 -	14·8	76·2
1912 - -	15·8	81·1
1913 - -	11·6	85·3
	(per cent. of gross profits)	

Broadly speaking, profits resulting from the purchase, holding or sale of securities appear under (1);
profits from the granting of short term credit and the
provision of other facilities under (2).   This statement
requires a good deal of qualification to make it accurate, but when all proper allowances are made the above
figures may still be said to show a shifting in the centre
of gravity of the banks' business away from large
'capital' transactions.

The foregoing developments in respect of the functions of the creditbanks were accompanied by hardly

[1] *Op. cit.* p. 217.

less important developments in their organization. Mention has already been made of the establishment of suburban sub-offices (*Depositenkassen*), of branches at the seaports and in foreign countries, and of affiliated foreign banks. But within Germany there was a wider movement, especially marked towards the close of the last century, in the direction of linking up all parts of the Reich in bank systems having their centres in Berlin.

Finance naturally tends to centralization. The unification of Germany removed the obstacles which had previously thwarted that tendency, while the selection of Berlin as the political capital of the Reich practically determined the location of the new centre. The Discontogesellschaft, Berliner Handelsgesellschaft, and Deutsche Bank, as well as the Königliche Seehandlung, had their headquarters in Berlin when the Empire was founded; and the new Reichsbank was established there soon afterwards. Then the Berlin Stock Exchange rapidly displaced that of Frankfurt a. M. as the chief investment market in Germany; the presence of this market and of the just mentioned banks assured the pre-eminence of Berlin as a short-loan market.

The first stage in the development of the modern German banking organization is marked by the attraction of the larger and more enterprising banks of the provinces to Berlin. The Darmstädter Bank led the way by opening a branch in the capital in 1871, and was followed two years later by the Mitteldeutsche Creditbank. These two, however, were rather ahead of the general trend; it was not until 1881 and 1892 that the Dresdner Bank and A. Schaaffhausen'scher Bankverein respectively appeared in Berlin. The Commerz- u. Discontobank (Hamburg) also opened a Berlin branch in 1892, extending its metropolitan connexions later (1904) by the absorption of the Berliner Bank. These Berlin offices were at first only branches

(*Filialen*) but they soon grew to be co-ordinate head-
offices which rather eclipsed the original head-offices.
In this way these five banks became Berlin banks.
Together with the four large banks established from
the beginning in the capital, they constituted the class
Berliner Grossbanken. As it is frequently necessary to
refer to this group, it may be convenient to set out the
names of its members in a list:

The Great Berlin Banks (1904-13)

Deutsche Bank.
Discontogesellschaft.
Bank für Handel u. Industrie (*Darmstädter Bank*) (Berlin
    and Darmstadt).
Dresdner Bank (Berlin and Dresden).
Berliner Handelsgesellschaft.
Mitteldeutsche Creditbank (Berlin and Frankfurt a. M.).
Nationalbank für Deutschland.
Commerz- u. Discontobank (Berlin and Hamburg).
A. Schaaffhausen'scher Bankverein (Berlin and Cologne).

It may be mentioned here that from 1905 to 1909
the Schaaffhausen'scher Bankverein had a close working agreement with the Dresdner Bank. Later, at the
very close of the pre-war period, the entire capital of
the Schaaffhausen'scher Bank was taken over by the
Discontogesellschaft; although left nominally in independent existence, the former bank then disappeared
from Berlin.

These nine banks left little room for the opening of
further branches in Berlin. Certain provincial institutions, such as the Allgemeine Deutsche Creditanstalt of Leipzig, sought to obtain a footing in Berlin
by entering into 'commandit partnerships' with
Berlin bankers; but this arrangement did not prove
very satisfactory. Accordingly the provincial banks
were impelled to seek contact with the money market of
the capital by forming friendly relations with one or
other of the leading Berlin banks. Now the needs of

the provincial banks in this respect found their counter-part in the desire of the Berlin banks to extend and diversify their contacts with German industry and to widen the area from which they could draw surplus balances and funds destined for investment. Such relations, therefore, were easily established. The Berlin bank assisted its provincial associate by re-discounting its bills and making on occasion other advances, by executing its Stock Exchange commis-sions, and by carrying out large financial transactions on behalf of its customers; the provincial bank, besides bringing the Berlin bank this business, passed on to it any funds for which local employment might be lacking; mutually they helped one another in the collection of bills and cheques. To give the arrangement a measure of permanence two means were commonly adopted. Firstly the Berlin bank was represented on the Board of Supervisors (for an account of which see next chapter) of the provincial bank; secondly it acquired a holding of the capital of the provincial bank. The participation and representation might be mutual, but the tendency was for the provincial bank to lose some of its independence to the Berlin bank.[1]

In this way each of the four D-banks—to a less extent some of the other Berliner Grossbanken also—came to be surrounded by a group of provincial banks (*Konzern*) working in harmony with it and more or less under its control. The composition of these groups in 1913 was given by the *Deutsch-Oekonomist* as follows:

---

[1] An arrangement based on an exchange of shares would give the Berlin bank more influence over the provincial one than the latter would acquire over the former, firstly because a given nominal amount in shares would represent a larger proportion of the capital of the provincial bank than of the capital of the Berlin bank ; secondly, because the Berlin shares would exchange at a premium in terms of the provincial shares—say two provincial shares to one Berlin share. In some cases the arrangement was altogether one-sided, as when the Discontogesellschaft acquired the whole capital of the Norddeutsche Bank of Hamburg (1897).

BANK GROUPS, 1913

Deutsche Bank

Deutsche Ueberseeische Bank.
Bergisch-Märkische Bank.
Siegener Bank.
Essener Creditanstalt.
Hannoversche Bank.
Hildesheimer Bank.
Osnabrücker Bank.
Oldenburg. Spar- u. Leihbank.
Rheinische Creditbank.
Schlesische Bankverein.
Deutsche Treuhand A.G.
Privatbank zu Gotha.
Niederlausitzer Bank.

Braunschweigische Privat-bank.
Anhalt-Dessauische Landes-bank.
Braunschweig Bank u. Credit-anstalt.
Chemnitzer Bankverein.
Commerz Bank, Lübeck.
Danziger Privat-Aktienbank.
Deutsche Vereinsbank.
Lübecker Privatbank.
Norddeutsche Creditanstalt.
Pfälzische Bank.

Discontogesellschaft

Barmer Bankverein.
Norddeutsche Bank (all capital owned by Discontogesell-schaft).
Rhein-Westfälische Disconto-gesellschaft.
Dürener Bank.
Süddeutsche Discontogesell-schaft.
Bayerische Disconto u. Wech-selbank.

Brasilianische Bank f. Deutsch-land.
Bank für Chile u. Deutsch-land.
Bank für Thüringen vorm Strupp.
Schlesische Handelsbank.
Geestemünder Bank.
Magdeburger Bankverein.
Oberlausitzer Bank.
Stahl, Federer A.G.

The Allgemeine Deutsche Creditanstalt, Leipzig, and the Bayerische Hypotheken- u. Wechselbank, Munich, were also supposed to have especially close relations with the Discontogesellschaft.

Dresdner Bank

Rheinische Bank.
Märkische Bank.
Oldenburgische Landesbank.
Mecklenburgische Bank.
Schwarzbergische Landes-bank.

Deutsch-Südamerikanische Bank.
Deutsche Orientbank.
Bankverein Gelsenkirchen.

Darmstädter Bank

Ostbank für Handel u. Gewerbe.	Vereinsbank, Wismar.
	Württemberg Bankanstalt.

A. Schaaffhausen'scher Bankverein

Westfälisch-Lippische Vereinsbank.	Mittelrheinsche Bank.
	Mülheimer Bank.

In the formation of these groups we see the second phase of the development of German banking organization—the extension of the influence of the Berlin banks throughout the provinces. The Berlin banks also expanded their organization by means of branches. Apart from the suburban sub-offices (*Depositenkassen*) —of which the number maintained by the Berliner Grossbanken increased from 18 in 1896 to 276 at the end of 1911 [1]—branches having a more independent status (*Filialen*) were opened in towns in which the banks had not previously been represented. The following tabulation, based on a larger table given by Adolf Weber,[2] shows the number of such branches possessed by the leading Berlin banks and nine leading provincial banks in 1913:

Bank.	No. of Branches.[3]	Bank.	No. of Branches.
Deutsche Bank	10	Mitteldeutsche Privatbank	60
Discontogesellschaft	12	Barmer Bankverein	21
Dresdner Bank	48	Rheinische Creditbank	24
Darmstädter Bank	49	Essener Creditanstalt	24
Berliner Handelgesellschaft	0	Rheinisch - Westfälische	
Nationalbank f. Deutschland	0	Discontogesellschaft	21
Commerz- u. Discontobank	6	Bergisch-Märkische Bank	20
		Pfälzische Bank	19
A. Schaaffhausen'scher Bankverein	12	Schlesischer Bankverein	20
Mitteldeutsche Creditbank	8	Norddeutsche Creditanstalt	19

[1] Riesser : *Von 1848 bis Heute*, p. 113.

[2] *Depositenbanken u. Spekulationsbanken*. Anlage I.

[3] Where a bank had more than one headquarters, the additional ones have been counted as branches.

Commonly these branches resulted from the absorption of a private banking business, less frequently from the liquidation of a provincial bank. It will be noticed from the above table that the provincial banks were by no means behind, but rather in advance of, the Berlin banks in building up a network of branches: but it must be remembered that almost all of the provincial banks enumerated were to some extent tributary to banks in Berlin.[1] From several instances in which Berlin banks merged provincial banks into their own organization[2] during the ten years or so before the War, it would rather appear that their preference was shifting from the ' group ' system of organization to a more centralized branch banking system. But down to 1914 the former system remained more characteristic of German banking organization.

To show what had been accomplished by this movement towards banking ' concentration ' in both its forms before the outbreak of the War, the following statistics may be given. The nine Berlin banks comprised with their groups 62 out of the 160 creditbanks having at least one million marks capital according to the *Deutsch-Oekonomist* statistics for 1913. These 62 banks had in their control at the end of this year 83% of the total working funds (capital and reserves, deposits and current account balances) of all the 160 banks taken together. Statistics covering the smaller banks are more difficult to obtain, but according to Lansburgh the Berlin banks without their provincial associates administered practically one-half of

[1] The Mitteldeutsche Privatbank, Magdeburg, which excelled in point of number of branches was supposed to have certain relations with the Deutsche Bank but objected to being considered a member of its group.

[2] Thus the Dresdner Bank absorbed the Breslauer Wechselbank and Württembergische Landesbank in 1909 : the Darmstädter Bank the Bayerische Bank für Handel u. Industrie in 1910 : while just before the War, in 1914, the Deutsche Bank absorbed the Bergisch-Märkische Bank.

the resources (49%) of all creditbanks large and small.[1]

The growth of the creditbanks in function and organization more than filled all the gaps in the German credit system.   At the outset—between 1850 and 1870, and even later—the existing institutions were inadequate for the work to be done.   In recognition of this, private bankers took an active part in the establishment of creditbanks, and the earlier credit-banks themselves assisted in the promotion of other such banks and of *Notenbanken*.   But by the beginning of the present century a considerable amount of over-lapping had become evident, and the competition of the creditbanks was being severely felt by private bankers, savings banks and the lesser note-issuing banks; at the same time the creditbanks began to complain of excessive competition amongst themselves.

The note-issuing banks faced this competition with the advantage of their special privileges.   None the less their position became in general a difficult one. In their own privileged field they were more and more hemmed in by the expansion of the Reichsbank; while in competing with the creditbanks they were handicapped by the restrictions which were the price of their privileges.   In this predicament most of them decided sooner or later to abandon their rights of note issue and become ordinary creditbanks—a development which, by adding to the number of the latter, partially offset the trend towards concentration previously described.[2]

The savings banks also had a special field, though they in their turn felt and resented the encroachment of the creditbanks in the sphere of deposit banking. But it was the private bankers, conducting a business

---

[1] See *Deutsche Banken, von 1907-8 bis 1912-13,* p. 7.

[2] The number of the lesser note-issuing banks declined from thirty-two in 1875 to four in the decade before the War.

of more nearly the same scope as that of the credit-banks, and having no transactions from which those banks were excluded, who suffered most from the new competition.

In banking, as in so many other branches of business, the joint stock association could show a balance of advantages over the private firm. Its two immaterial assets, permanence and publicity, were more effective in attracting deposits than the personal reputation of the private banker, which was somewhat diminished by the many failures of bankers in the years 1888-1890. The large sums of which the banks in this way acquired comparatively cheap use enabled them to be more generous in their terms for loans and discounts. Moreover the bankers found greater difficulty in increasing their own capital, and this two-fold limitation of their resources made it dangerous, if not impossible, for them to seek to meet the credit needs of large scale industry. Yet again, the unlimited liability of the partners of a private firm was an obstacle in the way of territorial expansion. To crown their difficulties the legislation passed at the end of the century relating to dealings in stock exchange securities had the effect of curtailing just those transactions which for most of the bankers were of chief importance.[1] Despite these drawbacks, some of the largest private bankers—

---

[1] Bourse law of 1896, Stamp Duty laws, particularly that of 1894, and to some extent the Dépôt law of 1896. (Law relating to safe keeping of securities.)

Beyond curtailing transactions of special interest to the bankers, certain provisions of these laws for a time actually gave the banks some advantages over the bankers in respect to the business that remained. Thus, firstly, the banks with their large clientèle were able to escape the tax on bourse transactions by balancing sale and purchase orders outside the Bourse ; and secondly, the provincial bankers, passing on orders to a Berlin correspondent, had at first to pay the tax twice. Subsequently, however, these inequalities were removed. For discussions of these laws and their influence on banking development, see Schuhmacher: *Ursachen und Wirkungen der Konzentration im deutschen Bankwesen, Weltwirtschaftliche Studien*, pp. 195-7 ; and Obst: *Bankgeschäft*, ii. pp. 461-3.

particularly those connected with the Berlin money market: S. Bleichröder, Mendelssohn & Co., Delbrück Schickler & Co., J. Dreyfus & Co.; but also certain provincial bankers: Warburg & Co., Hamburg; Deichmann & Co., Cologne—were able to retain a leading position.   But a greater number of the important bankers found that their best course was to sell their business to the banks before it was taken from them.[1]

Amongst the creditbanks themselves, competition between the Berlin banks and the provincial banks was partially, though by no means entirely avoided by the arrangements described above.   Between the Berlin banks, however, and between their groups, it became very keen, accentuated by the efforts of each bank to diversify its business by establishing contacts with new areas and new branches of industry.   Here we may observe a distinction between the amalgamations of the late seventies, which were mostly between banks of the same locality and tended to reduce competition, and the later forms of combination, which were mainly inter-local and brought the leading banks into direct or indirect competition throughout the country.   The limitation of this competition by agreement can hardly be said to have been begun before the outbreak of the Great War. (See, however, Chapter V, pp. 179-180.)

---

[1] In this way disappeared R. Warschauer & Co., Breest & Gelpcke and Jakob Landau of Berlin ; Erlanger & Söhne, of Frankfurt a. M. ; W. H. Ladenburger Söhne of Mannheim ; and A. L. Camphausen of Cologne. The famous firm, M. A. Rothschild & Söhne, Frankfurt, came to an end for lack of an heir, the Discontogesellschaft succeeding to its connexions. Hardy & Co., Berlin, converted into a private limited company (G.m.b.H.), came under the control of the Dresdner Bank.

CHAPTER II

THE CREDITBANKS AND INDUSTRY

IT is fairly generally known that the relations between banks and industrial firms are closer in Germany than in this country. This characteristic of German banking has already been emphasized in the Introduction to this book, and an account of its origin has been given in the preceding chapter. The purpose of the present chapter is to describe these relations in more detail, in order that vague ideas may be made precise and certain misconceptions removed. It is convenient to speak here of the relations of banks to industry, because the topics to be discussed are those commonly dealt with under the heading of 'the financing of industry'; nevertheless most of what is said will be equally applicable to the relations between banks and purely commercial firms, allowance being made for the smaller requirements of the latter in fixed capital. On the other hand, the operations of the banks in support of foreign trade, important though they were for industry, are reserved for treatment later.[1]

In the first section of this chapter, which deals with financial technique, it is possible to use the present tense very largely, because in this matter the War has not introduced much change. The second section, however, in which some of the consequences of the financial methods are considered, definitely relates to the period before the War.

[1] See chapter III.

I

From what has been said of the kinds of business performed by the creditbanks, it follows that the transactions between a bank and a particular customer undertaking may be very varied.   Generally speaking the complete relation between the two is to be regarded as an indivisible many-sided whole, rather than as a sum of separate relations.   But if this is clearly understood, it will be convenient to divide the typical relation into three main parts.

(1) *The Current Account Connexion*

The term ' current account ' may suggest to the English reader an account which can be drawn upon by cheque.   In Germany, however, the cheque account (*Scheckkonto*) is often distinct from the *Kontokorrent*, and the latter must be defined by reference to the legal peculiarities of the debtor and creditor relations with which it is associated.   According to German law, then, a current account relation exists between two parties—one at least being a trader (*Kaufmann*)— when money claims arise on both sides, and these claims are not settled individually, but are treated as items in an account of which the balance is struck periodically.   Once this balance is determined, the several debts on each side are considered to be settled, and there emerges in their place one claim and one (equal) debt.   Interest may be reckoned on both sides of the account, and the interest items are included with the other items in arriving at the final balance.[1]   The general practice of the German banks before the War was to allow interest at 1% or $1\frac{1}{2}\%$ below Bank rate when their customer was in credit and to charge

---

[1] For these and further details see Obst: *Das Bankgeschäft* (ed. 1924), i, pp. 229 *et seq.*; Leitner: *Bankbetrieb und Bankgeschäfte*, pp. 168 *et seq.*; Loehr: *Das deutsche Bankwesen*, p. 41.

interest at 1% above Bank rate (with a minimum of 5%) when he was in debit.[1] The accounting period was usually six months, but either party had the right to close the account and demand payment of a debit balance at any time.

In the ordinary current account connexion the customer sometimes owes money on the balance to the bank and sometimes has a balance to his credit. The extent to which he may be indebted to the bank, the maximum period for which the indebtedness may be outstanding and the security to be given, are fixed by agreement from time to time after a consideration of his general circumstances and the particular purposes for which he may require advances. The point of importance to be noticed here is that the average German firm has always depended to a remarkable degree upon obtaining current account advances, and that not merely to provide itself with working funds but also for the purpose of extending its permanent equipment (construction of buildings, acquisition of machinery and the like) in anticipation of recourse to the investment market.

On the opening of a current account the customer has to signify his acceptance of the General Terms (*Conditionen*) upon which the bank does business.[2] These General Terms, which are very elaborate and designed to protect the bank from all possible litigation, cover not merely the management of the current account itself but also the conditions upon which deposits are received, upon which discount, ' lombard,' guarantee and acceptance credit is given, and those on which the bank is prepared to act on behalf of its

---

[1] Interest was usually allowed or charged from day to day on the balance on one side or the other (*Staffel-Rechnung*), but other methods were also employed. See Obst: i, pp. 243 *et seq.*

[2] The signature of a regular agreement between the parties would in most States be subject to a stamp duty. To avoid this a declaration of acquaintance with the conditions imposed by the banks is substituted.

customer in various ways—such as the buying, selling, safeguarding and administering of securities, and making and receiving payments. As these various credits and services are ordinarily only given to those who have current accounts, to and from which any sums involved are passed,[1] the idea of the current account connexion (*Kontokorrentverbindung*) has been extended by common usage to include their provision. Riesser is using the term in this wider sense when he describes the bank in its current account business as 'a maid-of-all-work in the service of its customers.' (*ein Mädchen für alles im Geschäftshaushalt der Kunden.*)[2]

(2) The Promotion of Companies and their Equipment with Capital.

In Germany there are two methods by which a company (*Aktiengesellschaft* or *Kommanditgesellschaft auf Aktien*: see Appendix I.) may be promoted, namely, the *successiv* (or *Zeichnungs*) *Gründung* and the *simultan* (or *Uebernahme*) *Gründung*. In the former, which resembles the method commonly used in England, the promoters invite the public to subscribe the capital and so join with them in bringing the company into existence: in the latter the entire capital is taken over, in the first instance, by the promoters themselves. At the time of the first railway promotions, promotion by subscription was the general practice; but in later years it has been almost completely supplanted by the alternative method.

Five founders at least are legally necessary for the promotion of a company. In the case of a transformation of a private firm, the late owner will probably be

---

[1] Where a separate cheque account is kept for a customer payments made or received on his behalf will flow out of or into this. But it will be kept at the amount ordinarily required by transfers to and from the current account or 'conto ordinario.'

[2] *German Great Banks*, p. 259.

one of these; and, if it is his intention to retain the concern largely in his own hands, he may take over a large part of the new shares.   But where it is intended to place most of the shares amongst the public, the greater part of the capital is usually provided in the first place by one or more large banks or bankers— the remaining promoters possibly contributing only the minimum sum for one share each.

The general use of the ' simultaneous ' method of promotion can be explained in part at least by the rôle which the banks have played in the development of German industry.   At first, as we have seen, it was necessary for them to lead the investing public by themselves making the initial investment.   Later, as experience of industrial investment became more general, it should have become less necessary for this course to be taken; yet a reluctance to decide on parti- cipation in an undertaking before it is fully launched, and a preference for projects to which a leading bank has already committed itself, may have remained and still remain amongst investors, if only as the outcome of habit and tradition.

On this view the prevailing method of promotion is a consequence of the functions which the banks have assumed in connexion with investment.   Almost the reverse relation of cause and effect is suggested, how- ever, by Liefmann in the following passage.

' Although of course other factors have contributed, and it has also to be recognized that the legal processes of promotion have themselves been shaped by special economic circumstances, none the less it can be asserted that it is the German method of " simultaneous " promotion, in opposition to the " successive " method of English law, which has given the German banks their special character.'[1]

It may indeed be possible to reconcile these two views with the help of Liefmann's opening qualifica-

[1] *Beteiligungs- u. Finanzierungsgesellschaften*, ed. 1921, p. 476.

tions. But it seems probable that the choice between the two methods of promotion has in fact been influenced by certain legal requirements which cannot easily be derived from the economic circumstances of which we have already taken account. The requirements in question were introduced by laws passed towards the close of the last century in order to suppress various abuses in connexion with joint stock companies and bourse speculation—*Aktiennovelle* of 1884 (later reinforced in the *Handelsgesetzbuch*), *Börsengesetz* of 1896; and the most important of them are the following:

(*a*) The whole of the capital must be subscribed— and at least 25% paid up—before a company comes into existence. Resort to the method of subscription entails, therefore, a certain delay in bringing the company into being. Unless, further, the subscription is well underwritten, the project may fail because the subscription is not completed within a period which must be fixed in the prospectus.[1] The project may also fail in the case of a *successiv Gründung* through neglect of original subscribers to fulfil formalities required, or through their insufficient attendance at the opening general meeting.

(*b*) All promotion fees, etc., have to be disclosed, and reports of independent auditors in respect of the valuation of assets to be acquired by the new company have to be lodged in court.[2] Hence promoters are led to look for their profit not in what they receive from the new company itself, but in the difference between the price at which they take over the shares in the act of simultaneous promotion (which cannot be below par), and that at which they subsequently sell the shares to the public.[3]

---

[1] H.G.B. section 189.   [2] H.G.B. sections 186, 191-5.

[3] See Schuster's article in Ripley : *Trusts, Pools and Corporations*, p. 782.

(c) When a company is formed to take over an existing private business (*Umwandlung* as opposed to *Neugründung*) one business year must elapse and a Report and Balance Sheet showing that year's results be published, before its shares can be admitted to 'official' transactions on the bourses.[1] Shares which are not fully paid up are also excluded from official dealings—except in the case of insurance companies. In both cases the restriction of the market deters the general investor and favours a method of promotion which does not depend upon his immediate response.

The acquisition of large blocks of shares, even if only paid up in part, naturally calls for large resources, and the more so if, as is commonly the case with a 'conversion' transaction, the shares have to be held for some time. The use of the *simultan Gründung* means, therefore, that company promotion is the affair of the larger banks and bankers. This was largely the case already, before the passing of the new company

[1] As to the relative importance of *Umwandlungen* and *Neugründungen*, it is to be said that while in the last years of the nineteenth century they were about equal, in the years before the War the former very distinctly predominated. The following tables relating to shares of new industrial companies admitted to the Berlin Bourse in the years 1907-12, are given by Adolf Weber, *Depositenbanken u. Spekulationsbanken*, second edition, pp. 224-5.

	Conversions.	New Undertakings.
	(a) Number of promotions.	
1907 - - - -	13=72%	5=28%
1908 - - - -	12=86	2=14
1909 - - - -	32=84	6=16
1910 - - - -	22=81	5=19
1911 - - - -	14=87	2=13
1912 - - - -	29=91	3= 9
	(b) Nominal amount in million marks.	
1907 - - - -	58·8=71%	24·9=29%
1908 - - - -	83·8=85	15·0=15
1909 - - - -	100·3=85	17·1=15
1910 - - - -	123·6=87	17·5=12
1911 - - - -	78·3=86	22·5=14
1912 - - - -	96·7=78	26·7=22

and bourse acts: none the less this legislation can be held to have influenced the situation, in the sense that it provided new reasons for the intervention of the banks at a time when the original reasons were losing some of their force.

With the establishment of a new company and the acquisition of a greater or less portion of its capital, only the first step is completed so far as the promoting bank is concerned.   For the satisfactory termination of the whole transaction, the shares taken over at the time of promotion have to be placed amongst the investing public.   The *Gründungsgeschäft*, that is, is normally followed by an *Emissionsgeschäft*.

Here the bank may proceed in several ways:

(*a*) The shares may be offered for public subscription at a fixed price.[1]   This is a method by which large quantities of shares may be placed very quickly. If the issue is oversubscribed, the bank will be able in making allotment to give a preference to those who appear to be genuine investors and who are willing to undertake not to resell within a certain period. Usually the admission of the shares to ' official ' bourse transactions is obtained before they are offered for subscription, or a promise that this is to be sought is given in the prospectus.

(*b*) A second method is to obtain admission of the shares to one or more of the bourses without inviting subscription. The bourse authorities (*Zulassungsstelle*) have to be informed of the price at which the shares are to be offered at the time of introduction (*Einführung*) and the nominal amount so offered.   In the latter respect certain minimum quantities are fixed—before the War, 1,000,000 marks at Berlin, Frankfurt and Hamburg, 500,000 marks elsewhere; but in reality the initial supply is always elastic within the stated

---

[1] This subscription *after* promotion must not be confused with subscription *as part of* promotion.

amount, since the issuing house can always buy in again through agents. The gradual unloading of shares on the bourses, which is therefore possible by this method, gives it an advantage in some cases over the first method with its large sales at one time and price. This second method is also favoured where the amount of shares to be issued would not justify the public invitation of subscriptions.[1] But it may break down if the demand is great in relation to the supply, for in that case it may be impossible to bring about an initial price which is not higher than a responsible issuing house cares to accept.

(c) A third method of placing shares is by direct sale to customers or to banking firms with which the issuing bank stands on friendly relations ('*freihändige Verkauf,*' '*Aktien unten den Hand gebracht*'). This method is commonly used to supplement the two already described, sometimes as part of the original plan—part of the issue being earmarked for disposal in this way—sometimes because the original plan has not met with complete success. But shares may also be offered for sale without being introduced to a bourse and without there being any public subscription. In this way considerable expenses are saved and this is a determining consideration where the issue is very small and where an official quotation would be of little or no advantage—e.g. shares of Hypotheken-banken find a ready market amongst small investors without it. But in other cases the failure to seek admission to the bourse is apt to be attributed to an unwholesome desire to avoid the scrutiny of the *Zulassungsstelle*. The method of direct sale, it should be added, gives the bank most opportunity to ensure that the shares are placed permanently.

---

[1] It may be mentioned that introduction to a leading bourse at a good price is sometimes desired to ensure future saleability rather than as a means of effecting immediate sales.

The *Gründungsgeschäft*, as has been said, is normally followed by an *Emissionsgeschäft*, which forms with it a complete transaction.   But this is not to say, of course, that every *Emissionsgeschäft* is in this way linked to a *Gründungsgeschäft*.   New securities come into being in connexion with increases in the capital of existing companies and with loans to companies and public authorities; and these also are issued by the banks in the ways above described.   Occasionally the issuing bank acts merely as an agent receiving commission for its mediation; but the practice of taking over the securities at a fixed price and selling them, if possible, at a profit is much more general.[1]

In order to reduce the risk borne by a single bank and to create a wide interest in the success of an issue, it is very common for several banks (or bankers) to make themselves responsible for the issue collectively. For the purpose they come together in a loose, elastic association, called a *Konsortium*.   Where the securities to be issued result from a promotion, it is natural to find that the members of this association (the *Konsorten*) and the promoters are identical, but this is not always the case—a bank which took no part in the promotion, for instance, may at a later stage take up an interest in the emission.   To return to the working of the *Konsortium*, the details vary from case to case, but the following arrangement may be taken as typical. Each member pledges itself to accept a certain portion of the issue and to make payments in respect of it as required.[2]   One bank is chosen as director (*Leiter*) of

---

[1] An *Aktiengesellschaft* can only give out bearer obligations (*Inhaber-Schuldverschreibungen*) with the consent of the State government. This restriction is evaded, however, by the issue of *kaufmännische Verpflichtungs-scheine* in the name of a bank ' or order.' This is a further circumstance necessitating recourse to a bank when fresh capital is required. See Loehr : *Das Deutsche Bankwesen*, p. 125.

[2] In addition to the *Konsorten* proper there may be *Unterbeteiligten*, that is, firms which come to an arrangement with a member to share its portion

the common transaction, guided, if the *Konsortium* is a large one, by a small committee. For fear some of the members should act contrary to the general plan, the securities are not divided amongst them, but remain until definite sale in the hands of the managing bank (*Leiter*), which is thus constituted a central selling agency to which the *Konsorten* pass their orders. This bank also intervenes to regulate the price of older securities of the same origin, keeps the common accounts, and calls upon the members as necessary for contributions. On the termination of the *Konsortium*, the total profit or loss and any remaining securities are shared between the members in proportion to the participation which they have accepted in the issue. The *Konsortium* is generally formed for a certain period, but may be liquidated before this or renewed for a further term. Some *Konsortien* [1] are more or less permanent in the sense that one finds just the same banks associated time after time for transactions in certain securities—e.g. the *Konsortium* for Prussian loans, the Far East Syndicate, the group of banks acting for the Löwe Companies. So general is the use of *Konsortien* in transactions of any importance that it has become customary to speak of any transaction involving the taking over of securities for the purpose of emission as a *Konsortialgeschäft*, without it being ascertained that in the particular case a *Konsortium* really exists.

Contrary to what is often thought in this country, lasting participation in other enterprises has not been part of the general policy of the German creditbanks, at any rate in their modern period. Beyond finding a safe and liquid investment for part of their own

in much the same way as that in which the members share in the whole. These *Unterbeteiligten* must observe the general directions governing the *Konsorten* in respect of the issue transactions, must not undersell for instance, but otherwise they treat with a particular member not with the *Konsortium* as a whole.

[1] Plural of *Konsortium*.

resources in first class securities, the functions which they seek to perform in the investment market are those of middle-men. These functions involve holding securities for a certain length of time; and when an issue proves unsuccessful, or securities have to be bought back from the market in order to maintain their price, this period may be extended almost indefinitely.[1] But the participation which results in these latter cases may be regarded as involuntary and incidental.

In qualification of this statement, the banks have commonly participated as a matter of policy in other banks, in trustee companies (*Treuhandgesellschaften*) and in certain financial companies. The last named have mostly been either foreign companies, such as the *General Mining Company* of London and South Africa, or companies formed in conjunction with large industrial groups, like the *A.E.G.*, for the special purposes of those groups; the relations between the banks and both classes of company will be discussed again later.[2] Deliberate industrial participations of a more or less permanent character also occurred in a number of special cases, of which the most interesting perhaps was the ownership of the *Internationale Bohrgesellschaft* of Erkelenz by the Schaaffhausen'scher Bankverein. The *Bohrgesellschaft* was originally a company which undertook to drill for minerals on a commission basis, and was of use as such to the Bankverein in proving projects in which it was interested. Later it developed into an undertaking which prospected on its own initiative, acquired mineral leases, and sold these leases to companies formed for their exploitation by the Bankverein. Finally it became to a large extent a financial company itself. In all its stages it was used

---

[1] Examples : Deutsche Bank and shares of *Deutsch-Osterreich Mannesmann Rohrwerke* : Discontogesellschaft and those of *Dortmunder Union* and *Compagnie Parisienne de l'air comprimé.*

[2] Section 2 of this Chapter and Chapter III, pp. 101-102.

by the bank to increase its own connexions and influence in various departments of mining, outside Germany as well as within.   Somewhat similar were the participations of the Dresdner Bank and Berliner Handelsgesellschaft respectively in the *Elektrizitätsgesellschaft Lahmeyer* and the railway construction firm *Lenz & Co.*[1]   Lastly, it must be mentioned that a bank has often acquired a controlling interest in an industrial undertaking temporarily, in order to influence its policy at a particular juncture.   Generalizing for all these exceptions, however, it may be said that the object of deliberate participation has been to extend the bank's influence or acquire new connexions, but never to enlarge bank dividends by industrial profits.

Two other kinds of transaction which change the legal basis upon which undertakings work may be referred to here, namely, Fusions and Reconstructions. Both are frequently combined with recourse to the investment market; and for carrying through both the assistance of banks is commonly sought—if indeed the initiative does not come from that quarter.

(3) *Representation on Boards of Supervisors.*

The German Joint Stock Company (*Aktiengesellschaft*) has three governing organs: the Executive (*Vorstand*), the Board of Supervisors (*Aufsichtrat*), and the General Meeting of Shareholders (*Generalversammlung*).   In principle the relation between the three is that suggested by their names: the General Meeting is the legislative body and theoretically the ultimate authority within the limits set by the law and the Company's own articles; the Executive is charged with the current management of the Company's affairs; and the Board of Supervisors comes in between to keep

---

[1] Liefmann, *op. cit.* 1913 ed. p. 53.

a check on the Executive in the interest of the shareholders. The general duty of the Board of Supervisors, as defined in Section 246 of the *Handelsgesetzbuch*, is as follows: ' The Board has to watch over the
conduct of the Company's business in all its branches,
and for this purpose to keep itself informed of the
Company's affairs. It has to examine the yearly
balance sheet and any proposals brought before the
General Meeting, and to report thereon.' Beyond
the right to summon special General Meetings, the
law gives the Supervisors few powers of direct intervention in the Company's affairs; but more extensive
powers may be conferred upon them by the Company's articles. In fact the tendency has been to
require the concurrence of the Board of Supervisors
in the decisions of the Executive in an increasing number of matters, and thus to increase the
importance of the former at the expense of that of
the latter.

The banks commonly obtain representation through
the person of their own directors (sometimes through
Prokuristen or officials having powers to act for their
bank) on the supervisory boards of companies which
are their customers. By this means they seek to
strengthen their connexion with the undertakings in
question, and to gain more influence on their policy
and more insight into its execution. Incidentally they
are sometimes able to extend their connexions also in
this way, through the personal relations formed by
their representatives with other business men on the
boards. When representation is not ceded willingly,
the banks have not infrequently shown themselves able
to extort it by means of their financial power.

The table on p. 50, based on data in Riesser's work,[1]
shows the number of *Aufsichtratsstellen* occupied by
representatives of the six leading Berlin banks in 1911,

[1] *Die deutschen Grossbanken*, 4th edition, 1912, pp. 651-672.

classified broadly according to branches of industry. In elucidation it should be said that a bank has sometimes more than one representative on the Board of one company; and that commerce here includes banking.

REPRESENTATION OF THE BANKS ON INDUSTRIAL BOARDS OF SUPERVISORS, 1911

Branch of Business.	Deutsche Bank.	Dis-conto-gesell-schaft.	Dresdner Bank.	Darm-städter Bank.	Berliner Handels-gesell-schaft.	Schaaff-hausen Bank-verein.
Mining and Smelting -	17	22	13	11	26	25
Stone and Earth products	4	2	4	3	2	4
Metal-working - -	5	6	4	2	12	12
Machine and Instrument making - - -	15	10	6	9	6	18
Chemicals - - -	3	4	2	4	2	5
Oil and Fat products -	3	8	—	4	3	2
Textiles - - -	8	5	5	6	6	4
Paper - - - -	1	—	4	1	—	2
Rubber - - -	1	2	—	—	—	—
Food, Drink and Tobacco	3	1	3	11	5	2
Building - - -	1	—	3	—	—	5
Artistic products - -	2	—	—	—	—	—
Commerce and Finance -	32	38	25	16	10	28
Insurance - - -	7	6	3	6	1	5
Transport - - -	9	19	14	16	14	22
Foreign Companies -	24	10	12	14	16	6
Hotels and Restaurants -	—	—	1	—	—	—
Wood and Wood products	—	—	—	1	—	—
Plantation Companies -	—	—	—	—	—	—
Electricity - - -	15	7	8	11	12	4
Land Development Companies - - -	9	3	13	17	8	4
	159	143	120	132	123	148

Attendance to the affairs of the companies of which they are Supervisors must occupy much of the time of the banks' delegates. Usually certain of the directors of a bank specialize in this work. This leaves the others free, but means that a small number of directors have between them to keep watch over a large and diverse collection of companies. There is force, therefore, in the criticism that the bank members of the industrial Boards are unable to give as much time as might be desirable to studying the interests of the shareholders whom they are supposed to protect. Much can indeed be said from this point of view against the whole system of exchanging representatives, which has now become so common. On behalf of the representation of the banks it can at least be claimed, however, that the bank directors have a special contribution to make to the councils of other undertakings as a result of their general experience in finance.

As companies, the banks themselves have Boards of Supervisors, and on these are to be found not only representatives of associated banks, but also important leaders of commerce and industry. Usually the latter are invited by the banks to take up these positions in order that their interest may be won or relations further cemented. Just as the banks sometimes obtain these positions by force, however, so too—but much more rarely—the industrialists are able to intrude themselves on the Boards of banks. Speaking of the period before the War, this seems only to have happened in the case of small local banks.

The exchange of these representatives is an important link between the banks and industry, but it is somewhat inaccurate to describe it as an ' interlocking of directorates.' As has been shown, the functions of the *Aufsichtrat* are not those of an English Board of Directors, although in practice they may tend to approximate to the latter to a much greater extent than was intended when the organ was first created. Particularly misleading results are obtained when the industrialists sitting on bank *Aufsichträte* are regarded as bank directors and then all their connexions represented as ramifications of the banks' interests.[1]

---

[1] For an example of this mistake, see the U.S. *Report on Co-operation in the Export Trade*, I, p. 62 ; II, pp. 519 *et seq.*

The close relation between the German banks and industry is summarized by Dr. Jeidels with the statement that 'the banks attend an industrial undertaking from its birth to its death, from promotion to liquidation, they stand by its side whilst it passes through the financial processes of economic life, whether usual or unusual, helping it and at the same time profiting from it.'[1]　But the connexion has its beginnings as a rule not in an act of promotion, but in a current account relation.　As this develops the bond will probably be tightened by *Aufsichtrat* representations, and, as occasion arises, capital transactions—conversion into a company, raising of fresh capital, issues of bonds, reconstructions, etc.—will be undertaken by the bank on behalf of its customer.　At this stage still, however, the current account relation retains its primary importance.　In the first place, as a continuous relation and one which gives the bank an insight into most of the customer's money transactions, it provides much of the data required for estimating the risk involved in the intermittent capital transactions.　This, at any rate, is the case if each customer deals exclusively with one bank, as is insisted upon by the banks so far as is within their power.　Again current account transactions lead up to capital transactions even more directly, in the sense that improvements and extensions of plant, etc., are often undertaken by means of current account credit which is to be repaid later with the proceeds of a capital issue.　To quote Jeidels once more: 'The industrial current account is the *pivot* of all transactions between bank and industry; promotion and issue transactions, direct participation in industrial undertakings, and co-operation in management through Boards of Supervisors, these stand in very many cases in a close causal sequence with bank credit.'[2]

[1] *Das Verhältnis der deutschen Grossbanken zur Industrie*, p. 50.
[2] *Op. cit.* p. 33.

II

The foregoing outline of the technique of industrial banking in Germany reveals many opportunities for the banks to exercise influence on the policy of their industrial clients.   Some of these require that the bank should go out of its way to secure control, but others arise in the course of normal credit relations.   Thus, under the latter head, there are occasional opportunities of intervention when the assistance of the bank is sought for capital transactions, and more frequently there is the possibility of exerting pressure through the power to recall credit already granted and to refuse further credit.   The latter possibility is of sufficient importance to be illustrated by an extract from a letter sent by a bank to a firm which ventured to adopt a policy of which the bank disapproved.   As quoted by Jeidels,[1] the Dresdner Bank wrote to the Executive of the North West German Cement Syndicate under the date November 19th, 1900.

' According to the notice published by your Company in the *Reichsanzeiger* of the 18th, we have to reckon with the possibility that decisions will be taken at the General Meeting to be held on the 30th which are likely to introduce changes in the scope of your business of a kind not agreeable to us.   On this ground we are regretfully obliged herewith to withdraw the credit granted to you;   accordingly we ask you to make no further drafts on us and at the same time politely request that you will repay the balance due to us, at the latest by the end of the month.   Should, however, no decisions of this kind be taken at the General Meeting in question and safeguards be offered us in this respect for the future, we declare ourselves very ready to enter negotiations with you with a view to the granting of a new credit.'

That the banks should be able to exercise some influence on their customers through their power to grant or withhold credit is not, of course, peculiar to

[1] *Op. cit.* p. 126.

Germany, and is, further, to some extent necessary for the safeguarding of the banks' private interests. But the great dependence of German industrial undertakings upon bank credit gave the banks exceptional powers which they did not use exclusively for the purpose of protecting themselves from losses.

As an exceptional measure for obtaining control of a particular industrial concern, mention has been made of the acquisition of large shareholdings, whether temporarily or permanently. Here it should be added that considerable voting rights at a shareholders' meeting are often to be obtained in less expensive ways. Frequently, for instance, the investors amongst a bank's customers are willing to leave their voting rights, by proxy, at the bank's disposal—this being especially likely to happen when the shares are left with the bank for safe keeping or as pledges for loans. Moreover, in many cases where shares are purchased with bank credit they are not transferred to the customer's name until the credit is repaid; in such cases, and also when shares are taken in (on contango) from one stock exchange settlement to the next, the bank enjoys the voting rights for the time being. Again shares may be borrowed from friendly banks and bankers for the period round about a particular General Meeting.

Finally there is the direct influence of the bank delegates on industrial Boards of Supervisors. Much is made of this by foreign observers; reflection suggests, however, that the representation of banks on these boards is important not so much as an independent source of power as a means by which their other powers are rendered more effective.

Once a bank has obtained influence over a particular undertaking in one or other of these ways, the power to affect the distribution of its orders gives the bank a lever in dealing with other industrial concerns.

The position before the War, then, was that the ordinary industrial (or commercial) firm of moderate means found its freedom of action to a great extent conditioned by the good will of its bank, even when in a sound and fairly prosperous state.   If it happened to fall upon bad times, it was likely to lose this freedom entirely and be compelled to accept any scheme of reconstruction or fusion which the bank might choose to dictate.

In relation to the greater industrial undertakings and industrial groups (*Konzerne*), however, the influence of the banks was very much less.   Here the financial resources of the industrialists were larger, both absolutely and in relation to their needs; often they competed less amongst themselves than did the banks; whilst the very magnitude of their undertakings caused the banks to shirk the responsibility which would be involved in a high degree of control.   In the generation immediately preceding the War, moreover, leaders of outstanding ability were more often found in the ranks of the industrialists than in those of the bankers.

The financial strength of these larger industrial concerns showed itself, in the first place, in a comparatively small degree of dependence upon bank loans—indeed they were more often creditors than debtors of the banks.[1]   This is to be explained in turn, partly by the fact that they were better endowed than smaller undertakings with capital of their own, but also in some measure by the stringent terms of payment which they were able to impose on their customers.[2]   Their strength was also seen in the strong market for their shares and debentures, for the placing of which

[1] This was especially true of the great chemical concerns—Hoechst, Casselda, Badische Anilin u. Sodafabrik, see Schulze-Gaevernitz *Die Deutsche Kreditbank*, p. 155.

[2] This point applies particularly to the well-organized coal and iron industries.

they could often pick and choose between rival mediators.

In certain cases these industrialists were able at once to demonstrate and increase their independence by maintaining direct and regular relations with a number of banks—and even with several Grossbanken.   For the illustration of this point, we may quote the following paragraph from Adolf Weber's work:

'For years the Phoenix Mining & Smelting Co. (*A. G. für Bergbau u. Hüttenbetrieb*) dealt exclusively with the Schaaffhausen'scher Bank, now it has connexions also with the Discontogesellschaft, the Darmstädter Bank, the Deutsche Bank, the Dresdner Bank, and the Nationalbank.   Until 1905 the Gelsenkirchen Mining Co. (*Bergwerkgesellschaft*) was in touch with the Discontogesellschaft alone; since then the Dresdner, Deutsche and Schaaffhausen Banks have entered into relations with it.   The German-Luxemburg Mining & Smelting Co. (*Deutsche-Luxemburgische Bergwerks & Hütten A. G.*) is now attended by all four D-Banks (the Deutsche Bank having joined the circle quite recently), and the Rheinische Bank, the Schaaffhausen Bank and the Nationalbank as well;   ten years ago the Darmstädter Bank was the only banking connexion of this undertaking.   The small sewing machine factory founded by Ludwig Loewe in 1869 was supported by the private bankers, Born & Busse;   to-day the Loewe group of banks comprises the Discontogesellschaft, the Dresdner Bank, the Schaaffhausen Bank, the Darmstädter Bank, Bleichröder, and the Nationalbank—which has absorbed Born and Busse.'[1]

This division of the business of an industrial concern between several banks was brought about in several ways.   Sometimes it was the result of a fusion between firms having different banking connexions; sometimes of competition between the banks for a valuable connexion; and sometimes of a desire on the part of the banks to limit their individual risks in respect of a particular concern.   However brought about, the

[1] *Depositenbanken u. Spekulationsbanken*, ed. 1915, pp. 108-9 ; ed. 1922, pp. 127-8.

resulting position was one in which the banks usually found their influence diminished.

Motives of prudence appear also to have determined the attitude of the banks towards another innovation which appeared in German industrial finance in the first decade of the present century, namely the establishment by certain large industrial undertakings of their own financial companies.

This development occurred chiefly in the case of the great electrical concerns (A.E.G., Siemens, Loewe, etc.), but also in the case of certain companies engaged in the construction of light railways (Lenz, Bächstein). The characteristic of both classes of undertaking is that they depend for their activity upon new constructional or development work which requires considerable enterprise for its initiation. This enterprise not always being forthcoming from independent quarters on the scale required to keep the engineering concerns fully occupied, the latter were tempted to supply it themselves by promoting electricity supply or railway undertakings to be their own customers. The risks attending this course were reduced by the fact that public utility undertakings of these kinds usually enjoyed more or less monopolistic concessions. But on the other hand such undertakings could not be expected to reach their normal earning capacity for some time, even after the completion of their works. Hence these flotations involved difficult problems of finance, to solve which the new financial companies were formed.

The precise functions assumed by these financial companies varied from case to case, a concern like the A.E.G. having a number of such subsidiaries and using one more for one purpose, another more for another purpose, without, however, sharply delimiting the sphere of any of them. Some were concerned mainly with promotion transactions, some more with participation in already existing undertakings; again some were concerned chiefly with temporary participations and looked to sell their shareholdings as the undertakings in question developed, whilst others participated more permanently as holding or investment companies. The methods by which the financial companies themselves obtained their capital varied correspondingly, but the typical method was by the sale of debentures. In addition to their principal functions in connexion with promotion and investment, they also engaged to a certain extent in short term banking. In particular they kept current accounts for the companies belonging to their group and made advances on their shares.[1]

The initiative in this development came mainly from industry, but it received the support of the great banks. The latter agreed to a departure in these cases from the practice by which they themselves were responsible for the flotation of new undertakings, because to have adhered to that practice would have meant an excessive immobilization of their own resources and the danger of binding their fate to that of a particular industrial group.[2] It only remained, then, for them to assist the industrialists to solve their problem in their own way. By participating in the new financial companies the banks retained some of their influence; and by acting in co-operation with them in issue transactions, they retained a share in the business of the groups; but in both respects they lost a great deal. As Liefmann says:

' It is not to be supposed that the formation of such financial companies will increase the influence of the banks on industry,

---

[1] For full account of these financial companies see Liefmann's great work : *Beteiligungs- u. Finanzierungsgesellschaften.*

[2] These dangers are well illustrated in the failure of the Dresdner Kreditanstalt which had allowed itself to become unduly involved in financing the projects of the Kummer Electrical Group. See Chapter V.

but rather the contrary.   In opposition to a widely held opinion,
I have always disputed that one could speak of a growing influence of the banks on German industry as a general pheno-
menon, and anyone who has closely studied the history of the
investment banks in the period from 1850-1870, must agree
with me.   The development of the financial companies seems
to me now to be a further circumstance which tends in the
opposite direction of a greater independence of industry in
relation to the banks.   In the financial companies more or less
neutral institutions are created, which stand between both
parties, and render industrial undertakings more independent of
the banks in precisely that sphere in which heretofore they were
most dependent on them—in the raising of capital for permanent
investment.'[1]

Here Liefmann is speaking of a possible development
by which the banks would delegate the business of
promotion in general to more or less independent
financial companies; but what he says seems to apply
to the actual development so far as it went.

It has been remarked that in many branches industry had advanced further than banking towards the
regulation or suspension of competition.   In itself this
is a circumstance which may be regarded as having
increased the strength of industry *vis à vis* the banks.
The promotion of the industrial cartels and combines,
however, has not infrequently been represented as the
work of the banks and the crowning example of their
influence.   To complete this section it is necessary to
inquire how far this is true.

A bank doing business with a number of similar
industrial undertakings might be expected to encourage them to co-operate rather than to engage in
wasteful competition; and it is sufficiently certain that
many fusions and working agreements which were
desirable on technical grounds were promoted in this
way.   But it is another matter to say that schemes of
monopolistic combination were initiated from the side

---

[1] *Op. cit.* ed. 1921, p. 491.

of the banks. For this to appear likely it would be necessary to show either that all (or nearly all) the firms in a particular industry had one and the same banking connexion; or, failing this, that at the time the different banks were more ready to act in concert than the competing industrialists.

Since there were eight or nine great banks, besides several important provincial banks, the former hypothesis would imply that the banks specialized to a high degree with regard to the branches of industry to which they devoted attention. Now it is certainly true that these banks were not all equally interested in all industries; each had a field or fields in which its footing was peculiarly strong. Thus the coal and iron industries were especially important for the Schaaffhausen'scher Bankverein; the electrical industry for the Berliner Handelsgesellschaft and also for the Deutsche Bank; transportation undertakings for the Discontogesellschaft (which worked here first in conjunction with, later as successor to, M. A. Rothschild & Söhne); and the brewing industry for the Mitteldeutsche Creditbank and Darmstädter Bank. Similarly the Dresdner Bank was particularly strong in its connexions with the chemical industry and with the textile industries of Saxony; whilst the absorption of the Breslauer Diskontobank gave the Darmstädter Bank an exceptional position in relation to Silesian industries. But this differentiation, discernible in the business of even the largest banks (it was of course more marked in the case of the provincial banks) was a legacy from the first stage of their history, when their connexions were necessarily local, or an indication that their programme of expansion was but very incompletely carried out; the whole trend of their policy in their modern period has been in the opposite direction. Just as they sought to avoid too extensive commitments with respect to particular industrial concerns, so they aimed at a distribution of risks between industries. Largely for this reason they opened branches in new regions and entered into friendly relations with other banks which differed from themselves in the composition of their industrial connexions.[1] And in certain cases the penetration of new industrial fields was effected by more direct advances to particular undertakings—this most noticeably in the case of the coal and iron industries.

This expansion of the great banks *across industrial frontiers* was by no means completed at the time when the chief *Kartelle* were formed, but it had already proceeded far enough to leave the hypothesis we are examining very little application. A project for the formation of a cartel had usually to deal with undertakings having relations with different banks; and these banks had connexions in other industries, the interests of which might be adversely affected by the success of the project.

Again the efforts of the banks to diversify their industrial connexions aggravated the competition between them, thus invalidating also the second

[1] The latter point is well illustrated in the 'community of interests' established between the Schaaffhausen'scher Bankverein and the Dresdner Bank in 1903. The complementary character of the connexions of these two banks is clearly shown by the following table of their representation on *Aufsichträte* :

	Coal.	Iron Works (possibly combined with Coal).	Transport.	Textile.	Food.
Dresdner - -	6	12	47	25	36
Schaaffhausen -	55	38	19	12	19

It is true that the arrangement was dissolved in 1907. But this in no way diminishes the force of our argument. For after this date the Dresdner extended its contacts with the heavy industries of the West by other means ; while the highly localized Schaaffhausen'scher Bankverein lost its independence to the Discontogesellschaft in 1914.

hypothesis above.   In the coal and iron industries particularly the intrusion first of the Deutsche Bank and then of the Dresdner made this competition especially acute just when these industries were in the throes of re-organization.   Such co-operation as was to be found in the industrial policy of the banks would appear to be far more the result than the cause of progress in industrial combination.

It is mistaken then to ascribe the initiative in the industrial combination movement to the banks, at any rate as a general rule.   Rather as Jeidels says: ' The banks had first to let the industrial development take its own course; the process of concentration had first to create a situation in which the interests of their industrial customers were so clear that the banks were thenceforward both in a position and under a compulsion to formulate a definite policy in relation to it.' [1] But this does not mean that the banks had no part at all in the development.   At a very early stage they helped to prepare the way by encouraging fusions between individual undertakings and so reducing the number of competitors. Throughout their attitude was sympathetic, even while it remained passive.   Finally, once the plans for combination had reached a certain stage and were within measurable distance of fruition, the banks gave active support to ensure their success.

The last point may be illustrated by two of the more striking cases in which the banks intervened on the side of the cartels.   The first concerns the coercion of the *Phoenix Iron Co.* to join the Steel Works Association.   The transaction and its attendant circumstances are described by Jeidels as follows:

' When at the beginning of 1904 the Steel Works Association was to be set up as an organization embracing all branches of German steel production in place of the loose " Half

[1] *Op. cit.* p. 256.

finished products " association, the Phoenix (Co.) of Laar was opposed to joining, on grounds which can only be briefly indicated here : up to this time Phoenix produced comparatively little crude steel (half finished product), but had an extraordinarily varied production of rolled or finished products at its works in Laar, Erschweiler, Hamm, Lippstadt, Nachrodt and Beleche, chiefly of tram lines, plates and wire, the greater part of which it exported. In 1898 it had added to its plant for the production of these finished goods by the purchase of the works of the Westphalian Union with the express object of making most of the raw material (i.e. crude steel) for these products at Laar for itself. Since the execution of such plans, involving the construction of heavy plant, naturally proceeded slowly, at the time of the inception of the Steel Works Association, only the blast furnaces were ready, although the construction of the steel making plants was actively in hand. For the time Phoenix was the largest purchaser of crude steel in the world, and had therefore altogether different interests from those of an association which aimed at raising crude steel prices and which further would not wish to see its control over production threatened by a works taking to the production of its own raw material. In addition Phoenix had no interest whatever in the regulation of exports and the rationing of contracts which this involved, since it possessed old and firmly established connexions abroad. By entering the Association it would have to abandon once and for all plans, developed at great expense and with far-seeing view, already partly in operation, which would have made Phoenix the greatest iron works in Germany. But the absence of Phoenix would have made seriously questionable the possibility of an association in the formation of which not only the other smelting works but also the banks were interested. On the Board of Supervisors of the Phoenix Co. were represented, amongst others, Sal Oppenheim, Jnr., a Cologne banking firm in close contact with the Discontogesellschaft, the latter itself, the Schaaffhausen'scher Bankverein and the Darmstädter Bank. An extraordinary General Meeting was called, the Schaaffhausen'scher Bankverein, which had most interest in the matter, obtained a majority of the shares, and adhesion to the Association was voted against the most forcible arguments of the directors. From the point of view of the Association an immediate decision was of greatest importance, in view of the difficulty of the negotiations. A six months' delay until the ordinary General Meeting had to be avoided at all costs.' [1]

In the other case, which occurred about the same time, a number of banks used their combined financial strength to thwart an attempt of the Prussian Government to curb the power of the Rhenish Westphalian Coal Syndicate. To this end the Government had decided to acquire control of the important colliery undertaking, the *Hibernia Mining Co.*, and had commissioned the Dresdner Bank to purchase all Hibernia shares on the market on its behalf. On hearing of this plan, the Syndicate induced the three other D-banks, the Berliner Handelsgesellschaft and S. Bleichröder to take concerted action to forestall the Dresdner. The Syndicate's group succeeded in obtaining a majority of the shares, to hold which a special company, the Herne G.m.b.H. was formed; and the miscarriage of this plan discouraged the Government from again attempting this kind of intervention.

With regard to the question of leadership, it is always difficult to know how much is to be ascribed to personality and how much to circumstances. But it does seem significant that whereas in the period from 1850 to 1880, or thereabouts, the most outstanding men in business life were bankers—Hansemann, Mevissen—in the following years they were industrialists—Rathenau, Kirdorf. In part at least this may be explained by the fact that the banks, having played their pioneer rôle, were now becoming more stereotyped in their business, and thus offered fewer opportunities to men of initiative.

If on the whole there was a tendency before the War for the larger industrialists to become less dependent on the banks and to exercise greater initiative in their

[1] *Op. cit.* pp. 147-8.

own sphere, it cannot be said that there was any danger of the banks falling under industrial tutelage.   A few local banks were, it is true, dominated and perhaps owned by the big industrial concern of the neighbour-hood.[1]   But mostly the smaller banks escaped this servitude by becoming dependent on the big Berlin banks.   The latter, with their varied interests, large resources, and carefully placed share capital, were well able to guard their own independence.[2]

[1] The relations of Thyssen to the Rheinische Bank, Mulheim, and of Stinnes to the Mittelrheinische Bank, Coblenz, may be instanced.   Riesser : *German Great Banks*, p. 745.

[2] One case only is mentioned of the intervention of an industrialist in the affairs of the great banks.   Hugo Stinnes is said to have had a hand in bringing about the Dresdner-Schaaffhausen *Interessengemeinschaft*.   But, as we have already seen, important considerations of banking policy also favoured this arrangement : we have here, therefore, at the most but a partial exception to our general rule.

CHAPTER III

THE BANKS AND FOREIGN TRADE

I

THE industrial progress of Germany was very largely conditioned by the place which she could obtain in the world's markets. It has already been shown that to assist in the development of Germany's economic relations with other countries was one of the foremost objects of the creditbanks in the period after 1870. The purpose of the present chapter is to give a fuller account of their activities in this direction.

From the first it was realized that, in order to play an important part in furthering foreign trade relations, it was necessary to have better representation abroad than could be obtained by the appointment of foreign correspondents. The first task undertaken by the creditbanks was, therefore, to secure such representation, in some cases by the extension of their own organization to foreign places, in some cases by forming close relationships with foreign banking firms, and in some cases by the intermediate course of establishing affiliated foreign banks. The particular method adopted depended upon the character of the foreign place or region and the precise objects which the representation was intended to serve.

In the case of foreign financial centres, to which attention was first directed, the earliest method pursued was that of entering into ' sleeping ' or ' commandit ' partnerships with private bankers there established. Thus in its very earliest years the Darmstädter Bank acquired interests of this kind in banking firms in Paris and New York (1856) and in Vienna (1857). By this means a closer bond was formed than that which joins two correspondents; at the same time the risks were definitely limited, and there was no need to enter into competition abroad with existing institutions. The method was, therefore, eminently suited to the first tentative stage of German banking, and was resorted to later here and there. But its efficacy was limited by the fact that the management of the *Kommandit* (or firm in which the German bank participated) remained, and from the nature of the arrangement had to remain, in the hands of foreign partners, who were hardly likely to make the cultivation of German interests their first object, and who sometimes hazarded the German capital in speculations of their own. It was a further disadvantage that connexions of this kind could as a rule only be formed with firms of rather minor importance. Accordingly, when more ambitious plans came to be entertained after 1870, preference was given to other methods.

In London, because of its especial importance in international finance, three of the leading German banks opened branches: the Deutsche Bank in 1872, and the Dresdner Bank and Discontogesellschaft rather later, in 1895 and 1899 respectively.[1] Two other German banks obtained representation in London less directly, the Commerz- u. Discontobank by participation in the *London and Hanseatic Bank* from its

---

[1] ' Commandit partnerships,' it should be said, were in any case out of the question for legal reasons here. There was also some difficulty at first in obtaining permission to have branches in London, and in 1871 the Deutsche Bank resorted to another means of obtaining representation, i.e. the promotion of an English subsidiary, the German Bank of London, Ltd. Its shares in this company were sold in 1879.

establishment in 1872, and the Darmstädter Bank by a 'community of interest' arrangement with the *Bankers' Trading Syndicate* (allied to Japhet & Co.) from 1899 to 1909.

The method here adopted by the Commerz- u. Discontobank, namely, the promotion of a bank registered under foreign law in which a considerable shareholding was retained, was the one most usually employed in order to obtain a foothold in the money markets of neighbouring countries. Thus the Darmstädter Bank established the *Amsterdamsche Bank* in 1871 and the *Bank u. Wechselstube A.G. Merkur* Vienna, in 1903; the Discontogesellschaft the *Banque Internationale de Bruxelles* in 1898 (acting with certain Austrian and Swiss banks) and the *Compagnie commerciale Belge, anciennement H. Albert de Bary & Cie*, Antwerp, in 1900.[1] Perhaps in the same class may be placed the participation of the Dresdner Bank in the *Banque J. Allard & Cie*, Paris, although this began not with the establishment of the latter, but on the occasion of an increase in its capital in 1909.[2] However, the opening of branches in Brussels and Antwerp in 1910 by the Deutsche Bank and Discontogesellschaft respectively—not to mention the somewhat different case of the erection of a branch of the Deutsche in Constantinople in 1908—may be regarded as indication that the German banks were inclined to change their policy in this connexion just before the War.

As an alternative to the 'commandit partnership' as a means of obtaining a contact with centres which afforded little scope for new institutions, the more elastic form of a 'community of interest' was favoured in later years. An agreement was drawn up which

---

[1] H. A. de Bary was previously a *Kommandit* of the Discontogesellschaft. Strasser : *Die deutschen Banken im Ausland,* pp. 63-64.

[2] Further capital holding acquired in 1912. Strasser, p. 65.

provided for the co-operation of the German bank and the foreign institution in certain matters of common interest; but apart from these each retained full freedom of action, and as a rule there was no participation of either side. This arrangement was especially characteristic of the banking connexions between Berlin and New York: *Discontogesellschaft—Kuhn, Loeb & Co.*; *Deutsche Bank—Speyer & Co.*;[1] *Dresdner Bank—J. P. Morgan & Co.* Somewhat similar relations appear to have existed between German banks and some of the Swiss banks—particularly the *Schweizerische Kreditanstalt* and the *Schweizerischer Bankverein*.[2] The similarity consisted in the fact that the relations were those of equals and did not detract from the general independence of either institution concerned in each case. But the technical nature of the connexion is not properly to be described as a ' community of interest '; it was based on participations rather than on formal agreements.

In all these cases the aim was to establish a connexion with an already well-developed financial centre, and in some cases the international importance of the latter counted for as much as the possibilities of developing German trade with the country in which it was situated. Quite different problems arose when it was sought to advance German interests in distant and undeveloped regions; and for the solution of these problems the method resorted to was the formation of German overseas banks as subsidiary companies.

The regions in question were South America and the Far East. Although less remote, the Near East

---

[1] Such arrangements were facilitated by the fact that many of the New York bankers were of German origin. Apart from the above-mentioned community of interests ' with Berlin banks, close business relations based on family connexions existed between German and American private bankers. Strasser, *op. cit.* p. 167.

[2] *Ibid.* p. 88.

may also be included here in view of its economic character.

The first South American banks of German nationality—also the first German overseas banks—were founded in the early seventies: the *Deutsch-Belgische La Plata Bank*, in which first the Discontogesellschaft and then the Deutsche Bank were interested, in 1872, and the *Deutsch-Brasilianische Bank*, a subsidiary of the Norddeutsche Bank, in 1873. Both of these had to be liquidated, however, after a brief period of existence, and nothing further was done in this direction for about ten years. Then in 1886 the Deutsche Bank established the *Deutsche Ueberseebank*, with a head office in Berlin and a capital of 10 million marks. Under the title *Banco Aleman Transatlantico* an office was opened in Buenos Aires in 1887; and business here developing rapidly in the early nineties, the capital of the bank was increased to 20 million marks in 1893, the title being changed at the same time to that of *Deutsche Ueberseeische Bank* for technical reasons.[1]

In the Argentine Republic further branches were opened at Bahia Blanca and Cordoba in 1903, at Tucuman and Belle Ville in 1905, and at Mendoza in 1910. Before this the Ueberseeische Bank had extended its business to Chile, where the first branch was opened at Valparaiso in 1896 and was quickly followed by others. (Iquique and Santiago in 1897, Concepcion, Valdivia and Antofagasta in 1898, Temuco and Arica in 1912.) Branches were also established in Peru (Lima, Trujillo, Arequipa and Callao); Bolivia (La Paz, Oruro) and Uruguay (Montevideo) in the years 1905 to 1907; and in Brazil (Rio de Janeiro, São Paulo and Santos) in 1911 and 1912. Outside South America branches were opened in Mexico City in 1901

---

[1] It was necessary to form a new company in order to raise the nominal capital without paying up the original capital in full. Riesser: *Die deutschen Grossbanken*, p. 354 note.

and Barcelona in 1904. In 1906 the Mexican branch was handed over to the *Mexikanische Bank für Handel u. Industrie*, formed by the Deutsche Ueberseeische Bank, with the assistance of non-German capital; but, on the other hand, the direct representation of the Deutsche Ueberseeische Bank in Spain was increased by the conversion of the firm *Guillemo Vogel*, Madrid, previously a *Kommandit* of the Deutsche Bank, into a branch.

Meanwhile the Discontogesellschaft, in conjunction with the Norddeutsche Bank, had founded first the *Brasilianische Bank für Deutschland* in 1887, and then the *Bank für Chile und Deutschland* in 1895. The capital of each was originally 10 million marks—that of the Brasilianische Bank was raised to 15 million in 1912—and both had their head offices in Hamburg. They were alike again and in contrast to the Deutsche Ueberseeische Bank in that each was devoted to business with one country particularly—a point in which they resembled the English South American banks of the time, such as the London & Brazilian Bank. Yet another common feature was that each had a principal foreign office—at Rio de Janeiro and Valparaiso respectively—which supervised the other branches and had the advice of a strong local committee. The other branches of the Brasilianische Bank were at São Paulo (1893), Santos (1895), and Porto Alegre (1904); those of the Bank für Chile at Santiago (1897), Concepcion (1848), Temuco (1905), Antofagasta (1905), Victoria (1907), and Valdivia (1907). As a small exception to what has been said above, this bank also opened two branches in Bolivia—La Paz and Oruro (1905).

A fourth German-South American Bank was set up in 1905 with the title *Deutsch-Südamerikanische Bank*. The parent banks in this case were the Dresdner Bank, the A. Schaaffhausen'scher Bankverein, and the Nationalbank für Deutschland. The capital of the

new bank was fixed from the first at the comparatively
high figure of 20 million marks, and it early set about
cultivating a wide field.   In addition to its head office
in Berlin and a branch at Hamburg, branches were at
once opened at Buenos Aires and Mexico City, followed by others at Valparaiso in 1910, and at Santiago
and Rio de Janeiro in 1911.

The interest of the German banks in the Far East
was hardly later in manifesting itself than their interest
in South America.   In the seventies the Deutsche
Bank experimented with branches at Yokohama and
Shanghai at the same time that it participated in the
La Plata Bank; and in the eighties plans were being
discussed for the establishment of a German Asiatic
bank while the Deutsche Ueberseebank was being
brought into existence.   In the case of the Asiatic
project the initiative came from the Discontogesellschaft, but the co-operation of most of the leading
banks and bankers in Germany was obtained, and the
Imperial Government also gave considerable encouragement.   Certain difficulties as to the legal status of
the proposed institution and as to the form in which it
should be endowed with capital delayed the completion
of the plans; but finally these were surmounted and
the *Deutsch-Asiatische Bank* was founded in 1889.
The failure in the same year of the *Comptoir d'Escompte
de Paris*, one of the most important European banks
having offices in the East, made this starting point
especially opportune.

A peculiar feature of the Deutsch-Asiatische Bank
was that the unit in which its capital and all its
accounts were expressed was not the mark but the
Shanghai tael—a weight of silver used in the East
as 'money of account.'   The capital of 5 million
Shanghai taels—paid up in marks on the basis of
the prevailing price of silver [1]—was contributed by

[1] The first 25 % was paid at the rate of 4·5 marks to the tael.

the numerous firms which combined in the promotion as follows:

Discontogesellschaft - - -	805,000 taels
Königliche Seehandlung - -	175,000 ,,
Deutsche Bank - - - -	555,000 ,,
S. Bleichröder & Co. - - -	555,000 ,,
Berliner Handelsgesellschaft - -	470,000 ,,
Jacob S. H. Stern - - -	470,000 ,,
Bank für Handel u. Industrie -	310,000 ,,
Robert Warschauer & Co. - -	310,000 ,,
Mendelssohn & Co. - - -	310,000 ,,
A. M. Rothschild & Söhne - -	310,000 ,,
Norddeutsche Bank - - -	380,000 ,,
Sal. Oppenheim jr & Cie - -	175,000 ,,
Bayerische Hypotheken- u. Wechsel-bank - - - - -	175,000 ,,
	5,000,000 ,,

Another peculiarity of this bank was that its head office was located abroad at Shanghai;[1] owing to Germany's possession of territorial rights, however, this did not bring the bank under Chinese law. This head office and a branch at Tientsin were opened in 1890. In the course of the next twenty years an organization was steadily built up which covered China fairly completely—with further branches at Hankow (1897), Tsingtao (1897), Peking (1905), Tsinan (1910), and Canton (1910); and extended to Hong Kong (1899), British India (Calcutta, 1896), Singapore (1906), and Japan (Yokohama 1905 and Kobe 1906).[2]

The first German bank carrying on business in the Near East was the *Deutsche Palästina Bank*, formed in 1899 by the Berlin firm, Von der Heydt & Co. This

---

[1] Following example of the British Hongkong & Shanghai Banking Corporation, except that this had its head office at Hong Kong.

[2] The capital was also raised to 7·5 million taels.

bank originally depended upon business with pilgrims and other visitors to Jerusalem, but came to take an active part in financing trade after branches had been opened at Jaffa, Beirut, and other commercial centres in the Levant. During its early years, however—and indeed, so long as it remained primarily interested in this region—its capital was small, 450,000 marks raised to 1 million in 1907; and it was only after the establishment of the *Deutsche Orientbank* in 1906, that Germany was represented in this quarter by an institution in any degree capable of competing with the French and British banks.

The history of the Deutsche Orientbank begins really with the collaboration of the Nationalbank für Deutschland with the Banque Nationale de Grèce in the promotion of the *Banque d'Orient* of Athens in 1904. The latter was conceived with a twofold purpose, namely, to fill a gap in the internal credit system of Greece and to represent the commercial and financial interests of Germany in the Levant. In practice, however, it was found somewhat difficult to reconcile these two tasks, and accordingly it was agreed, after about a year's experience, that the Nationalbank für Deutschland should withdraw from control of the Banque d'Orient and that, with the goodwill of the Banque Nationale, a new bank should be established for the cultivation of German interests.

The Deutsche Orientbank, which was the outcome of this arrangement, had an original capital .of 16 million marks, raised to 32 million in 1910, and a head office in Berlin. In its promotion and the subsequent ownership of its capital, the Nationalbank was joined by the Dresdner Bank and the A. Schaaffhausen'scher Bankverein. From the Banque d'Orient, in addition to general support, it received a branch which the latter had opened in Constantinople and an agency in Hamburg; and it further succeeded to the Banque d'Orient's part in agreements with the Deutsche Palästina Bank and the *Deutsche Levant Linie*. New branches were soon opened at Brussa, Alexandria and Cairo; and in 1909 the two Egyptian branches were supplemented by a number of agencies in order to extend their already important business in financing the export of raw cotton. Where political interests predominated, the bank met with certain reverses; thus a concession to open a branch in Persia, obtained at the instigation of the German Government, had to be abandoned owing to the opposition of the Entente Governments; and two branches opened in Morocco (Tangier and Casa Blanca) in 1909 were closed in 1913.[1] But expansion was continued in the Levant and European Turkey by the opening of offices at Messina (1909), Adana (1910), Aleppo (1910), Adrianople (1910), and Dedeagach[2] (1910). In May 1914 the Orientbank agreed to purchase the Levant branches of the Deutsche Palästina Bank, which had now joined the Hohenloe group of undertakings and transferred its interest to the affairs of this group in Germany; but the outbreak of the war and the subsequent course of events prevented the completion of this transaction. It should be added that from 1908 the Deutsche Bank was directly represented in the Near East by a branch at Constantinople, of which a Baghdad sub-office was opened in 1914.

Although 'foreign' banks, in the sense that they carried on most of their business abroad, all these overseas banks, not excepting the Deutsch-Asiatische Bank, were German companies. In several cases the statutes or articles contained provisions which ensured that they should remain in German control, and actually (if we neglect the little Deutsche Palästinabank) the

---

[1] After the Franco-German agreement, French competition became too keen ; the offices were sold to the Société Générale.

[2] Last-named given up in 1913 owing to the Balkan War.

entire capital was in every case retained by the parent home banks.

After this common feature, certain less fundamental but nevertheless important points of contrast between the several overseas banks are worth emphasizing. Thus whilst in the Far East the representation of all German interests was concentrated in the Deutsch-Asiatische Bank,[1] the four South American banks continued abroad the competition between the Deutsche, Disconto, and Dresdner-Schaaffhausen groups. In this respect an intermediate state of affairs existed in the Near East, the Orientbank and the Constantinople branch of the Deutsche Bank competing in small matters but co-operating in larger transactions. These, it may be said, particularly large issue and promotion transactions, were much more important in the business of the Eastern banks (Orientbank and Asiatische) than in that of the South American banks, which was more purely commercial; and underlying this difference may be discerned the greater importance of the political element in Germany's Eastern interests. Finally, along quite different lines, a distinction may be drawn between the banks which only confined their operations within a broad region: South America, Far East or Near East, and those which restricted themselves to one country—Brazil, Chile (with Bolivia) or Palestine.

The histories of the individual banks are bound up with the histories of their particular regions or countries, into which it is impossible to enter here. But a brief reference may be made to certain common difficulties with which they had to contend.

One of the most obvious of these, but not the least troublesome, was that of finding for the staffs of the foreign branches men who combined the requisite

---

[1] The Dresdner Bank, Schaaffhausen'scher Bankverein and Nationalbank, not amongst its promoters, joined the *Konsortium* later.

qualifications of personal integrity, a training in banking technique, and a knowledge of local conditions. A second was that of winning business at the expense of, or at any rate in competition with, English and French banks which had been established considerably longer and generally enjoyed high prestige.[1] But perhaps the greatest difficulties were those occasioned by the instability of the foreign currencies with which they were concerned, due in the East to the depreciation of silver, and in South America to the unregulated issue of paper currency.[2]

Possibly this element of uncertainty would not have been really serious for banks engaged exclusively in foreign exchange business, for against its restrictive influence on foreign trade might be set an access of business in 'forward' exchange. But it was serious for the German overseas banks, because their programme included the making of advances abroad, and these in connexion with local, as well as international, trade. The purely local business may have been more necessary to them than it was to their English rivals, because their share in the international business was smaller; but it was also of considerable advantage in giving them an insight into the affairs of local firms. In any case the problem arose of preventing the depreciation of their own resources with that of the local currency.[3] Their simplest course to this end was to

---

[1] In many cases German firms abroad adhered to their English banking connexions after the services of the German banks had become available. Thus, according to Strasser (*op. cit.* p. 128 footnote), ' Die ersten deutschen Chinafirmen befanden sich, z.b. noch 1914, im Board der Hongkong & Shanghai Banking Corporation.'

[2] The *Orientbank* does not seem to have been troubled with difficulties of this kind. Minor wars, the prelude to 1914, were its chief vexation.

[3] This problem did not arise so directly in the case of the Deutsch-Asiatische Bank : for since its capital was in terms of silver, the depreciation of silver could not occasion an ' open ' loss. But for this bank also the problem existed in so far as it recognized an obligation to maintain the gold value of its own resources by increasing its reserves or to compensate its shareholders by high dividends and bonuses.

make only 'valorised' loans, i.e. loans repayable in
local currency but by an amount of that currency
varying with the rate of exchange. This practice was,
in fact, adopted at times by the South American banks,
and protected all but their 'till' money; but by
transferring the exchange risk to the borrowers it
seriously restricted business. A less complete solution, but one more satisfactory so far as it went,
consisted in using their credit to economise the employment of their own capital. The Deutsch-
Asiatische Bank in China and, for a time, the Deutsche
Ueberseeische Bank in Argentina, were able to do this
by issuing banknotes, but the more general method
was to obtain the use of foreign money by attracting
deposits. For the rest, it was common to provide a
kind of insurance cover for exchange risks by the
purchase of 'forward' sterling. It should be added
that the high rates of interest which prevailed in
South America, particularly during the periods of
stabilization, enabled the banks engaged in business
there to set aside large sums out of profits for
depreciation.

Judged by financial results the Deutsche Ueberseeische Bank and the Brasilianische Bank were the
most successful. The Bank für Chile also maintained
a good average in its dividends, but these were more
variable in sympathy with the fluctuations of Chilian
trade. The Deutsch-Südamerikanische Bank had
hardly reached the profit-making stage by 1914,
suffering in its first years from the repercussions of the
1907 crisis, and perhaps also from a desire to realize
its programme too quickly. The Deutsch-Asiatische
Bank paid good silver dividends, although the outcome
in marks was not very satisfactory. However, since
all the capital of these banks was in the hands of
the banks at home, their profit-making capacity was
of less importance than their co-operation in the

work which is described in the later sections of this chapter.

Overseas banks of a broadly similar type were also established for the German colonies in Africa; the *Deutsche Afrika Bank* by the Discontogesellschaft in 1906 for German South-West Africa; the *Deutsch-West Afrikanische Bank* by the Dresdner Bank in 1904 for Togoland and the Cameroons; the *Handelsbank für Ost Afrika* by the *Deutsch-Ostafrikanische Gesellschaft* and a number of the leading banks at the end of 1911 for German East Africa.[1] These, however, were of much less importance.

Finally, the German banks found yet another kind of field for the expansion of their influence in certain of the less developed countries in Europe, namely, Italy, Roumania, and Bulgaria.

In these cases, also, new banks were promoted, but these were foreign in the sense of being constituted under foreign laws, resembling in this the banks established in Brussels, Amsterdam, etc.[2] They were foreign again in that a part—and sometimes the larger part—of their capital was drawn from indigenous and other non-German sources. The extent to which in practice they were under German influence was apt to change—usually to diminish—in the course of time and is often difficult to determine; but they were never expressly devoted to German interests.

An opportunity to intervene in the development of Italian banking was provided by a severe financial crisis in 1893, which entailed the failure of the Banca Generale and Credito Mobiliare and left all the existing banks in a weak condition. To utilize this opening a *Konsortium* was formed by the Discontogesellschaft,

---

[1] The *Deutsch-Ostafrikanische Bank*—founded 1905—was primarily a note-issuing bank. The *Deutsche Afrika-Bank* was an ordinary company, the others 'colonial companies' (*Kolonialgesellschaften*) under a special law.

[2] See p. 68 above.

which comprised the Deutsche Bank, the Darmstädter Bank, the Berliner Handelsgesellschaft, and S. Bleichröder & Co., and was later joined by some half-dozen Austrian and Swiss banks and certain Italian interests. By this *Konsortium* the *Banca Commerciale Italiana* was established at Milan in 1894 with a capital of 20 million lire. In 1898 the capital was increased, and on this occasion the *Banque de Paris et des Pays Bas* was admitted to participation.

The Banca Commerciale developed rapidly and became in many ways the most important bank in Italy. It was characterized by the large number of industrial undertakings which it promoted, and in which it participated; and in many of these, particularly in electrical undertakings, it co-operated with German capital and enterprise. In the course of time the *Konsortium* was modified by a decline in the German share and an increase in the Italian, Swiss, and French holdings; but German representation in the council of administration did not decline in the same proportion. The facts here are shown by the following table given by Strasser [1]:

Country.	No. of Shares.		Representation in Council, 1914.
	1895.	1914.	
Italy - - -	6,814	195,544	17
Germany and Austria	29,711	7,411	9
Switzerland - -	3,475	64,097	3
France - - -	—	42,922	4
	40,000	309,974	

It may be added that, until the entry of Italy into the late war, the position of General-Director was held by Otto Joels, a naturalized Italian of German parentage.

Another Italian bank, the *Credito Italiano*, which stood little behind the Banca Commerciale in impor-

[1] *Op. cit.* p. 69.

tance, was also to some extent subject to German influence. The syndicate by which it was formed included the Nationalbank für Deutschland and R. Warschauer & Co. amongst other foreign banks; and while Warschauer & Co. early relinquished its holding, that of the Nationalbank was retained until the War and secured a place in the administrative council for one of its directors until his death in 1914.

The interest of the German banks in Roumania was due mainly to her undeveloped oil resources, but also to her potentialities as an exporter of grain to Germany and an importer of German manufactures. As in the case of Italy, they were able to take advantage of the weakness of the national banking system in order to establish powerful banks under their own tutelage. Of these there were two: the *Banca Generala Romana* (capital 10 million lei) promoted by the Discontoge-sellschaft, S. Bleichröder, and representatives of Roumanian business in 1897; and the *Banca Marmorosch Blank & Co. S.A.* (capital 8 million lei) which resulted from the amalgamation of the private firm Marmorosch Blank & Co. and the Société de Crédit, Bukarest, in 1904. Marmorosch Blank had up till then been a *Kommandit* of the Darmstädter Bank, and the latter and the Berliner Handelsgesellschaft joined with Hungarian and Roumanian capital in the formation of the new bank. French interests, again represented by the Banque de Paris et des Pays Bas, were introduced when the capital was raised to 10 million lei in 1905. Both the Banca Romana and the Banca Marmorosch Blank became flourishing ' mixed ' banks, engaging alike in short-term banking, particularly in connexion with the grain trade, and the largest capital transactions. In the latter, especially in financing the oil industry, they co-operated extensively with the parent banks in Germany. Until 1905 the Banca Romana remained entirely in the ownership of the original promoters and, therefore, almost completely under German control. Obscurity surrounds the subsequent distribution of its shares; additional capital was raised from the Roumanian and German publics in 1906, and the holdings of the Discontogesellschaft seem gradually to have been reduced in the following years; but the bank is generally considered to have remained under German predominance until 1914 and later. The Banca Marmorosch Blank was always more international in the composition of its capital, the distribution of this between nationalities in 1905 being: 36% Roumanian, 24% German, 20% Hungarian, and 20% French. As a consequence German interests were not here predominant, but they were favoured in comparison with the other foreign capital in the allocation of places on the *Aufsichtrat*—receiving 4 against 2 assigned to the Hungarian shareholders and 1 to the French, out of a total of 16.[1]

In Bulgaria the Discontogesellschaft, S. Bleichröder, and the Norddeutsche Bank took the initiative in promoting the Banque de Crédit (*Kreditna Banka*), Sofia, and provided two-thirds of its capital.

Of all this foreign banking organization the branches in financial centres (particularly London) and the subsidiary overseas banks may be considered to have been the most important parts. In comparison with pre-war English banking organization, with its independent foreign banks, the feature which stands out is the closer integration between the organs dealing respectively with domestic and foreign trade. The advantages of this closer connexion appear to be recognized in the post-war tendency of the English banks to open branches abroad and participate in overseas banks.

[1] Strasser, *op. cit.* p. 79.

II

THE FINANCING OF FOREIGN TRADE

In the methods adopted for financing foreign trade and in the incidental services rendered to exporters and importers, the German banks and their subsidiaries followed very closely the practices which were already general and had largely been perfected by English bankers. On this ground an exhaustive account of the technique employed would appear to be superfluous, and the following outline [1] of the more typical transactions is chiefly designed to illustrate the working of the organization described in the previous section.

With regard to the export trade, financial assistance was given mainly by way of advances to bridge over the interval between the shipment of goods and the arrival of the purchaser's remittance. This interval was, of course, frequently a considerable one; for it would hardly ever be less than the time required for the double voyage to and from the country to which the goods were sent, and generally it would be longer by a period during which the importer was given credit. In some cases the advance was given in the form of current account or 'acceptance' credit with the home bank on the strength of the exporter's general standing: and this was the only method available when the exporter gave 'open' or 'book' credit to his foreign customer. But more usually the advance was secured by the rights of the exporter arising out of the transaction in question and embodied in a draft upon the importer. This draft, made out to order and accompanied by the 'documents' relating to the consignment, was handed over to the bank for collection, and on the

---

[1] Largely based on A. J. Wolfe, *Foreign Credits*, U.S. Dept. of Commerce and Labour, Bureau of Foreign and Domestic Commerce, Special Agent Series, No. 62, 1913.

strength of the authority thus acquired to receive payment and control the disposition of the goods meantime
(or at least until the importer formally acknowledged
his obligation to make the payment), an advance would
be made of a certain proportion of the invoice value of
the goods.[1]　In such cases the exporter's home bank
might either make the advance itself or arrange for it
to be made by a filial overseas bank.[2]　Recourse might
also be had to an overseas bank in the more rare cases
when exporter's drafts were sold outright (or discounted)[3] and when advances were sought against
goods not definitely sold but shipped to agents on
consignment.

In the regions in which they operated it was
generally a branch of an overseas bank to which the
documents were sent for delivery to the importer.
According to the exporter's terms—which determined
the wording of the accompanying draft—this delivery
took place either against payment of the draft or against
its acceptance payable after a certain interval.　It may
be said that the latter arrangement was more usual in
the German export trade.[4]　Even where the draft was
made payable on receipt of documents (English d/p
drafts) it was possible and not unusual for the goods
to be released to the importer under an agreement by
which he handled them only as an agent of the bank
until payment was completed.　Concurrence in
arrangements of this kind called, of course, for careful
exercise of discretion on the part of the overseas bank.

---

[1] Varying from 60 to 80 %, according to circumstances.

[2] Both courses were common, but one may suppose that the latter was
more usual in the cases in which the importer was given credit for a time.

[3] Apparently the Deutsch-Asiatische Bank engaged especially in this
form of transaction.

[4] Brandt mentions that in China it was the practice to keep control of the
goods after receiving the importer's acceptance, releasing them in instal-
ments against payment. *Zeitschrift für Handelswissenschaft*, 1914, Heft 3,
p. 78.

In the event of the importer failing to comply with the exporter's conditions when the documents were offered to him, the local officers of the overseas bank provided for the storage of the goods until further instructions were received; and they also supervised the storage and release of goods sent abroad ' on consignment.'[1]

The payment to be made by the importer (on receipt of documents or on maturity of the draft accepted by him) might be fixed either in terms of his own currency or some other currency, such as marks or sterling. In the latter case, which was the typical one in trade between Germany and countries outside Europe, his debt might be discharged by handing to the bank acting for the exporter—i.e. in most cases, the branch of an overseas bank—a mark or sterling draft for the value of the goods. But it was more customary for the importer to pay in his own currency the price of the appropriate draft, and this would be provided for in the first draft drawn by the exporter by making the sum named in marks or sterling payable in the importer's currency at the ' drawing rate ' of the bank acting for the exporter abroad. In the majority of cases, therefore, the latter made itself responsible for the transference of the value of the goods from one country to another, and for this purpose had either to provide and remit a draft or to arrange otherwise for its European branch or correspondent to credit the exporter with the sum due to him.

A further point to be noticed about the importer's payment is that it did not necessarily amount to an immediate discharge of his debt at its full value as given by the invoice. On the contrary the exporter's terms commonly allowed payment to be made by a bill for the amount owing payable after an interval of (say) three months after sight—so that one time draft might

---

[1] The Deutsch-Asiatische Bank had its own warehouses in China. Brandt, *loc. cit.*

be paid by another time draft. Where the first draft was drawn in marks or sterling the same effect might be achieved by making it payable in the importer's currency at the ninety days drawing rate; in such a case the second draft would not necessarily come into actual existence (i.e. the transactions could be settled between the overseas banks and the home banks by book entries). Wherever the second draft was actually created, it would commonly be discounted.

The chain of transactions here outlined would be somewhat simplified when a bank in the importer's country wrote a ' letter of credit ' on his behalf, by which the exporter was authorized to draw directly upon it or upon some other bank—perhaps one in Germany or London. This would usually make the exporter's draft at once saleable. It is mentioned by several German writers that German overseas banks performed this service for importers from Germany, although Mr. A. J. Wolfe in his report on *Foreign Credits*[1] says that German banks made less use of this practice than those of England and France. The German overseas banks also assisted foreign importers with credit in other forms (e.g. if a draft was payable in marks at ninety days drawing rate, they allowed payment to be deferred for ninety days and then made at sight rate).

Less need be said about the methods used in financing imports into Germany. Here the rôles of the home bank and the overseas bank were largely reversed, the former opening credits against which the exporter could draw and the latter making advances upon these drafts.

In all this, as has been said, there was little if anything that was new. The methods and forms adopted in assisting German trade were those of the English foreign trade banks and, it may be added, had been

[1] *Op. cit.* p. 37.

used by these, not in the service of British trade alone, but to a great extent also in the service of the commerce of other countries—including that of Germany. But the application of these methods to German trade became more effective when carried out within a co-ordinated national system with its own organs abroad. Moreover, if the technique was essentially that of the English banks, there was, as must now be indicated, an important difference in the way in which it was used.

This difference related to the length of credit terms, to some extent also to the standing of firms to which credit was given, in the export trade. In both respects the German banks assisted the exporting merchants to be distinctly more accommodating than their chief competitors. As Mr. Wolfe says: ' The lengthy credit terms granted by Germans to customers in many markets where Americans and even British fear to trade except on a basis of cash against documents, puzzle and worry their competitors.' [1] According to the point of view, the departure might be described as one either in the direction of greater enterprise or greater recklessness; and particular instances might doubtless be found to justify either description. But it can hardly be doubted that this credit policy con-tributed to the growth of the German export trade, and, judged on the whole, as a policy applied to the trade of a country which came late into the world's markets, it seems to have justified itself by its results.

[1] *Op. cit.* p. 12.
Speaking of English methods Wolfe says : ' With regard to credit accommodation to foreign customers, the export merchants of Great Britain and the British overseas banks meet the demand adequately, but the ten-dency is to keep down the length of credit terms. Where foreign com-petition seeks to gain trade by offering longer credits, other things being equal, the British export merchant and manufacturer is apt to let the trade go rather than encourage a policy recognized in England as harmful.' P. 55.

We have left to the last consideration of the change
attempted, and in part effected, in the way of substituting the mark for the pound sterling as the basis of
trade between Germany and overseas countries.
Actually this was one of the first objects which
the German banks set before themselves in this
field.

The general facts with regard to the pre-war position of sterling bills as something like international
currency are too well known to need recapitulation.
So far as German trade is concerned one may say that,
prior to the establishment of the German overseas
banks, the use of sterling was general in dealings with
countries outside Europe (except those bordering on
the Mediterranean—Morocco, Egypt, Asia Minor—
where the franc had an international standing).

The disadvantages attending the interposition of a
third currency—that of a country not concerned in the
trading operation—may be looked at from the point
of view of the merchant or from that of the banks.
From the standpoint of the former, there was in the
first place the expense of remitting to London to meet
his obligations or of cashing his claims on London, as
the case might be. And secondly, there was the
circumstance that two, instead of one, exchange risks
entered into transactions with his foreign customers.
It is true that the German merchant usually bore only
one of these risks, and that the smaller one connected
with the mark-sterling exchange; but had he been
able to trade in marks, there would have been no
exchange risk at all. When, as at first, dealing in
sterling meant seeking the assistance of foreign banks
and finance houses, the German trader might be at a
further disadvantage in comparison with rivals who
could entrust their business to banks of their own
nationality. From the standpoint of the German
banks, the predominance of sterling was resented

because it helped to maintain the leading position of the English banks and enabled these to earn coveted profits. Some of these disadvantages, it is clear, might be obviated through the services of the German banks in London. Moreover, it must be pointed out that the use of sterling as the unit of value or account in foreign trade transactions did not in every case necessitate the employment of sterling bills; the Argentine importer, for instance, might pay in his own pesos on the basis of the peso-sterling exchange rate and the German exporter might receive payment in Germany in marks on the basis of the mark-sterling rate, and here the only drawback to the use of the sterling basis would be the introduction of the extra exchange risk. But despite these qualifications, it was thought that neither the trader nor banker in Germany would be quite on a par with his English competitor until they had become independent of sterling and the London money market.

For the attainment of this end most was expected from the development of the overseas banks. It was hoped that as they grew themselves they would introduce the use of mark bills more and more widely, and establish an active market for such bills around each of their branches. This hope, however, was only realized to a limited extent. The greatest measure of success appears to have been achieved in the German-South American trade. Here, according to Wolfe,[1] the mark came to be used more often than sterling, although, in qualification of this, it is generally agreed that the latter was almost exclusively used in Chilean trade.[2] But in any case sterling continued to be the basis of a considerable volume of business between Germany and this continent, while in other overseas

---

[1] *Op. cit.* p. 50.

[2] Cf. Strasser, *op. cit.* p. 50. Presumably the case was the same with Peruvian trade, since the Peruvian pound was identical with sterling.

markets, particularly the Far East, its use remained
the rule.

In explaining the failure to make greater headway
in this direction, due weight must be given to the
influences which constitute economic inertia—the preference of men for practices to which they are accus-
tomed, the necessity of beginning a new development
on a small scale, with its attendant disadvantages, etc.
But it may be suspected that progress was also impeded
by other causes of a more permanent character. Some
qualifications have been suggested to the disadvantages
which appear at first sight to have been involved in
trading on a sterling basis; it may now be pointed out
that there were certain advantages in using sterling
bills and the services of the London money market.

(1) The payments to be made on each side between
any two countries never exactly balance and are usually
very far from being equal. Consequently it is very
convenient that one financial centre should act as a
kind of international clearing-house in which credit and
debit differences can be offset. Before the War
London occupied this position, and for this reason it
was advantageous that many payments should be made
through London which had no connexion with English
trade.

(2) The use of sterling bills was bound up with the
use of the London Discount Market; this market was
the most efficient and reliable in the world so far as
foreign trade bills was concerned, and if not actually
the cheapest was distinctly cheaper—usually by about
1% per annum—than that of Berlin.

This second point is especially important because
it reminds us of the fact that the trade of Germany—as
of other countries—was largely financed by lenders in
London. The value of the service thus rendered was
sometimes overlooked by German writers, who were
apt to calculate what Germany had to pay for the

mediation of London and present the result as though it were simply a burden on German commerce, without taking into consideration that the sum arrived at included the interest on capital which Germany could ill afford to provide herself.[1]   Assuming that the payment of acceptance charges, etc., to English bankers could be avoided by using the German offices in London, the net disadvantage to the German economy of having to use sterling bills in settling with other countries may be expressed thus:

the disadvantage of the extra exchange risk *plus* the expense of maintaining offices in London *plus* British stamp duties *minus* the saving of interest owing to the cheaper rates prevailing in the London money market.

Now the pre-war variations in the mark-sterling exchange were not great, and the German offices in London were useful for other purposes, particularly in connexion with the Stock Exchange.   The saving in interest is not easy to calculate.   On the one hand the acceptances of the German branches in London (which for the moment we are supposing to be used in all German trade financed through London) may not have received the most favourable treatment in the London bill market; on the other hand—and this appears to be a more important consideration—the difference between the London and Berlin rates would have been greater than it actually was, if fewer demands had been made on the London market and more on that of

---

[1] Hauser, *Die deutschen Ueberseebanken,* p. 17, quotes Heiligenstadt to the effect that the gross profit (*Gewinn*) of English banks in Interest and Charges out of the mediation of payments between Germany and other countries amounted to 3-3½ million marks (per annum ?).

Riesser, *German Great Banks,* p. 538, says : ' Thus, for instance, as late as 1888 according to consular Reports the commercial exchanges between Germany and Chile, valued in the aggregate at 60,000,000 marks yielded about 500,000 marks of profit to British bankers, merely because all acceptances by means of which these exchanges were effected had to be liquidated in the British market.'

Berlin. On this basis the net disadvantage would not appear to have been much and, at times at least, might have been negative. The calculation needs, of course, to be modified in so far as the use of sterling bills led in practice to the mediation of English banks; but it is not clear that this ' invisible ' import meant a loss for the country as a whole.

III

THE CREDITBANKS AND THE EXPORT OF CAPITAL

At the outbreak of the War Germany came third amongst the nations of the world, following England and France, in respect of the amount of capital invested abroad. With regard to this broad fact there seems little question; but when we look for precise figures for any of the countries we find estimates which show considerable divergence from one another. In the case of Germany, Helfferich [1] estimated the foreign investments in 1913 at 20 milliard marks (20,000 million marks). A more recent estimate by Lenz,[2] however, relating to the same year (or perhaps 1914) gives a figure of 31 milliards. For the foreign investments of England and France immediately before the War Lenz quotes estimates of 80 and 42 milliards [3] respectively (authority not named). The former, equivalent to £4000 million roughly, is nearly double the amount given by Mr. C. K. Hobson—£2,332 million.[4] Even allowing for possible differences in what is covered by the figures, it would appear that Lenz's estimates are all too high.

Since the accumulation of these investments was spread over different periods in the case of each

---

[1] *Deutschlands Volksvermögen*, p. 112.
[2] *Weltwirtschaftliches Archiv*, Bd. 18, p. 48. [3] *Ibid.* p. 49.
[4] *Export of Capital*, p. 207.

country, estimates of the annual amounts of new foreign investments are in some respects more significant. According to Mr. Hobson (writing in 1914)

' Great Britain has for some years past never invested less than £100,000,000 per annum in the Colonies and foreign countries, and recently the amount has been in the neighbourhood of £200,000,000. The yearly flow of French investments to other lands is now estimated by M. Neymarck at from 80 to 100 millions sterling; German foreign investments, judging from the values of securities admitted to quotation on the German bourses, must amount to from 40 to 60 millions per annum.'[1]

The following table[2] gives statistics of security issues, domestic and foreign, admitted to quotations on the German Stock Exchanges since 1886, and shows the proportion which the foreign issues formed of the total.

Years.	Million Marks.			II % of III.
	I Domestic Issues.	II Foreign Issues.	III Total.	
1886-90	4,360	2,322	6,682	34·7
1891-95	4,833	1,462	6,295	23·2
1896-1900	8,216	2,420	10,636	22·7
1901-1905	8,339	2,147	10,486	20·5
1906-1910	12,615	1,497	14,112	10·6
1911	2,249	460	2,709	17·0
1912	2,751	270	3,021	9·7

It will be observed that the relative importance of the foreign issues was greatest in the first quinquennium here covered, and subsequently declined steadily. But the relative decline was due to the great increase

[1] Op. cit. p. 161.

[2] Strasser, op. cit. p. 26, based on Helfferich, op. cit. p. 117.

in home investment which accompanied the industrial development of Germany after 1890.   Taken by itself, the rate of foreign investment was well maintained throughout the whole period, and it is probable that the total amount invested abroad was doubled during the generation before the War.   The beginning of the nineties may also be regarded as a turning point in the character of German foreign investment.   Before that time, in the desire to escape the unfavourable conditions of the home capital market, money was lent anywhere where high rates were offered with but little consideration of the risks involved.   Later, projects were more carefully scrutinized or prepared, and investment was concentrated more in certain fields.   The change, which probably made the presence of German capital abroad more conspicuous, was largely a result of the policy of the banks.

Germany's foreign investments were naturally effected in several different forms.   Here two main forms will be distinguished, namely, loans to foreign governments and investment in foreign business undertakings—although the distinction is weakened by the fact that, in many of the most important cases coming under the latter heading, foreign governments gave concessions, guarantees or even capital contributions.   The importation of ' ready-made ' securities —the least active form of foreign investment—will not be considered.

(A) The first foreign government to receive active assistance from German banks in its loan transactions appears to have been that of Austria.   The more or less international house of Rothschild had made itself very early the principal banker to this government, with a group of Austrian banks as satellites; and in 1862 the Darmstädter Bank participated in a transaction of this group.   Two years later the Discontogesellschaft also took up part of an Austrian loan issue.   Next in order comes the Russian Government, which was assisted by the Berliner Handelsgesellschaft for the first time in 1868.   In the early seventies considerable sums were raised by the Discontogesellschaft for the Government of Roumania.   In the later seventies and the eighties foreign loan transactions became especially important, the governments most largely assisted being those of the South American Republics—particularly the Argentine—and Portugal.

Through the transactions of the latter years considerable losses were incurred, and this circumstance, together with the improvement in home prospects, led to the adoption of a more restrained and cautious policy in foreign lending.   The Discontogesellschaft remained, however, an important member of Rothschild's Austrian group and also engaged in further transactions for the Roumanian Government.   At the same time, after 1890, considerable financial assistance was given to governments which had not previously had relations of this kind with Germany, namely, Italy, Turkey and Bulgaria, China (1887, 1896, 1898, and 1912), and Japan (1905).   Participation in South American public loans became less common; but they did occur—as, for instance, in the Peruvian Loan of 1905, São Paulo (Brazil) State Loan of 1906, and the Chilian Loan of 1907—and on these occasions the overseas subsidiary banks were useful intermediaries.

In carrying out these foreign loan transactions, it was common for several banks to work together; and where transactions in connexion with the same country or group of countries were fairly frequent, this resulted in the formation of more or less permanent *Konsortien*. Of these the best known was the *Asiatische Konsortium*, composed as follows:

> Deutsch-Asiatische Bank,
> Discontogesellschaft,
> Deutsche Bank,

S. Bleichröder & Co.,
Darmstädter Bank,
Berliner Handelsgesellschaft,
Jakob S. H. Stern,
Norddeutsche Bank,
Sal. Oppenheim jr & Cie,
Bayerische Hypotheken- u. Wechselbank,
Königliche Seehandlung,
Dresdner Bank,
A. Schaaffhausen'scher Bankverein,
Born & Busse,
Nationalbank für Deutschland,
L. Behrens & Söhne.

In some cases, e.g. the Italian and Russian *Konsortien*, the *Konsortium* was made up partly of German banks and partly of banks of the borrowing country.[1]

The participation of German banks in foreign government loans sometimes meant the penetration of fields which had previously been monopolized by English institutions, which only yielded a share after a struggle. This was particularly the case in China, where the dominance of the *Hongkong and Shanghai Banking Corporation* was almost unchallenged until the middle of the nineties. In 1895, however, all the Powers competed for the Chinese Indemnity Loan; and on being defeated then by a Russian-French combination, the Hongkong and Shanghai Banking Corporation formed an alliance with the Deutsch-Asiatische Bank which succeeded in securing the loans of 1896 and 1898. This alliance was soon extended to co-operation in railway projects, and marked the definite admission of Germany to a leading part in Far Eastern finance. Another country from which German finance was for long excluded was Peru. Here the English *Peruvian Corporation* enjoyed a monopoly of government loan business which was

---

[1] The Rothschild Austrian *Konsortium* was predominantly Austrian with a few German members.

only broken by the Deutsche Ueberseeische Bank in
1905.[1]

(B) In the promotion of business undertakings
abroad a large part was played by the great electrical
groups: the *A.E.G.*; *Siemens & Halske*, etc.   Indeed
it is probable that these were responsible for the
greater number of German promotions of this kind.
As we have seen, these groups comprised their own
promoting and holding companies; and while some of
the latter restricted their interests to projects within
Germany, others were specially devoted to ventures
abroad,[2] and yet others combined German and foreign
interests. Consequently the participation of the
creditbanks in the promotion of electrical undertakings
abroad was usually subordinate, as in the case of
similar developments at home.   In certain important
instances, however, this was not so, and we find the
banks concerned in foreign electrical projects as principal promoters.[3]

The other outstanding cases of the promotion of
foreign undertakings by German enterprise and capital
relate to transportation and mining, particularly railways and petroleum mining.   Here the initiative was
chiefly provided by the banks.

Although German capital had assisted in the construction of foreign railways in the previous decade,

[1] On this occasion the German bank seems to have acted very much as a
blackleg, the Corporation having decided to boycott the Government
until it had satisfied certain outstanding claims.

[2] *Deutsch-Ueberseeische Elektrizitäts Gesellschaft* (A.E.G.) ; *Syndikat für
die Finanzierung elektrischer Unternehmungen in Russland* (A.E.G.) ; *Die
Bank für elektrische Unternehmungen*, Zurich (A.E.G.) ; *Kontinentale
Gesellschaft für Elektrische Unternehmungen* (Schuckert) ; *Schweizerische
Gesellschaft für Elektrische Industrie* (Siemens u. Halske).

[3] Thus the Deutsche Bank was primarily responsible for promoting
electrical works in Barcelona and Seville in 1894, and in the Rand (S.
Africa) in 1895 ; in 1903 it promoted an electrical tramway undertaking in
Valparaiso.   The Dresdner Bank was promoter of the Victoria Falls Power
Company in 1906.

the first examples of German banks taking a part in the initiation of enterprises of this kind occurred at the beginning of the seventies. In 1871 the Discontogesellschaft and several other German banks joined an international syndicate for the promotion of the St. Gothard Railway Co., to build and operate the line tunnelling under the pass of that name. Switzerland and Italy were the other countries represented in the project, and each country provided one-third of the privately raised capital. In the same year the Discontogesellschaft formed a company to complete and operate an important line in Roumania, which had already been commenced with German capital. This transaction may best be described as a reorganization of a half-finished project in the interests of German bond-holders. Dr. Strousberg, the original promoter, had found himself unable to pay the interest on the bonds, and the Roumanian Government held itself to be absolved from a guarantee which it had given because the programme of construction was not being carried out to time. In these circumstances the Discontogesellschaft formed a new company to take over the concession, gave shares in this company in exchange for the bonds, and brought in new capital for the completion of the construction. Some years later, in 1888, this same bank joined with Krupp's in the formation of a company to exploit an important railway concession in Venezuela with a guarantee of interest from the Venezuelan Government. The project was carried through successfully so far as the German part was concerned, but serious difficulties were encountered later with the Venezuelan Government over the fulfilment of its guarantee.[1]

---

[1] This difficulty led to diplomatic action and very nearly to war. In the end the matter was settled by a compromise, but the German shareholders had to go without dividends for several years and finally obtained much less than they had been promised.

After this the Discontogesellschaft yields prominence for some time to the Deutsche Bank. The latter began with the promotion of the Anatolian Railway (Constantinople-Angora) in 1889. This transaction is of interest as the first promotion undertaken by the Deutsche Bank independently; but it concerns us more here as the first of a series of great transportation projects initiated by this bank in the Near East. It was followed by the promotion of the Macedonian Railway (Salonika-Monastir) in 1891, of a company to develop the harbour of Haidar Pasha— the terminal port of the Anatolian Railway—in 1902, and finally of the great Baghdad Railway in 1903. The last named was to connect Baghdad with the Anatolian Railway, covering a distance of 3,000 km. Contributions were made to the capital by Swiss, Austrian, Italian and, eventually, French finance, as well as by the Turkish Government; and a portion of the line was built by a Swiss company; but German finance, led by the Deutsche Bank, provided the initiative and retained the greater part of the control. To assist it in all these projects, the Deutsche Bank had formed a financial company in 1890, the *Bank für Orientalische Eisenbahnen*, with its headquarters at Zurich.

Meanwhile the Syndicate for Asiatic Transactions had been engaged in similar transactions in the Far East. The chief of these was the promotion of the Shantung Railway in 1899. This was an exclusively German project, and indeed, it was expressly provided that three-fourths of the Board of the Railway Company should be of German nationality. At the same time the Shantung Mining Co. was formed with a concession to exploit all the coal deposits within a certain distance of the railway. Later a scheme for continuing the Shantung Railway north and south was elaborated in conjunction with the Hongkong and

Shanghai Banking Corporation. Loans were made to the Chinese Government for the purpose in 1908 and 1910-11, and a German Company, the *Deutsch-Chinesische Eisenbahngesellschaft*, was formed to undertake the construction of the northern portion.[1]

German enterprise in the petroleum industry was chiefly concerned with the exploitation of the Roumanian oil fields, where we find its first and most important manifestation in the relations between the Deutsche Bank and the *Steaua Romana*. The latter was the largest petroleum company in Roumania, and the Deutsche Bank seems to have had an interest in it from some time early in the nineties; but the active control was at first exercised by the *Wiener Bankverein* and its subsidiaries, the *Ungarische Bank für Handel und Industrie* and the *Internationale Petroleumindustrie A.G.* The position was changed in 1903, when the banks were threatened with losses through difficulties into which the Steaua Romana had fallen; to remedy the situation the Deutsche Bank then stepped in with a scheme of reorganization. An essential feature of the scheme was the improvement of the commercial side of the organization, so that the Roumanian and other European producers might be able to compete with more success with the Standard Oil Co. For this purpose a number of affiliated trading companies were formed in different countries.[2] At the same time arrangements for transportation by sea were made with the Shell Company. In the following year (1904) the Deutsche Bank, assisted by the Wiener Bankverein, the Darmstädter Bank, the Nationalbank für Deutschland, the Mitteldeutsche Creditbank, and Jakob S. H.

---

[1] Strasser, *op. cit.* p. 124. Diouritch : *L'expansion des banques allemandes à l'étranger*, p. 350.

[2] *Petroleum Produkt* A.G. ; *Dänische-Deutsche Petrol Cie.* ; *General Petroleum Co.* ; *Deutsche Petroleum Maatschapyi* ; *Schweizerische Petroleum Produkte Lagergesellschaft*, Zurich.

Stern, promoted the *Deutsche Petroleum A.G.*, a controlling and holding company for the whole group. The concatenation of interests was further extended in 1906 by an agreement between the Deutsche and Nobel-Rothschild groups for the linking of their sales organizations. As a result of that agreement, three further trading companies were established—one for Germany, one for Britain, and one for the rest of Europe.[1]

In the meantime the Discontogesellschaft, working as so often in conjunction with Bleichröders, had also entered this field. In 1903 it acquired considerable holdings in two oil-producing companies—the *Telega Oil Company* and the *Buschtenari Petroleum Industrie A.G.*; in the following year it promoted a refinery—the *Vega Rumanische Petroleum A.G.*—and an important trading company—the *Crédit Pétrolifer*; and in 1905 it united all these interests in a holding company, the *Allgemeine Petroleum Industrie A.G.*[2] With regard to the part played by the German banks in the Roumanian petroleum industry in general, it is interesting to notice the opinion of Jeidels:[3]

'The petroleum undertakings, particularly those of Roumania, represent the most active intervention of the German banks in the direction of taking up and developing a new industry.'

As further examples of the participation of German capital in foreign undertakings, and that under the leadership of the banks, we may mention the promotion of two large holding companies for shares in South African gold mines. The first was *A. Goerz & Co.*,

---

[1] *Deutsche Petroleumsverkaufgesellschaft, m.b.H.*, the *British Petroleum Co.* and the *Europäische Petroleum Union, G.m.b.H.*

[2] This does not exhaust the interests of the German banks in foreign oil mines. For the Schaaffhausen'scher Bankverein through the *Internationale Bohrgesellschaft*, was part owner of the *Petroleum A.G., Campina*. Diouritch, *op. cit.* p. 247.

[3] *Op. cit.* pp. 389, 390.

established by the Deutsche Bank as a small syndicate (G.m.b.H.) in 1893, and enlarged to a limited company under Transvaal law with a capital of over a million sterling in 1897.   The second was the *General Mining and Finance Corporation* (capital £1¼ million), promoted by the Dresdner Bank, Discontogesellschaft, and S. Bleichröder in 1895.   In these cases, however, German finance was merely seeking to share in the gains from developments for which it was not itself responsible.

An important feature of the banks' policy with respect to the ' Export of Capital ' was their insistence, wherever possible, that the capital should be received in the form of German products.   Where investment was being made in private undertakings, this could usually be accomplished through their influence in the governing organs of the companies concerned; when for any reason this was not possible, and again in the case of public loans, it was not unusual for an express stipulation to be made to this effect before the loan was granted.   This matter seems to be of sufficient interest to justify some concrete examples.

According to Diouritch:[1]

' tout le matériel pour la construction du chemin de fer du Vénézuèle fut fourni par la maison allemande Krupp.   Si nous examinons la construction du chemin de fer d'Anatolie, nous trouvons pour le seul embranchement d'Ismidt à Angora, les chiffres suivants: le poids total des rails, traverses, éclisses, boulons, etc., est de 70,000 tonnes; 90% de ce matériel fut fourni par les maisons métallurgiques allemandes, en particulier par Krupp, la Gutehoffnungshütte et le Aachener Hüttenverein.   Quant au matériel de roulement, toutes les locomotives viennent des usines d'Esslingen ainsi que les wagons.[2]

---

[1] *Op. cit.* pp. 221-2.

[2] Later on, p. 400, Diouritch gives further particulars with regard to these orders : ' on peut se rendre compte de ces commandes : jusqu'a 1893, les usines allemandes avaient déjà reçu pour 4½ millions de commandes pour le matériel de roulement.   Elles avaient également fourni pour 9 millions

Nous pouvons faire les mêmes constatations à propos du chemin de fer de Shantung. Les matériaux métalliques nécessaires pour la construction de ce chemin de fer pesaient en total 100,000 tonnes. Cette commande fut faite en entier à des fabriques métallurgiques allemandes; elle fut répartie entre les firmes suivantes:—Fried. Krupp à Essen; Bochumer Verein à Bochum; Gutehoffnungshütte à Oberhausen; Hoerder Bergwerks u. Hüttenverein à Hoerde; la Dortmunder Union et les Vereinigte Königs u. Laura Hütte, Berlin. Quant au matériel de roulement, il vient de même en totalité de l'Allemagne. La valeur totale des matériaux de construction du chemin de fer du Shantung est estimée à environ 25 millions de mark.'

The same writer states that the Chinese Railway Loan of 1887 (negotiated apparently by Warschauer & Co.) was made

' sous condition expresse que tout le matériel necessaire à la construction de ces chemins de fer serait commandé en Allemagne ';

and again that similar conditions were attached to the 1909-10 loans.

With regard to the Baghdad Railway, our information is not equally complete. But it may be assumed that the bulk of the materials for the first stretch of 200 km. (*Konia-Eregli-Bulgurlu*) which was built by a German company came from Germany; while with regard to the much larger second stretch (*Bulgurlu-El Helif*) which was constructed by a Swiss company, S. Wolff [1] says: ' The rails for the whole 840 km. were ordered from the German Steel Works Union and the contract for shipping of all the material was given to a German shipping company.'

To conclude with illustrations from another field: the Dresdner Bank obtained orders for German elec-

---

de francs environ de matériaux de construction. Et à cette date la première ligne seulement était construite ; pour la seconde qui nécessitait environ 14 millions de francs de matériaux de construction, des commandes furent également faites aux usines allemandes.

[1] *Das Gründungsgeschäft*, p. 121.

trical works as promoter of the Victoria Falls Company;[1] the electrical equipment for Haidar Pasha Harbour was provided by *Siemens u. Halske*; orders in connexion with works on the Danube were obtained by the Discontogesellschaft for the *Luther Machine Factory*.[2]

It may be contended that this policy of fostering the export of goods in connexion with the export of capital was largely superfluous. Increased capital exports (i.e. imports of investments) usually lead automatically to increased commodity exports, and in a free world capital market it is hardly possible to impose conditions as to how investments shall be spent, unless they agree very closely with what the parties would voluntarily choose. But it must be remembered that any adjustment which foreign lending necessitated in the rest of Germany's balance of payments might in part have taken the form of a diminution of imports;[3] and further that competition had often little scope in the case of projects, such as those for the construction of railways, which were based on public concessions. The banks' policy might also be defended on the ground that it mitigated the temporary disturbances in the exchanges which are apt to accompany large foreign loan transactions. But on the other hand it is open to criticism as being liable to push trade into unnatural channels: assuming that the natural adjustment consequent on increased foreign lending requires increased commodity exports, this need not mean that the exports should be destined for the countries receiving the loans.

The whole practice of foreign investment was much discussed in Germany, with special reference to that

---

[1] Strasser, *op. cit.* p. 24.   [2] Jeidels, *op. cit.* p. 217.

[3] We may leave out of account two other ways in which foreign lending might be balanced, i.e. bullion exports and short term foreign borrowing, as being of merely transitional importance.

country's position, and in the present century the trend of opinion appears to have been in its favour. The immediate encouragement given to the commodity export trade was one important consideration on this side of the argument, and another was that the sums accruing abroad to Germany's credit in the future—interest and dividends—would help to pay for her increasing imports of foodstuffs and raw materials. On the other side critics argued that the risk of loss, particularly through default and international complications, was especially great in the case of foreign investments; and further that the capital sent abroad was required for use at home. The first of these arguments lost force as the unfortunate experiences of the early nineties receded into the past and failed to be repeated; while the misgivings aroused by the second were to a great extent allayed by the decline in the relative importance of foreign investments already referred to. It might, perhaps, have been argued that the domestic supply of short term capital was unduly sacrificed to lending abroad, but this point does not appear to have been put forward. With the political aspects of the German export of capital, we are not here concerned. (It is interesting to notice, however, that writers like Schulze-Gaevernitz considered that *insufficient* attention was given to political considerations in making foreign loans. Certainly much German money was invested in countries which eventually became hostile. One might venture the suggestion that German statesmen were inclined to over-estimate the political effect of economic penetration.)

CHAPTER IV

THE CREDITBANKS AND THE MONEY MARKET

I

THE transactions of the creditbanks in direct connexion with trade and industry arise, as has been shown, out of standing relations, and are apt to be influenced in each case by the special circumstances of those relations. In money market dealings, on the other hand, the individuality of the parties is comparatively a matter of indifference; each transaction is significant as one of a more or less standardized class, and not as an incident in a continuous relation between the parties. In the present chapter we have to study the transactions of the Berlin money market before the War and the influence of the creditbanks on the development of that market.

In Berlin, as elsewhere, the short loan market had two parts, those concerned respectively with the discounting of bills and the making of loans upon first class stock exchange securities.

The development of the creditbanks affected the bill market in two ways. On the one side they provided it with considerable funds and tended to depress the rate of discount for the best bills. This had the incidental effect of driving from the market many private bankers whose business was carried on chiefly with their own money. On the other side they provided the market with new material in the form of bank acceptances.

According to an estimate by Prion,[1] bank acceptances increased from 16% of the total German bill
circulation in 1885 to 31% in 1905. In part this
change was due to the substitution of bank paper for
commercial paper, because the banks enjoyed greater
credit than commercial houses and consequently their
bills received more favourable treatment. In such cases
the bank accepting the bill simply gave a guarantee to
a debt already existing between two other parties.
But the change was also due in some part to the substitution of acceptance credit for current account credit.
Instead of making an advance, a bank would accept a
bill drawn by the customer, who could then obtain the
money he required by discounting the bill. The advantage of this course from the customer's point of
view lay in the fact that acceptance credit and discount
credit together cost less than current account credit.
While the interest payable on the latter was 1% *above*
Bank rate, with a minimum of 5%, bank acceptances
could usually be discounted in the market 1% *below*
Bank rate; charges had to be taken into account in
both cases, and in the case of the bill there was also
a stamp duty, but the net result was a difference in
ordinary times of about 1% in favour of getting a bill
accepted and discounted.[2] To some extent, of course,
what was here an advantage to the customer was a
disadvantage to the bank; but there were circumstances in which the substitution of the cheaper form
of credit would be favoured by the bank as well. The
bill, once accepted, was either discounted (or re-discounted) with another bank, or it was held in the portfolio of the accepting bank. In the former case the
first bank would have accommodated its customer and
earned an acceptance charge without parting with any

---

[1] *Wechseldiskontgeschäft*, p. 51.

[2] For calculations, see Prion, *op. cit.* p. 114 and Weber, 'Depositenbanken,' etc., 1915 edition, pp. 151-2 ; 1922 edition, pp. 185-6.

money; in the latter case the substitution of a bill for an advance might make the bank's assets appear more liquid.[1] Bills originating in this way embody a debt only existing between the accepting bank and its customer and are ' finance ' bills. One of the disadvantages of the general use of bank acceptances is that it has become difficult or impossible to distinguish between these finance bills and bills based on mercantile transactions.

Bank money and bank acceptances created the private discount markets of Berlin, Frankfurt, and one or two other large towns. The material of these markets, the *Privatdiskonten*, consisted in form of bills for not less than 5,000 marks, payable in German money at a place at which the Reichsbank had an office, and with a currency of from eight weeks to three months. ' Domiciled ' bills were excluded. With respect to the quality of the acceptance—ordinarily the acceptor's name alone was considered—three classes were recognized:

(1) The acceptances of first class banks and bankers. (*Prima Akzepte.*) For this purpose Prion defined this group as consisting in 1905 of the four D-banks, the Berliner Handelsgesellschaft, the A. Schaaffhausen'-scher Bankverein, and the private firms Bleichröder, Mendelssohn, and Warschauer.[2] Obst, writing since the War, includes here all the Berliner Grossbanken and the bankers Bleichröder, Mendelssohn, Delbrück, Hardy, and Dreyfus—Warschauer having been absorbed.[3] Treasury bills would also come into this class.

(2) The acceptances of provincial banks and of well established bankers of second rank. The acceptances

---

[1] Until, that is, the introduction of the standard balance sheet form in 1912, which necessitated the specification of ' own acceptances ' in separation from other bills.

[2] *Op. cit.* p. 31.   [3] *Das Bankgeschäft*, 1924 I, p. 275.

admitted to this class differed from one bourse to another, only those of the largest provincial banks and bankers being eligible in Berlin.

(3) The best commercial acceptances, together with acceptances of provincial banks (in Berlin) and bankers not considered good enough to be placed in class 2.

Bills of the first class possessed to a high degree the characteristics of standardized market staples. (*Vertretbar* is the adjective applied to them in German, i.e. ' representable ' or ' fungible.') All the acceptances of any one firm were considered equally good; and whilst differences were recognized in the quality of the acceptances of different firms (the acceptances of the Discontogesellschaft, Bleichröder, and Mendelssohn seem to have enjoyed the highest esteem), with corresponding differences in the discount applied, these differences were more or less stereotyped. Further, these bills were treated in this way on all German bourses. Bills of the second class were treated similarly, but only locally. Those of the third class, on the other hand, were always subject to a more individual appraisal.

The demand side of the Berlin private discount market was provided by banks and bankers, including the *Preussische Zentral-Genossenschaftskasse*—the State-supported central institution for the co-operative credit system—insurance companies and savings banks. In addition to these more or less regular purchasers, intermittent demands came from many quarters at which temporary surpluses of cash collected from time to time—mortgage banks, municipalities, private firms and individuals. Mortgage banks, like foreign investors, usually entrusted the employment of their funds in the market to the creditbanks, but others made use of certain private bankers as brokers to establish a connexion with the supply side of the market. These brokers, it may be mentioned, were also used at times by the large banks, sometimes to place bills which they wished to unload on the market surreptitiously, sometimes to withdraw their acceptances when an excessive quantity was on the market. The *Königliche Seehandlung*, having the often considerable surplus funds of the Prussian Government to invest, was often a large buyer of first class bills, but it bought from the great banks almost exclusively—re-discounts, very often their own acceptances.

Official machinery for fixing and publishing the private discount rate did not exist on the Berlin Bourse: but informally a central bureau (*Zentralstelle*) had been formed to which prospective buyers and sellers, or their brokers, could turn when unable to find their counterpart elsewhere. Here the firm, F. Meisner & Co.'s successors,[1] acted practically—though not officially—as *Kursmakler*, i.e. as brokers charged with adjusting the rate so as to equate supply and demand; and here the rate was daily posted up at 2 p.m. (1.30 on Saturdays). Owing to the large sums which they controlled, it was really the great Berlin banks which fixed the rate by agreement amongst themselves. Prion has described the proceedings as follows:

'The representatives of the banks meet together during bourse hours, discuss the figure at which the rate should be fixed in view of the position (dispositions) of their principals, and report their views to the central bureau. Here anyone interested in the private discount rate can obtain information as to the rate in prospect and intervene, if he desires, with offers or bids. At the bureau orders are received up to 2 p.m. when the agreed rate is announced, unless the orders received require it to be modified. Meantime orders will have been received by the individual banks which may make an alteration of the rate necessary. In this case a further discussion between the representatives will take place, as also when the proposed rate has attracted an excess of bids or offers at the bureau. The

---

[1] Obst, *op. cit.* I, p. 226.

banks then decide, according to their circumstances, to take up the excess supply or meet the excess demand, or to make the necessary adjustment in the rate.' [1]

The rate fixed in this way was a price-basis rather than an actual price, since allowance had to be made for differences in quality and currency of bills coming within the class *Privatdiskonten*. The published rate was a maximum for the higher grade or 'represent-able' (*vertretbares*) paper (Class 1 above), and a minimum for the lower grade 'unrepresentable' paper (Class 3). Differences in currency—within the limits of eight weeks and three months—were only taken into account at certain times; in the years immediately before the War the practice grew up of quoting two rates at such times—one for bills with about 56 days currency and the other for bills with something like 90 days to run.

Although the central bureau in the Bourse building was the pivot of the market, the centre at which the necessary adjustments of demand, supply, and rate of discount were made, a very considerable part of the *Privatdiskonten* were bought and sold at the market rate over the counters of the banks. The extent of the bourse discount market has to be defined rather by the nature of the transactions than by the place in which they were carried out. As has been explained, it is the dealings which were discontinuous so far as the past and future relations of the parties were concerned, but which bore the closest relations to similar dealings being carried on at the same time between other parties, which are to be regarded as market transactions.

Within certain limits, the fixing of the private dis-count rate lay in the discretion of the banks. Their interest in the matter did not necessarily consist, however,

---

[1] *Op. cit.* p. 74.

in keeping the rate high, nor in following a policy of monopolistic charging, according to strict theory. The influence of money market conditions upon their other transactions had to be considered, particularly when large capital issues were pending. At times the interests of the leading banks and bankers were at variance; and on at least one occasion it was found impossible to fix a rate for this reason. This was in 1905, when the Deutsche Bank wanted an easy money market to facilitate the emission of a Japanese Government loan and was opposed by Mendelssohn & Co., the financial agents of the Russian Government.

The private rate was usually about 1% below the Bank rate (Reichsbank rate of discount), seldom being more than $1\frac{1}{4}$% below or less than $\frac{3}{4}$%. The difference naturally tended to deprive the Reichsbank of such bills as were eligible for the private market, and for a certain period in the last century the Reichsbank endeavoured to meet this competition by itself applying a rate below its official one in discounting the best bills (according to some authorities this was never done in Berlin owing to an arrangement come to with the Berlin banks). This discrimination in the treatment of bills, however, was generally condemned by public opinion as contrary to the proper policy of a public (or semi-public) institution; and consequently, although upheld as legal in a case before the *Bundesrath*, the ' private ' rate of the Reichsbank has been dispensed with since 1896.[1]

Since that date, therefore, the Reichsbank has had only one discount rate applicable to all bills sufficiently good to be discounted at all. A certain quantity of the best bills continued to go to the Reichsbank, despite the disadvantage of the relatively high discount

[1] The Bank (Renewal) Act of 1899 permitted the use of a ' private ' rate when the official rate was 4 % or lower : advantage was not taken, however, of this permission.

rate, because the terms on which the Bank kept *Giro* (let us here call them 'cheque') accounts made it advantageous for those having such accounts to do as much of their business with the Bank as possible.[1] But in general the Bank's portfolio came to hold—apart from re-discounts—good second class bills, or bills which because of their amount or currency were not eligible for the private market.

The margin between the Bank rate and the private discount rate tended to be limited by the conventional relationship which existed between the Bank rate and the banks' deposit rates. If this were not sufficient, the Reichsbank could influence the private rate by buying or selling Treasury bills (*Schatzanweisungen*). More usually the intervention took the form of selling Treasury bills to tighten market rates, for the desire of the banks to keep their share in the market usually ensured that their rates followed the official rate in its downward movements. Only in exceptional circumstances did the private rate stand above Bank rate: in times of great strain, when there were many finance bills on the market which were ineligible for discount at the Bank, or when a rise in the Bank rate was imminent.[2]

The leading Berlin banks generally professed not to re-discount bills from their portfolios. An acknowledged exception existed in connexion with the use of the Reichsbank to collect payment on bills accepted in 'Bank towns' other than that in which they were discounted. These bills were re-discounted at the

---

[1] The arrangement was that those using the Reichsbank system of making payments by book transfers had to maintain a certain minimum balance at the Bank, on which no interest was paid. The size of this balance was determined for each customer, primarily on the basis of the volume of payments made on his account (to or from different Reichsbank offices). But the amount determined on this basis was reduced according to the amount of profit yielding business brought to the Bank. See Appendix II.

[2] Prion, *op. cit.* p. 101. Obst, *op. cit.* I, p. 278.

Reichsbank for the minimum period—five to ten days according to the value of the bill.[1]   Apart from this, however, the profession cannot be taken seriously; indeed it was very largely the possibility of re-discount which caused the banks to regard bills with such favour as investments.   All that can truly be said is that the banks did not re-discount openly if it could be avoided. Three ways in which they could often turn bills into ready money were the following:

(1) By sale to their own customers, or through the mediation of brokers on the bourse.

(2) By re-discount at the Seehandlung, or by pledging the bills with this institution for loan.   The latter course (*Wechsellombard*) was perhaps the more usual.

(3) By re-discount abroad.   French banks, particularly the *Crédit Lyonnais*, were frequently used for this purpose before 1911.[2]

In cases of serious cash shortage, however, these means did not suffice: then bills with more than the minimum period to run had to be taken to the Reichsbank either for re-discount or as pledges for loans.   The possibility of having to take this course was a further circumstance tending to keep the Bank rate and the private discount rate in a certain relation to one another.

II

Loans in the money market raised on the deposit of stock exchange securities were taken up mainly, although not exclusively, by stock exchange speculators.   With one exception (to be dealt with below), the securities were pledged to the lender, and the loan

---

[1] These days, therefore, were always charged at the Bank rate when such a bill was discounted, even if a lower rate was applied for the rest of its currency.

[2] As an alternative to re-discounting, the German banks also raised money abroad by the sale of their own acceptances.   It is said that this was done very largely in the London market.

was, therefore, what is called in Germany a 'lombard loan.' In the case of these market lombard loans, the rate of interest depended almost entirely upon the duration of the loan; the quality of the pledge—possibly in some cases the standing of the borrower also —was taken into account in fixing the amount of margin required.

With regard to duration, and therefore rate of interest, the loans were of three kinds:

(1) *Tägliches Geld* or money at call. Here money was lent from day to day, and on notice being given before 1 p.m. on one day, had to be repaid before noon on the following day. The possibility of calling in the loan at such short notice was, of course, a great advantage to lenders in the position of the banks, and consequently the rate of interest charged was usually lower than the private discount rate. At times of temporary stringency, however—as at the end of the quarter—it might rise above the private discount rate; for those in need of money would prefer to pay a very high rate for a few days only rather than a moderately high rate for two months or more. The lenders, on their part, were influenced by the prospects of the market in distributing their funds; if the discount rate was likely to fall in the near future, they would prefer to discount bills, and this preference would tend to raise the day to day rate. So far as bourse speculations were concerned, *Tägliches Geld* was used by those engaged in cash dealings as opposed to dealings for the settlement; but it was also extensively exchanged between one bank (or banker) and another.[1] Between the big banks pledges were dispensed with.

(2) *Monatsgeld* (monthly money) or money lent between one bourse settlement and the next, these settlements then (before the War) taking place at the end

---

[1] For *Tägliches Geld*, see Prion, *op. cit.* pp. 83-5. Obst, *Bankgeschäft*, I, 326.

of each month. *Prolongation* money was another name given to money lent for such periods, and its purpose was to enable those engaged in time dealings as speculators for a rise (bulls) to ' carry over ' their transactions. It was offered in two forms as (*a*) *Ultimogeld* and (*b*) *Reportgeld*.

(*a*) *Ultimogeld* was simply a lombard loan from the end of one month to the end of the next. The speculator ' took up ' the securities which he had bought and then pledged them with a bank for a loan to be repaid, unless renewed, a month later. His hope was, of course, that the price of the securities would rise sufficiently before the next settlement to enable him to sell at a profit for that date and repay the bank. The rate of interest charged for *Ultimogeld* was normally rather higher than the private discount rate. This is to be explained partly by the fact that money so lent could not in an emergency be realized by re-discount, and partly by the fact that the lending of *Ultimogeld* meant the paying out of money at rather inconvenient times—at the end of the quarters indeed at very inconvenient times. (The arithmetical difference between an interest rate and a discount rate has also to be remembered.)

It may be mentioned here that under the same name *Ultimogeld* the banks also received money for like periods from private persons as well as from banks and bankers, paying for it a rate a little less than their lending rate for *Ultimogeld*, but rather higher than that which they paid on ' current account ' balances.

(*b*) *Reportgeld* was not strictly a loan at all. In all essentials the process of *Reportierung* corresponded to the continuation or carrying-over process on the London Stock Exchange. The ' bull ' speculator sold the securities which he had purchased to the *Reporteur* for the same settlement at the official settling price, thereby offsetting his original purchase and limiting his liabilities, so far as this settlement was concerned, to the payment of the difference between the settling price and his purchase price, if the latter were the higher. But at the same time he re-purchased the same securities from the *Reporteur* for the following settlement at the same price with the addition usually of a sum called the *Report* (contango). The *Report* represented—economically though not legally—the interest paid to the *Reporteur* for the loan of the settling price for one month.

Recourse to *Reportierung* or an *ultimo* loan were alternative ways by which a bull might continue his transaction. The *Report* charge might correspond to a rate of interest slightly higher than the rate for *ultimo* loans; for the *Reporteur* paid out the full value of the security without protecting himself with a ' margin,' and therefore took a bigger risk than the lombard lender. But the *Report* did not necessarily work out higher than the *ultimo* rate and might be very much lower. This was because the bulls wishing to carry over their transactions might be accommodated by ' bear ' speculators in the same security who were equally anxious to postpone the conclusion of their deals. Bulls and bears pairing, as it were, recourse to outside loans would become unnecessary, and the *Report* rate would be determined by the relative strength of the bull and bear positions. At times when there was heavy bearing in the market, the *Report* might become negative—a *Deport*—just as ' contango ' may be replaced in London by ' backwardation.'

The brokers charged with fixing the official price of each security (*Kursmakler*—see below), also acted as intermediaries between those who wished to carry over their transactions, and fixed the *Report* or *Deport* to suit the state of the market. This—stated always as a percentage of the nominal value of the security—was published in the official price list, but was not strictly an ' official ' rate automatically governing a number of transactions: speculators were free to make their own arrangements with or without the aid of unofficial brokers, bankers, etc.[1]

The banks, one may suppose, would not give out money ' on report ' unless interest was to be obtained in this way at a rate equal to if not above their rate for *ultimo* loans. This, however, would usually be the case with a considerable number of securities at any time. In other cases they doubtless acted as intermediaries between ' bull ' customers and ' bear ' customers, or, where *Deports* were being offered, lent out securities. At times they borrowed securities in order to be able to lend them again in this way.[2]

In ' taking in ' securities as *Reporteur*, the bank became for the month their owner. It was therefore free to pledge them and (in the case of shares) to exercise voting rights in respect of them. These were advantages which it did not ordinarily enjoy when lending on pledged securities (lombard loans): and it was not difficult to find ways of neutralizing the special risks of the *Reporteur* owing to the absence of a margin. The *Report* method of continuing a transaction also seems on the face of it the more convenient for the speculator. But just because it involved technically a change in the ownership of the securities, it came under the stamp duty on bourse transactions (*Schlussschein-stempel*): and notwithstanding the compromise by which the two transactions essential to the process were treated for this purpose as one, this was a handicap which greatly favoured the use of *ultimo* loans. Prion tells us

' On German bourses the *Report* process has lost much of its importance in favour of that of *ultimo* loans. Even the balancing of bull and bear transactions in the same paper

[1] Obst, *op. cit.* I, p. 330.   [2] Obst, *op. cit.* p. 331.

assumes more the form of *ultimo* loans, whereby the same purpose—the continuance of the transactions—is attained with a saving of stamp duties. The rate of interest can in these cases be adapted to the prevailing *Report* rate.' [1]

In the balance sheets of the banks, *Reports* and *Lombards* figured under the one heading, so it is not possible to trace this tendency statistically or to see how far it had gone before the War. By all accounts the volume of *Reportierte Effekten* remained considerable.

To return to our classification of lombard loans with respect to duration, there remains:

(3) *Fixes Geld* or money lent up to a certain date fixed for each loan. There was no regular period for the duration of these loans—one might be for 19 days, another for 41, and so on. Sometimes the loan was fixed up to a certain date and thereafter terminable daily.

Fixes Geld attained special importance in the Berlin market because it was the Seehandlung's favourite way of employing the surplus funds of the Prussian Government.[2] The date at which this money would be required again by the Government (for interest payments, salaries, etc.), was fixed and known with certainty: what the Seehandlung wanted, therefore, was not so much an investment which would be liquid at all times, as one which would last precisely until the time when the money would be called for. The predilection of the Seehandlung for these loans was shown by the fact that it only charged interest thereon at its discount rate, which meant giving them a slight preference over bills. As to margins and kinds of securities to be pledged, however, it was very strict in its requirements: it dealt indeed, in lombards as in bills, practically with the great banks and bankers exclusively. These very largely used the money so

---

[1] *Op. cit.* p. 88.　　　　[2] Obst, *op. cit.* I, p. 327.

obtained in making advances on the bourse—a fact
which justified the assertion that the money of the
Prussian Government was used to further speculation.

Lenders of *Fixes Geld* other than the Seehandlung
charged rates of interest varying with the actual term
of the loan, but usually between the private discount
rate and the Reichsbank lombard rate (i.e. 1% over
Reichsbank discount rate).

The banks and bankers provided a large part of the
money lent in these various ways: and in Berlin at any
rate they seem to have acted in close concert in fixing
the rates at which they lent.   Usually their rates were
a little higher than those charged for similar loans by
mortgage banks, insurance companies, and the *Preussische Zentral-Genossenschaftskasse*: but these were
stricter on the other hand in their requirements as to
margins.

In addition to making loans to speculators, the banks
were associated in two other ways with the business of
the bourse in shares and bonds.   Firstly, they helped
to provide a large part of the material dealt in: secondly,
they bought and sold securities, not only on their own
behalf, but also on behalf of their customers.   Strictly,
these branches of business were concerned with the
capital market rather than the money market proper;
but as the two markets were so closely connected in
practice, it seems not inappropriate to speak of these
transactions here.

Reference has already been made in Chapter II to
the work of the banks in taking over the shares and
obligations (debentures) of companies before they were
issued to the public.   It has now to be added that the
same course was adopted when public loans were to be
issued—whether those of the Reich, the German states
and municipalities, or foreign governments. (Here
also *Konsortien* or syndicates were formed to reduce the
risks of the individual banks.   There was a standing

Konsortium for the loans of the Prussian Government.) It may be said then that practically all new securities coming into the German market passed first through the hands of the banks. Normally the part of the latter was that of an intermediary: but upon their willingness to play this part the possibility of making new issues very largely depended. This, however, is not all. For securities to be dealt in on the bourse officially, that is, through official brokers with an official price quotation, it was necessary not only that they should be issued but that they should be formally ' admitted ' by the bourse authorities: and it was usually the banks who acted as the necessary sponsors in obtaining this admission. Altogether, therefore, the assistance of the banks was required at several stages before new securities came into the market.

In connexion with their issuing business the banks sometimes found it necessary to intervene as buyers on the bourse, in order to maintain the price of securities with which their name was associated (*Kursregulierung*). The greater part of their buying on the bourse, however, as well as of their selling, was done on behalf of their customers (*Kommissionsgeschäft*).

In Germany members of the general public wishing to deal in stock exchange securities usually gave their orders to a bank or banker. There were many bankers who specialized in this business and were practically stockbrokers, but it was perhaps most usual for the private investor or speculator to give his orders to the bank with which he dealt for other purposes. The banks were themselves members of the bourse; and in Berlin each of the big banks had several representatives in each important section of the market, whose duty it was to deal for their bank, both on its own account (*Propregeschäft*) and on behalf of its customers (*Kommissionsgeschäft*). In principle the bank representatives used the services of a broker on the bourse—those of an official broker in the case of securities officially dealt in—in concluding a deal on behalf of a customer. Consequently the customer was always charged the bourse brokerage in addition to the bank's own commission.   But in practice it was not necessary for the banks to resort to a broker for more than a part of these transactions.   Their representatives were always free to make bargains directly on the bourse without the help of a broker.   Moreover, in the case of securities having an official quotation, the bank might itself complete the deal with its customer by buying the securities he wished to sell, or supplying those he wished to buy; or, as was more common, it might offset the purchase and sale orders of different customers.   Thus recourse to the bourse might be entirely avoided.[1]

The growing practice of 'compensating' customers' orders outside the bourse was obviously very advantageous to the banks, since it enabled them to pocket the brokerage as well as their own commission.   It was much criticized, however, from the point of view of its effect on the bourse, the objection being that it deprived the latter of part of the material on which its judgment should be based and impaired its representative character.

To measure the truth in this criticism it is necessary to know something of the methods by which prices were determined and quoted on the German Exchanges.

---

[1] These possibilities resulted from a development of the commission relationship—itself always involving more extensive powers and duties than a mere agency—by which the *Kommissionär* (or person charged with executing the order) was given the right to complete the deal himself. (*Selbsteintritt.*)   The banks appear always to have stipulated in their general conditions of business that they should have this right.   It should be said, however, that the general obligation to get the best possible terms for the customers remained and was enforced by various legal provisions.

See Article by Walther Schmidt-Rimpler—*Kommissionsgeschäft*; *Handbuch des gesamten Handelsrechts*.   5th Bd.   1 Abt.   1 Hälfte, pp. 563-588 ; 977-1047.

Taking Berlin as our example (the methods were not uniform in all the bourses) the ' single price ' system (*Einheitskurs*) was adopted for ' official ' transactions upon a cash basis. That is to say, one price was fixed for each security at the end of each session to govern all transactions during that session; this uniform price was fixed by the official brokers (*Kursmakler*), to whom all orders had to be given, at the point at which demand and supply were in equilibrium. The same system was used in determining the opening and closing prices for time dealings; but time dealings in the course of the session were carried on under the varying price system; that is, the price varied, as in London, during bourse hours—some dealings taking place at one price and some at another—and the quotation was in the form of a list of prices. The varying price system was also applied in the case of cash dealings in securities not officially quoted. Now where the one price (*Einheitskurs*) system prevailed, it is hard to see how the practice of offsetting orders outside the bourse could have in any way impaired the efficiency of the price-fixing process. All orders received by the banks were executed, whether in the bourse or not, at the official ' unit ' price; and since the transactions within and without the bourse balanced one another at this price, it answered all the requirements. Any surplus of supply or demand, so far as unlimited orders were concerned, and (presumably) all orders to which a price limit was attached, would necessarily be transmitted by the bank to the bourse; no more than this would seem to have been necessary for the determination of a correct price. But the case was different when the varying price system applied. Here the withdrawal of part of the orders from the bourse would at least tend to increase the range of variation in prices. And the fact that the bank could in practice (if not in strict law) execute an order at any one of the several quoted prices, would enable it to act in a rather arbitrary way towards its customers. Assuming that the bank would not so far violate the law as to make a profit for itself in this way, it might still benefit one customer at the expense of another.

In the case of customers making speculative purchases of securities, the commission transaction was commonly linked with a credit transaction. Here again there were the two possibilities; either the bank could arrange for the carrying over of the transaction for a *Report* (assuming time dealings took place in the security in question); or it could lend the greater part of the purchase price, keeping the securities as pledge. The latter course was probably the more usual. When unpaid-for securities were pledged in this way, the bank commonly evaded the strict provisions of the *Depôtgesetz* (law relating to the safeguarding of securities) by placing the securities to a general account (*Stückekonto*) instead of to the *Pfandkonto* or *Depôtkonto* of the customer.[1] The effect of this was that the customer did not acquire property in particular (numbered) certificates, but only a claim to securities of a certain kind and of a certain nominal value; and in the event of the bank becoming bankrupt, this would rank as a general, not a special claim, with no priority over other debts. But the bank obtained by this means the right to raise money itself upon these securities, as well as possible voting rights—neither of which it would have had in the case of a lombard loan in the ordinary form. Loans of this kind tended to be somewhat indefinite in duration, although nominally terminable at any time.

In addition to its association with these credit transactions, the commission business of the banks was of considerable importance in connexion with their issue business. Customers who used the banks as their

---

[1] Kalveram, *Bankbilanzen*, p. 80. Obst, *op. cit.* I, p. 501.

agents for bourse dealings naturally tended to turn to them for advice in respect to those dealings; and this gave the banks opportunities to urge the merits of their own issues and exercise a general influence on the demand side of the security market. Further the insight obtained through handling their customers' security business must have assisted the banks in selecting the best time for an issue, and in discriminating between demands for investment purposes and those for speculation. It may be observed that these advantages resulting from the combination of functions were attended by certain dangers or possibilities of abuse. On the whole, however, it appears that these have been prudently avoided during the present century.

III

The growth of the creditbanks contributed very greatly to the activity and importance of the Berlin money market. At the same time, however, it rendered that market less stable and added to the difficulties of the central institution. Relegated to a somewhat subordinate position so long as conditions were easy, the Reichsbank found itself called upon more frequently to assist the market through periods of stress.

The variable character of the demands made upon the Reichsbank and the increase, both absolute and relative, in the range of variation within each year are shown in the first three columns of the table given on page 126.

The immediate explanation of this feature of the Reichsbank's business is mainly to be found in the demands made upon it at the end of the four quarters of the year, especially at the end of September and the end of December. At these times a large volume of

	Total Investments.			Average Uncover'd Note Issue.	Ratio of Cash Reserve to Note Issue.[1]	
	I. Annual Average	II. Spread between Maximum and Minimum.	III. II. as percentage of I.		I. Average.	II. Lowest.
	Mil. Mks.	Mil. Mks.		Mil. Mks.		
1876 - -	454·2	137·1	30·2	120·0	82·5	66·1
1877 - -	416·0	129·6	31·2	117·9	83·0	70·3
1878 - -	394·2	123·2	31·2	88·6	85·7	71·5
1879 - -	397·3	160·8	40·5	78·5	88·2	73·0
1880 - -	410·7	144·7	35·2	106·2	85·5	72·1
1881 - -	425·3	237·5	55·8	125·4	83·0	65·1
1882 - -	441·8	230·3	52·2	152·0	79·6	65·2
1883 - -	425·7	233·9	54·9	97·7	86·7	71·3
1884 - -	452·3	351·6	77·7	105·1	85·7	64·1
1885 - -	466·1	230·4	49·4	105·2	85·6	66·5
1886 - -	485·1	329·1	67·8	77·7	90·3	69·4
1887 - -	523·9	209·5	40·0	55·2	93·6	72·8
1888 - -	492·1	198·8	40·4	− 1·0	100·1	80·8
1889 - -	589·5	406·9	69·0	85·8	91·3	65·9
1890 - -	637·4	314·1	49·3	152·1	84·5	64·3
1891 - -	637·8	225·5	35·4	46·1	95·2	75·4
1892 - -	645·6	158·8	24·6	8·7	99·1	75·8
1893 - -	681·9	316·8	46·5	108·8	88·9	70·0
1894 - -	634·8	175·2	27·6	30·6	96·9	78·3
1895 - -	665·0	474·6	71·4	50·2	95·4	66·5
1896 - -	759·3	411·2	54·1	158·2	85·4	66·0
1897 - -	759·8	415·3	54·7	180·4	83·4	61·2
1898 - -	823·4	526·3	63·9	238·7	78·8	57·5
1899 - -	909·2	616·7	67·8	281·1	75·4	51·9
1900 - -	900·3	557·8	61·9	284·7	75·0	53·9
1901 - -	971·8	475·1	48·9	243·0	79·6	60·3
1902 - -	921·8	621·4	67·4	211·4	82·8	53·7
1903 - -	1,001·6	654·4	65·3	306·2	75·5	52·4
1904 - -	988·8	605·1	61·2	316·5	75·4	51·5
1905 - -	1,086·5	891·7	82·1	316·5	76·3	45·3
1906 - -	1,190·2	985·3	82·8	438·5	68·4	41·1
1907 - -	1,302·4	979·1	75·2	531·0	64·1	41·7
1908 - -	1,208·7	723·1	59·8	415·3	72·8	49·9
1909 - -	1,285·0	871·0	67·8	441·0	72·0	47·3
1910 - -	1,209·8	906·7	74·9	462·2	71·2	47·4
1911 - -	1,201·5	1,174·0	97·7	453·4	72·7	45·4
1912 - -	1,359·8	1,272·1	93·5	512·0	71·3	42·3
1913 - -	1,317·2	965·6	73·3	548·5	72·0	50·5

[1] See note opposite.

payments fell due in respect of rents, salaries, interest, etc., in addition to those necessary at the end of every month in connexion with stock exchange settlements. Now with the development of deposit banking, the cash reserves of individuals and firms passed very largely from their own keeping into that of the banks, and it was to the banks, therefore, that the demand for cash with which to make the quarterly payments was directed in the first instance. But the banks kept very little more money on hand or at the Reichsbank than was strictly necessary at ordinary times—till money and the minimum balances required by the Reichsbank in connexion with its *Giro* system. Consequently they were compelled to find the money required by borrowing, either by way of re-discounting bills or on the pledge of securities; and lenders being hard to find at such times in the open market, it was largely to the Reichsbank that they turned. Within the course of each trade cycle there was a waxing and a waning of the end-of-the-quarter demands upon the Bank; but the underlying trend was for these demands to grow with the concentration of balances in the hands of the creditbanks.

Faced with these demands, there was not much that the Reichsbank could do to protect its position. Simply to have refused credit would have been contrary to its policy; as a matter of principle it held itself ready to lend to all who could satisfy its more or less rigid credit conditions and were prepared to pay the price fixed by its published discount and interest rates. To have raised these rates just for the short periods when

---

[1] The cash taken as one term of the ratio here includes the notes of other German banks of issue. These notes are excluded from 'cash' in the rule requiring a cash backing of at least $33\frac{1}{3}$ % for the Reichsbank notes. Complete figures for the cash ratio in this sense are not available : it was usually 1 or 2 % lower than the ratio given, the difference being greater in the earlier years than in the later.

the pressure was greatest would again have been considered a bad policy for an institution expected to
promote stability in credit conditions; and in any case
this course would not have been very effective because
of the inelasticity of the demand for credit at such
times.[1]   There remained the unpleasant alternative of
restricting credit throughout the quarters, in order to
be able to meet the peak demands without strain.
This way out the Reichsbank did not take: rather the
credit granted apart from quarter-day requirements
was also allowed to increase, particularly during periods
of expanding trade.[2]   The consequence was that the
resources of the Bank were often seriously taxed, and
the reserves reduced to a proportion uncomfortably
near the minimum $33\frac{1}{3}\%$.[3]   Especially was this the
case when heavy end-of-the-quarter credit demands
happened to coincide with unusual borrowings on other
accounts.

This occurred at the end of 1906 and again, in
circumstances in some ways more alarming, at the end
of the following year (see table, p. 126).   1906 was a
year of exceptional business activity, accompanied by
growing stringency in the money market.   Extensive

---

[1] The demand was most inelastic for lombard loans, because here the
borrower could ordinarily make the period of the loan as short as suited his
convenience—whereas a bill had to be discounted for the remainder of its
currency.   In recognition of this, the Reichsbank prescribed a certain
minimum period for lombard loans taken up at the end of the quarter—at
first three days, later eight days. But even this proved an insufficient
deterrent.

[2] In this connexion the expansion in the average figures for the uncovered
note circulation after 1895 is to be particularly noticed.   Prior to this date
the uncovered note issue showed a decided tendency to become more
variable within each year, but no continuous tendency to grow from
year to year.

[3] The note issue of the Reichsbank was restricted in relation to its reserves
in two ways.   (1) The absolute amount of uncovered notes was limited.
(2) The cash cover was to be at least 33·3 % of the outstanding issue.   The
former restriction could be infringed subject to the payment of a tax on
the excess uncovered note issue : the latter could not be violated without
breaking the law.

demands for credit during the autumn combined with unusually large end-of-the-quarter demands to reduce the Reichsbank to a very weak position at the end of the year.[1]   Conditions remained rather strained during 1907, and when some relaxation might have been expected through the slackening of trade, a crisis was precipitated by the financial collapse in New York. This occurred in November, and at once produced an exodus of gold from the leading European centres. Everywhere rates of discount were raised, that of the Bank of England passing in the course of a few weeks from $4\frac{1}{2}\%$ to 7%, and that of the Reichsbank from $5\frac{1}{2}\%$ to $7\frac{1}{2}\%$.   But nowhere did this means avail to stay the foreign drain during this first month, and consequently critical conditions were for the time general.   London, as one would expect, was the first to feel the shock, and during November the market rate of discount was slightly higher than that of Berlin —$6\cdot7\%$ on average against $6\cdot6\%$.[2]   But in December the relative position of these two markets changed completely.   While in London conditions steadily improved, the difficulties of the Berlin market rather increased until they again reached their climax at the end of the year.[3]

The events of these years engendered a general feeling of dissatisfaction with the credit system and the way in which it was managed.   The first result of this feeling was that von Koch was induced to retire in favour of Havenstein as President of the Reichsbank; and the second result was the convening of a Committee of Inquiry (the *Bank-Enquête*) to investigate the possibilities of reform.   The Committee, which was set up in 1908, was composed of prominent bankers and

[1] Cash cover, as calculated for purpose of minimum $33\frac{1}{3}\%$ rule, $40\cdot3\%$ of note issue on Dec. 31st.

[2] Lansburgh. *Die Massnahmen der Reichsbank*, p. 19.

[3] Reserve percentage, $41\cdot3$.

business men and two economists,[1] with Havenstein as chairman. To provide a basis for their deliberations an elaborate questionnaire was drawn up, of which we may summarize the subject matter as follows:

(1) The desirability of increasing the capital or reserve fund of the Reichsbank;

(2) The desirability of increasing the tax-free 'note contingent' of the Reichsbank (i.e. the total amount of uncovered notes which the Bank might issue before the 5% tax on excess issue came into operation);

(3) The means by which an inflow of gold into Germany might be promoted, or an outflow restrained;

(4) The desirability of concentrating cash in the Reichsbank coffers at the expense of its circulation amongst the general public—the void being filled by Reichsbank notes, perhaps as legal tender and in small denominations, or bridged by the development of methods of payment which do not require the use of cash (*Bargeldlose Zahlungsverkehr*).

(5) The possibility of restricting the demands made upon the Reichsbank, especially at the end of the quarters.

(6) The desirability of controlling by legislation the investment of monies received upon deposit; or short of actual control, of influencing this by exacting the publication of balance sheets at certain times and in certain forms.

The first three of these topics concerned the constitution and policy of the Reichsbank alone, and the fourth was not interpreted so as to refer to particular institutions

---

[1] Lexis and Wagner. Perhaps Riesser should rank as a third, since he was an honorary professor of Berlin University ; but his chief qualification for membership was doubtless his previous experience as a bank director.

other than the Reichsbank: but the fifth and sixth related especially to the creditbanks, and the sixth in particular, with its suggestion of a law governing deposit banks similar to those governing note-issuing and mortgage banks, brought home to the bank directors the necessity of vindicating themselves before public opinion.   In the course of the inquiry they were fairly successful in showing the difficulties in the way of legal intervention, and in the end no recommendations were made on this or any of the other matters. But as a concession to critics a number of the more important banks agreed to publish five interim balance sheets a year, relating to their position at the end of alternate months, in addition to the annual balance sheets relating to their position at the end of the year.[1]

The years from 1908 to 1911 saw the renewal and amendment of the Bank Act[2] and various attempts on the part of the Reichsbank to strengthen its own position (particularly by the acquisition of gold and foreign bills), but no real change in the relations between the creditbanks and the Reichsbank.   During this interval the deposits—including current account balances—of the creditbanks increased by 30%,[3] and for most of the time conditions in the money market were easy; so long as this was the case the demands upon the Reichsbank did not seriously tax its resources.   But from the middle of 1910 they began to increase again with the increase in general trade activity, and then in the summer of the following year came the threat of war over the Moroccan question.

---

[1] The interim balances were called *Zwischenbilanzen* or *Zweimonatsbilanzen*.   Under the general company law only one balance sheet a year had to be published.

[2] The Act, i.e. regulating the Reichsbank and the four minor note-issuing banks.   The amendment made Reichsbank notes legal tender, and increased the tax free contingent from 472·8 to 550 million marks at ordinary times and 750 million marks at the end of the quarters.

[3] Lansburgh, *Die Massnahmen der Reichsbank*, p. 43.

The war scare does not seem to have affected the money market much until September, but in the course of that month heavy demands had to be met for the repayment of foreign credits and balances—particularly those received from France—and there were also considerable cash withdrawals by nervous depositors at home. (Comparing August with October *Zwischenbilanzen*, the Deutsche Bank lost $12\frac{1}{2}\%$, the Dresdner $8\cdot4\%$, and the Discontogesellschaft 7% of their deposits and current account balances,[1] and by the end of October there may have been already some recovery.) Between August 23rd and September 30th, the Reichsbank parted with nearly 25%[2] of its stock of gold, besides placing foreign bills at the disposal of the market on a large scale; but despite the large end-of-the-quarter demands which were to be expected quite apart from the crisis, the Bank rate was only raised from 4% to 5% (Sept. 19th). At this price the market was given extensive assistance. On September 30th the uncovered note issue reached a new maximum at $1\cdot25$ milliard marks; yet, thanks to the previous accumulation of gold, the cash ratio did not fall below 44%. With this last point in view, it might be held that the position never became really serious. Against this, however, is to be set the assertion that, in seeking to avoid overstraining the Reichsbank, the other banks recalled credits from their customers in a very drastic fashion, thus intensifying the crisis on the bourse.[3] In any case it was regarded as unsatisfactory from a political standpoint that the money market had not greater reserve powers for facing a crisis of this kind.

After 1911, therefore, the defects of the credit system acquired a new political significance, which was

---

[1] Lansburgh, *op. cit.* p. 43.

[2] 24·8 %—see tables in *Die Reichsbank 1901-1925*.

[3] Lansburgh, *op. cit.* p. 44.

enhanced by the Balkan wars and the general increase
in international tension.   At the same time it came to
be more generally accepted that the next step towards
reform must be made by the creditbanks.   Accordingly Havenstein now addressed to them three definite
demands:

(1) A limitation of advances made to speculators;
(2) More restriction in granting their acceptances
    and in the sale of their acceptances abroad;
(3) A strengthening of cash reserves (including re-
    serves at Bank), to be carried out gradually
    until they amounted to 15% of their deposits
    (instead of about 7·5%).

He also proposed a new form for the two-monthly
balance sheets, designed to make the composition of
assets and liabilities clearer.

The last proposal was at once adopted, and from the
beginning of 1912, 86 of the leading banks published
balance sheets every two months in the prescribed
form.[1]   The only important bank which failed to
conform to this practice was the Berliner Handelsgesellschaft.   The conference of banks and bankers
(*Bankiertag*) held in Munich in the same year, also
agreed in principle to accede to the other demands,
including that for larger reserves.   But here they
found excuse for delay.   In the first place, as the
Reichsbank itself was bound to recognize, the circumstances were exceedingly unfavourable for reform; as
the upward movement of trade approached and reached
its limit, money became scarce and deposits ceased to
increase.   In the second place they regarded it as
impossible to increase the sums held in idleness unless
they could exact compensation for the loss of interest

---

[1] 100 in 1914.   Since 1910 pressure had been brought to bear on the
banks to publish the interim balance sheets by instructing the bourse
authorities not to recognize the new issues of those failing to do so.

in the form of increased charges or decreased allowances to their customers; and to arrive at an understanding amongst themselves for this purpose, they
required time. As a result, no improvement had been
made by the end of 1913; indeed, at that date reserves
were proportionately rather lower than at the end of
1907.

Before attempting to probe more deeply for the roots
of the difficulties here described, one consideration
should be mentioned which sets the development of
the credit system in a more favourable light. There
is some reason to think that in the years before the
War the banks had come to recognize more generally
that the safest course to pursue in the face of a crisis
was to give generous assistance to customers whose
business was sound, rather than to husband carefully
their own resources. In the given circumstances, a
change of policy in this direction would probably lead
to a greater expansion of Reichsbank credit at times of
crisis, even if the change was on the part of the other
banks. And so far as due to this cause, neither the
greater demands on the Reichsbank nor the deterioration in its reserve ratio can properly be regarded as a
sign of greater weakness in the credit system as a
whole, but rather the contrary.

This consideration does not appear, however, to
dispose of more than part of the problem. In particular it does not explain the peculiar degree to which
these difficulties were experienced in Germany. Other
lines of explanation must, therefore, be examined.

1. *Inadequacy of Bank Reserves.*

Since the inconvenient demands for Reichsbank
credit were largely emergency demands from the other
banks, it is natural to find the root of the trouble in the
inadequacy of the latter's cash reserves. It was on
this view that Havenstein's demands for reform were

based.   It is clear that larger currency reserves, either
in the form of larger holdings in actual cash or of
greater reserve note issuing rights, would have eased
the situation at critical times.   And since the actual
reserves maintained by the creditbanks were very low
in comparison with those kept, for instance, by the
English banks—less than $7\frac{1}{2}\%$ of deposits on average
of Berlin banks at end of year and little over 5% at
other times [1]—it may be concluded that it was their
duty to provide the necessary increase.

If the practice of England is not accepted as setting
an unquestionable standard for Germany—and it is to
be noticed that a comparison with the French banks
would be less unfavourable to the German [2]—the
proper size of the banks' reserves becomes largely a
question of private interests between the Reichsbank
and the creditbanks.   Given that it was required to
form larger reserves by withdrawing currency from
circulation at normal times, this could be done either
at the expense of the creditbanks or of the Reichsbank.
In the former case the creditbanks could have held the
currency themselves or paid it into the Reichsbank,
which could then have increased its cash holdings
or diminished its note circulation by a like amount;
in the latter case the Reichsbank would have had to
curtail its normal loans and note circulation, thus increasing its reserve powers of issue.   In connexion
with the second possibility, it will be remembered that
the credit given by the Reichsbank had increased apart
from the end-of-the-quarter loans.   In all the circum-

[1] See Publication of Statistisches Reichsamt. *Die deutschen Banken,
1924-26*, p. 12.

[2] According to Kaufmann, *Das französische Bankwesen*, p. 305: on
the average of six annual balance sheets, 1904-1909, the cash reserves of
the three *sociétés de crédit*, the *Crédit Lyonnais*, the *Comptoir National*, and
the *Société Générale*, were respectively, 9·12, 9·83, and 13·10 % of their
demand liabilities. *Banques d'Affaires*, such as the *Banque de Paris et des
Pays Bas* and the *Banque de l'Union Parisienne*, usually kept smaller cash
reserves.

stances, the Reichsbank was probably justified in thinking that the sacrifice ought to be made by the creditbanks rather than by itself. But the issue was not as simple as it may at first appear; for it concerned not only the interests of two sets of shareholders, but also those of the Reich—as participating to about 60% in the Reichsbank's net profit—and of the customers of the creditbanks—threatened with having to bear the cost of the larger reserves in higher charges.

From a more general standpoint, the alternative of a restriction of the regular credit given by the Reichsbank might be deprecated on the ground that this would weaken its influence on the money market, whilst on the other hand an increase in the reserves of the creditbanks would strengthen it in this respect. This view appears to be correct if it is contemplated that the creditbanks would have raised their standard of what should be their minimum reserve percentage. If, on the other hand, they had merely increased their actual reserves without raising this minimum standard, they might have become more independent of Reichsbank influence because less in need of re-discounts.

But there need be no dispute as to the desirability of greater cash reserves in the system as a whole, if we leave out of account the possibility of relaxing the restrictions on the note issue.

2. *Deficiencies in the Technique of Payments.*

The practical purpose of bank reserves is to provide the means of meeting exceptional demands either for home currency or for the means of making payments abroad. Now the maintenance of such reserves usually involves costs; and further the increasing of reserves by withdrawing money from circulation is accompanied by risks of widespread disturbance. Attention should not be devoted exclusively, therefore, to providing reserves against any demands likely to arise; efforts should also be directed towards preventing the occurrence of exceptional demands. From this point of view the German banking system was open to considerable criticism in respect of the demands arising at the end of each quarter.

As we have seen, these demands were occasioned by the concentration at these times of a great number of payments. In the circumstances the concentration of payments produced this result. But the result was not a necessary consequence of the concentration of payments. On the contrary, in other circumstances the concentration of payments at certain times would rather reduce the need for cash, by increasing the opportunities for offsetting payments. In Germany the practice of making payments by cheques and other means which avoid the use of cash, was not sufficiently developed to take advantage of these opportunities; and thus what might have been an advantage became a disadvantage. Cheques were used, of course, to some extent, and the Reichsbank maintained clearing-houses (*Abrechnungstellen*) for their settlement; there were also *Giro* or transfer systems for economizing the use of cash, of which the Reichsbank system was the most important.[1] But it is generally agreed that the different systems together did not effect that the proportion of payments settled by transfers in bank accounts was anything like so high as in England or the U.S.A. Further—to account for the tendency for conditions at quarter days to become worse—the use of these methods of payments by customers of the banks, although growing, did not grow fast enough to counteract the effect of the increasing concentration of balances in the hands of the banks.[2]

[1] See Appendix II.

[2] The proportion of payments by bank customers which was actually made in cash may have declined, but the absolute volume of such payments increased.

That the extension of the *Bargeldlose Zahlungs-verkehr* (i.e. the making of payments without the use of cash) in one or other of its forms would provide at least a partial remedy for the difficulties of the money market was fairly widely recognized.   Its desirability was discussed and generally endorsed during the Bank Enquiry of 1908, and in the same year an Act was passed to regularize the legal position of the cheque. The directors of the Reichsbank continuously advocated advance along these lines, although in this they appear to have been concerned with the possibility of concentrating the supply of cash in their own hands rather than with that of reducing the demand for cash at the end of the quarters.   Finally, the importance attached to the subject by professional banking opinion is shown by the first of the five proposals for reform adopted by the Munich Conference of 1912:

'an improvement in the system by which payments are made through the development of methods which dispense with the use of cash, particularly of payment by *Giro* transfer and cheque; as a condition of the success of efforts in this direction we recommend the abolition of the cheque stamp which has demonstrably prejudiced the introduction of the use of the cheque amongst wider sections of the community.' [1]

Opinion, however, was not quite unanimous in this matter, and those who urged that more rapid progress should be made in economizing the use of cash met a stout opponent in Alfred Lansburgh, the editor of the monthly periodical, *Die Bank*.   In his brochure on the policy of the Reichsbank he went so far as to say:

'The surest means for avoiding monetary crises would be not the extension, but on the contrary, the gradual abolition of the practices which dispense with the use of cash in payments.' [2]

[1] *Deutsch-Oekonomist* Annual for 1912, p. 32.   The reference to the cheque stamp was occasioned by the introduction of a stamp duty in 1911.

[2] *Op. cit.* p. 50.

His main argument was that such practices are liable to break down in times of panic, and then the banks are exposed to greater demands than would be the case if individuals were in the habit of paying in cash and keeping their own cash reserves.

It will be observed that this argument was really directed against the concentration of funds in the hands of the banks rather than against improvements in the way in which these funds might be disposed of by their ultimate owners.   It may be admitted, however, that greater development of improvements in the methods of payment through the agency of banks would, in all probability, have been accompanied by a further concentration of money in the hands of the banks; and it then follows that the possible demands for repayment which could have been made in a crisis would have been increased.   Perhaps we may say further that the actual demands occasioned by a crisis would have increased absolutely, although not in proportion to the increase in bank balances, since experience has shown that balances subject to cheque are less likely to take flight in a panic than savings balances. But panic demands were only part of the total demands made for cash during such periods of stress as occurred in 1907 and 1911; another important part consisted of demands which would have been made apart from any crisis in view of the end-of-the-quarter currency requirements.   Not in themselves particularly alarming, these had a serious effect when superimposed upon the other causes of stringency; and to some extent their imminence prolonged the operation of the other causes.   The elimination of these recurrent quarterly demands for cash might be expected to have more than counterbalanced any increase in panic withdrawals and perhaps also to have shortened the period of strain.

But the question of economizing the use of cash in

payments and that of increasing cash reserves cannot
properly be considered apart from one another, because
progress in regard to the former would have considerably modified the problem presented by the latter.
On the one hand, the extension of the practice of
making payments by book transfers instead of in cash
would have tended automatically to increase the banks'
cash reserves.   The money no longer needed in circulation would have accumulated in their hands or those
of the Reichsbank, and *if they had not extended the
amount of credit given to their customers*, the cash cover
for their liabilities would have risen absolutely and
relatively; and this with no disturbance to trade and
at a comparatively small cost to the banks.[1]   But this
does not mean that reserves might have been left to
look after themselves.   Parallel with the substitution
of book transfers for cash payments, it would have been
possible for *the banks to have granted more credit to their
customers*, whilst keeping the proportionate cash cover
for their liabilities as high as before—or perhaps increasing it a little.   This would not merely mean that
an opportunity for improving reserve ratios would have
been missed; it would also have exercised an influence
in the direction of raising prices, which would have
been very undesirable in view of the already existing
tendency for the exchanges to be unfavourable.   To
prevent such an adverse development it would have
been necessary to insist that the opportunity should be
used to increase reserves rather than to extend credit.
Our conclusions are, then, that the economy of cash in
payments would have facilitated the building up of

---

[1] The cost to the banks is difficult to estimate closely.   According to the
general custom interest at a low rate would be paid on the increased
balances ; but this custom might have been abandoned.   On the other
hand, the banks would probably have increased their turnover and so
earned more in ' charges.'   How far their expenses would have risen with
the extra bookkeeping, it is hard to say.   But certainly this would have
been a relatively cheap way of increasing reserves.

larger reserves, which would have been of value in emergencies; that it would have greatly reduced the end-of-the-quarter demand for cash; and that it would have provided new reasons for keeping reserves at a higher level at all times.

The Bank Renewal Act of 1909 attempted to deal with the quarterly difficulties in another way, by extending the Reichsbank's tax free note contingent for end-of-quarter balance sheets from 550 million marks to 750 million. This concession enabled the Bank to meet the demands arising on ordinary quarter days without incurring the tax; but the more serious difficulty remained in the danger that when heavy quarterly demands were supplemented by other more exceptional demands, the reserve ratio for notes might fall near to the rigid minimum percentage. In the absence of other remedies, this difficulty might have been removed and the Reichsbank given a freer hand for dealing with crises, if the percentage cover requirements had been made more elastic. As may be known, this has since been done in the Bank Act of 1924.

3. Banking Policy, Over Investment and the Trade Cycle.

In one of the first attempts to study the difficulties of the German money market, Dr. Heiligenstadt advanced the thesis that these were due to a shortage of liquid capital, the result of over-investment in fixed plant, etc., for which the banks were primarily responsible.[1] He wrote with the conditions of 1906 before him, and it rather appears that he failed to make allowance for the normal characteristics of the particular phase of the trade cycle through which German industry was then passing. It is widely, although not universally, accepted that excessive investment in permanent forms produces a shortage of liquid capital towards the peak of a trade cycle: the evidence of such

[1] 'Die deutsche Geldmarkt,' in *Schmollers Jahrbuch*, 1907.

misdirection of investment in Germany seems to be of the same kind as is available in the case of other countries and to relate only to this phase of the trade cycle. However, this is only to shift the question to that of the responsibility of the banks for the general trade movements.   To this question, upon which no direct evidence seems to be available, a return will be made in the Conclusion.

CHAPTER V

THE BUSINESS OF THE CREDITBANKS AS A WHOLE

THE preceding chapters have been occupied with the part played by the banks in three main fields. We may now conclude this first part of our work by returning to the study of the banks as individual undertakings, and examining in more detail than was before possible the constitution of their business.

We may begin by taking as an example the balance sheet of the Deutsche Bank for December 31st, 1913, reprinted on pp. 144 and 145. This is in the form adopted by all the leading banks—with the exception of the Berliner Handelsgesellschaft—in the previous year. A short explanation of the meaning of the items will therefore be of general value.

AKTIVA. ASSETS

1. *Nicht eingezahltes Aktienkapital.*
   Unpaid share capital.

No figure appears against this heading, the Deutsche Bank, in common with the other leading German banks, having its capital entirely paid up.

2. *Kasse, fremde Geldsorten, und Kupons.*
   Cash, foreign currencies and coupons.

The greater part of the amount appearing here consisted of money in the tills of the bank's offices. ' Coupons ' means coupons due for payment.

BILANZ DER DEUTSCHEN

Aktiva.			per Ende	
1. Nicht eingezahltes Aktienkapital - -			—	—
2. Kasse, fremde Geldsorten und Kupons -			90,348,302	23
3. Guthaben bei Noten- und Abrechnungs- Banken - - - -			37,100,602	57
4. Wechsel und unverzinsliche Schatzanwei- sungen				
(a) Wechsel (mit Ausschluss von b, c und d) und unverzinsliche Schatz- anweisungen des Reichs und der Bundesstaaten - - -	639,001,793	25		
(b) eigene Akzepte - - -	—	—		
(c) eigene Ziehungen - - -	400,418	85		
(d) Solawechsel der Kunden an die Order der Bank - - -	—	—	639,402,212	10
5. Nostroguthaben bei Banken und Bank- firmen - - - - -			61,734,630	78
6. Reports und Lombards gegen börsen- gängige Wertpapiere . -			233,226,705	30
7. Vorschüsse auf Waren und Warenver- schiffungen - - - -			216,769,036	64
davon am Bilanztage gedeckt				
(a) durch Waren, Fracht- oder Lager- scheine - - - -	66,928,823	46		
(b) durch andere Sicherheiten - -	60,648,745	63		
8. Eigene Wertpapiere				
(a) Anleihen und verzinsliche Schatz- anweisungen des Reichs und der Bundesstaaten - - -	131,693,780	06		
(b) sonstige bei der Reichsbank und anderen Zentralnotenbanken beleihbare Wertpapiere - -	9,703,933	37		
(c) sonstige börsengängige Wertpapiere	18,008,185	80		
(d) sonstige Wertpapiere - -	1,795,723	35	161,201,622	58
9. Konsortialbeteiligungen - - -			53,462,472	22
10. Dauernde Beteiligungen bei anderen Banken und Bankfirmen - - -			82,469,426	35
11. Debitoren in laufender Rechnung				
(a) gedeckte durch börsengängige Wert- papiere M. 348,735,293. 64 gedeckte durch andere Sicherheiten M. 163,705,560. 11	512,440,853	75		
(b) ungedeckte - - - -	126,019,341	87	638,460,195	62
Ausserdem : Aval- und Bürgschaftsdebitoren -	142,300,710	51		
12. Bankgebäude - - - -			31,500,000	—
13. Sonstige Immobilien - - -			—	—
14. Sonstige Aktiva - - - -			1	—
Summa der Aktiva Mark			2,245,675,207	39

BANK   (nach dem neuen Formular)

Dezember 1913   Passiva.

1. Aktienkapital - - - - -			200,000,000	—
2. Reserven - - - - - -			112,500,000	—
3. Kreditoren - - - - -				
(a) Nostroverpflichtungen - -	1,824,562	81		
(b) seitens der Kundschaft bei Dritten benutzte Kredite - - -	—	—		
(c) Guthaben deutscher Banken und Bankfirmen - - - -	129,702,478	83		
(d) Einlagen auf provisionsfreier Rechnung				
1. innerhalb 7 Tagen fällig M. 626,563,918.34				
2. darüber hinaus bis zu 3 Monaten fällig M. 181,717,653.70				
3. nach 3 Monaten fällig M. 90,725,167.98	899,006,740	02		
(e) sonstige Kreditoren				
1. innerhalb 7 Tagen fällig M. 315,246,966.52				
2. darüber hinaus bis zu 3 Monaten fällig M. 97,694,128.61				
3. nach 3 Monaten fällig M. 136,570,913.65	549,512,008	78	1,580,045,790	44
4. Akzepte und Schecks				
(a) Akzepte - - - - -	284,078,810	78		
(b) noch nicht eingelöste Schecks -	16,624,283	89	300,703,094	67
Ausserdem :				
Aval- und Bürgschaftsverpflichtungen - - - -	142,300,710	51		
Eigene Ziehungen - - -	400,418	85		
davon für Rechnung Dritter M. 242,102.50				
Weiter begebene Solawechsel der Kunden an die Order der Bank	—	—		
5. Sonstige Passiva				
Dividende unerhoben - - -	34,134	—		
Dr. Georg von Siemens-Fonds für die Beamten - - - - -	7,565,162	90		
Rückstellung für Talonsteuer - -	1,960,000	—		
Uebergangsposten der Zentrale und der Filialen untereinander - -	7,121,618	45	16,680,915	35
6. Reingewinn - - - - -			35,745,406	93
Summa der Passiva Mark			2,245,675,207	39

3. *Guthaben bei Noten- und Abrechnungsbanken.*
   Balances with note-issuing and clearing banks.

This includes besides balances at the head office and branches of the Reichsbank—and possibly with other note-issuing banks—those with the Reichpost in connexion with its cheque system and with the *Bank des Berliner Kassenvereins*. Balances with foreign banks of similar type are only included here if placed through a foreign branch of the German bank, e.g. the deposits of the London branches at the Bank of England. This item represents the free reserve of the bank, although it must be remembered that in practice it was not altogether free, since the Reichsbank required the maintenance of a certain minimum reserve from members of its *Giro* system. Until 1912, items 2 and 3 were put together as one.

4. *Wechsel und unverzinsliche Schatzanweisungen.*
   Bills and non-interest-bearing short-term Treasury bonds.

The Treasury bonds are not shown separately, nor with regard to the other bills is it shown what proportion is made up of domestic bills and what proportion of foreign bills. On the other hand separate sub-heads are given for the bank's holdings of its own acceptances, of bills drawn by itself and of promissory notes given to it by its customers. Publicity with regard to these was first exacted by the new model balance sheet, and is particularly important because they are the least desirable elements in the portfolio—having as a rule only one outside signature. It is also valuable as a check on the practice of converting book debts into bills in order to improve the appearance of the balance sheet; although this may still be covertly resorted to by means of an interchange of acceptances between the banks. In the balance sheet before us it will be noticed that an entry—and that a comparatively small one—only appears against one of these sub-heads; but this establishes rather the efficacy than the uselessness of requiring them to be given.

5. *Nostroguthaben bei Banken und Bankfirmen.*
Balances with correspondent banks and bankers.

This item requires some explanation, because it does not include all the money that is owed to the Deutsche Bank by other banks, but shows only the debt to itself which the Deutsche Bank has created by paying money into other banks. When two banks, let us say A and B, have regular dealings with one another, it is common for each to keep two accounts—a *konto nostro* and a *konto loro*. A books to ' B bank, konto nostro ' all transactions with the B bank in which it takes the initiative, and to ' B bank, konto loro ' all transactions in which the B bank takes the initiative. Thus if the A bank obtains a credit balance with B by paying to B, this is for A a *Nostroguthaben*—a balance to A's credit in the account which it keeps ' B bank, konto nostro.' The B bank records this relation in the account which it keeps ' A bank, konto loro,' and has in respect of this account a *Loroverpflichtung* or debt, equivalent of course to A's *Nostroguthaben*. Now had this indebtedness of B to A arisen otherwise, by B overdrawing its account with A, it would have appeared in A's books in the account ' B bank, konto loro,' in respect of which the A bank would have had a *Loroguthaben*; while in B's books it would have appeared in the account ' A bank, konto nostro ' as a *Nostroverpflichtung*. The term *Nostroverpflichtung* will be found on the other side of the Deutsche Bank's balance sheet, amongst the liabilities; the other terms *Loroguthaben* and *Loroverpflichtung* do not appear, the *Loroguthaben* being merged in the *Debitoren*—item 11—whilst the *Loroverpflichtungen* are either described as *Guthaben deutscher Banken und Bankfirmen*, or, if due to foreign banks, are

included amongst the general *Kreditoren*. It should
be added that the *Nostroguthaben* include balances with
foreign as well as with domestic banks.

6. *Reports und Lombards gegen börsengängige Wert-
     papiere.*

The meaning of the terms *Reports* and *Lombards*
was explained when we were dealing with stock
exchange transactions in Chapter IV (pp. 115-117). A
lombard loan may in the widest sense be any loan given
against the surrender of a pledge, but here it is confined
to loans against stock exchange securities. It is not,
however, restricted to such loans given in connexion
with stock exchange dealings, and hence it is difficult
to draw a clear line between lombard loans and advances covered by the deposit of securities as collateral
—between *Lombards* and *gedeckte Debitoren*. In principle the distinction is that in the former case the loan
is based exclusively on the security, whilst in the latter
case it is based partly or perhaps primarily on the
personal credit of the borrower. A further distinction
which usually goes with the first is that in the case of
the pure lombard loan the transaction stands by itself
and the debtor is debtor for a fixed amount until repayment; whilst the outstanding advance against the
deposit of securities may vary in amount within limits,
and even change into a credit balance. But such distinctions are not always easy to apply in practice, and
a bank which wishes to make out that its position is
liquid may give itself the benefit of the doubt by booking as 'lombards' loans which would be more properly
described as 'covered advances.' It should be said,
however, that when speculating customers buy securities through their banks, paying a small margin and
pledging their purchases for the remainder of the price,
the transaction is usually entered as a 'covered
advance.'

7. *Vorschüsse auf Waren und Warenverschiffungen.*
   Advances against goods and shipments.
   (*a*) covered by goods, bills of lading and warehouse warrants.
   (*b*) covered by other securities.

Little explanation seems to be required here.   The
advances are mostly, although not exclusively, made in
connexion with foreign trade transactions, and are
often given in the form of an acceptance.   In the case
(*a*) the goods are hypothecated to the bank in one or
other of several possible ways.

8. *Eigene Wertpapiere.*
   Own securities.

These are sub-divided into four classes:
   (*a*) Loans of the Reich and the Federal States.
   (*b*) Other securities upon which the Reichsbank
        may make advances.
   (*c*) Other securities quoted officially on the Stock
        Exchange.
   (*d*) Other securities.

For the most part we have here securities held as
remunerative but easily realizable investments.   At
the same time, the holdings serve to some extent as a
kind of stock-in-trade for the bank's dealings on its
own account with its customers.   More will be said,
however, as to the scope of this heading in dealing
with the next.   We will only add that the securities
are commonly written down below their current
value.

9. *Konsortialbeteilungen.*
   Participations in issuing syndicates.

The nature of the *Konsortien* has been explained in
Chapter II (pp. 45-46). Taking the name of this account
strictly, it should show what the bank has paid to
syndicates which are still in existence—less, of course,

any writing down which may be thought proper.   On
this view, when a syndicate is wound up and any surplus
of securities is divided amongst the members, the latter
should transfer the securities received to the *Wert-*
papiere account.   Again, securities taken over by a
bank in the course of an issuing transaction carried out
independently would also appear under 8 and not as
Konsortialbeteilungen.   Many writers, however, think
that all securities acquired not because they are desirable as investments for the bank but as a stage in a
financing transaction, should be kept apart from ' own
securities ' and therefore shown here.   As the term
Konsortialgeschäft is commonly used as synonymous
with ' financing transaction,' it is probable that this is
usually done.

10. *Dauernde Beteilungen bei anderen Banken und*
     Bankfirmen.
     Permanent participations in other banks and
     bankers.

Participations in both joint stock banks and private
partnerships, domestic and foreign, are given here.
Permanent participations in industrial concerns, in the
rare cases in which they occur, would be given under
7 or 8.   So far as is known the Deutsche Bank had
none, unless we so classify its participations in financial
companies concerned with particular branches of
industry.

11. *Debitoren in laufender Rechnung.*
     Current account advances.

These are distinguished as covered and uncovered,
and the former are further sub-divided into those
covered by securities quoted on the Stock Exchange
and those otherwise covered—as by mortgages, insurance policies, personal guarantees or surrendered
book-debts.

Under the heading *Debitoren*, but not added into the total, the claims of the bank on its customers in return for certain guarantees given on their behalf are shown (*Aval- und Bürgschaftdebitoren*). The liabilities involved in these guarantees are similarly shown on the other side of the balance sheet. The guarantees in question are for the punctual performance by the customer of his part in a contract, it may be the making of a payment—as for taxes or freight—or the delivery of goods, or the completion of work undertaken (fidelity guarantee).

12. *Bankgebäude.*
    Bank buildings.

13. *Sonstige Immobilien.*
    Other real property.

14. *Sonstige Aktiva.*
    Other assets.

PASSIVA. LIABILITIES

1. *Aktienkapital.*
   Share capital.

2. *Reserven.*
   Reserves.

Under this heading it is usual to give only the general reserve—the statutory reserve which every German company has to keep for the purpose of meeting possible deficits on the profit and loss account, and voluntary general reserves. Reserves ear-marked for special purposes—for providing staff pensions, for the payment of certain taxes, etc.—are then entered lower down in the balance sheet, either, as in this case, under the general heading ' other liabilities,' item 5, or under a special heading.

3. *Kreditoren.*
   *Sums standing to the credit of others in the books of
   the bank.*

This is the most important part of the bank's
liabilities, and is divided into five classes:

    (*a*) Debts incurred with other banks (*Nostrover-
        pflichtungen*).

    (*b*) Credits which the bank has obtained for its
        customers with another bank.

    (*c*) Credit balances of German banks and bankers.

    (*d*) Deposits not subject to charge or commission.

    (*e*) Other sums standing to the credit of customers.

The last two classes are further sub-divided in
respect of the terms of repayment into:

    1. Those which can be withdrawn within 7 days.

    2. Others which can be withdrawn within 3 months.

    3. Those which can only be withdrawn after 3
       months.

The classes (*a*) and (*c*) have already been accounted
for in dealing with the *Nostroguthaben*; (*b*) covers debts
to other banks which the bank has incurred on behalf
of its customers; a counter-entry is included amongst
the advances (*Debitoren* or *Warenvorschüsse*) on the
other side. Although no information is given on this
point, it may be assumed that the debts of the bank
under these first three headings are due for repayment
within a short period.

We come now to (*d*) and (*e*), the sums standing in
the bank's books to the credit of its customers. Until
the uniform balance sheet was introduced, as from the
beginning of 1912, the banks usually returned two
kinds of credit accounts—in place of the present
five—called *Depositen* and *Kreditoren,* but the distinction drawn between the two varied from case to case
and was often very arbitrary. Sometimes the criterion
was whether the money had been paid in by cash or

credited by transfer from another account; sometimes, whether it had been paid in at a *Depositenkasse* or at an ordinary branch; sometimes whether or not notice of withdrawal was necessary; and sometimes no guiding principle was ascertainable. The need for a consistent classification was recognized by the Bank Inquiry of 1908-9, and several proposals were put forward which aimed at finding a basis for this in the economic character of the credit balances. The difficulty of finding a basis, however, which was generally acceptable and could at the same time be easily adopted in practice, prevented any result being reached along these lines; and those responsible for drawing up the uniform balance sheet two years later contented themselves—after providing for the first three classes—with adopting the somewhat external distinction between deposits and credit balances not subject to charges (*Provision*) and the others which were so subject.

In the main the sums included under the former heading (*Einlagen auf provisionfreier Rechnung*) answer to the description of ' Monies which are entrusted to the bank on the customers' own initiative with a view to earning interest, and which are placed to accounts in which the customers are always in credit '—that is to say, they are real deposits. On the other hand, the ' other credit balances ' (*e*) comprise for the most part the customers' balances in current account (as defined in Chapter II, p. 37). But this division is not carried out consistently. For in the first place, when separate cheque accounts are opened they are free from charges and therefore come under (*d*). And secondly the ' other credit balances ' subject to notice of withdrawal have really the character of deposits, a higher rate of interest being paid to compensate for the levying of the charge.[1] The most useful information to be

[1] True current account balances must from their very nature be withdrawable at any time. Presumably the ' other credit balances ' subject to

gathered from these two headings (*d*) and (*e*) would appear to be, therefore, firstly, the amount of real current account balances (*e* 1), and secondly, the division between credit balances withdrawable within 7 days (*d* 1 and *e* 1 together) and those requiring longer notice of withdrawal (*d* 2 plus *d* 3 plus *e* 2 plus *e* 3).

4. *Akzepte und Schecks.*
   Acceptances and cheques.

Nothing need be said about acceptances in addition to what has been said in Chapter IV (p. 107). The liability they occasion is of course offset by obligations on the part of the customers, which are entered on the other side either under *Warenvorschüsse* or *Debitoren*.

The cheques are those which have not yet been presented for payment, but of which the bank has received notice. For this to be given the cheques must be for large amounts individually, but together they do not make up a big item. In this case also there must be an offsetting entry on the other side of the balance sheet.

After 'acceptances and cheques' comes a statement of certain contingent liabilities which are not added into the balance sheet total: the *Aval- und Bürgschaftsverpflichtungen* or guaranty liabilities of which we have already spoken; bills outstanding upon which the bank has a liability as drawer—distinguishing those drawn on behalf of a third party; and promissory notes of customers which have been discounted—in this case none.

5. *Sonstige Passiva.*
   Other liabilities.

Various items may appear under this miscellaneous heading. Here we have a small obligation in respect of uncollected dividends, the sum standing to the credit

notice of withdrawal represent special balances—as for instance the proceeds of an issue which are not immediately required—for which it is not considered worth while to open a deposit account.

of a staff pension fund and a reserve for the payment of coupon tax. There is also an entry for ' Transitional items between the bank's offices.' This is a correcting entry which may appear on either side of the balance sheet. At the time when the balance sheet is made up transactions are in course between the offices which are booked as completed in one but not yet so booked in the other. This entry is made to correct the balance of errors thus arising.

6. *Reingewinn.*
  Net profit.

Some balance sheets show the carry forward from the previous year separately, others, as this, merge it in the year's net profit. Some balance sheets, e.g. that of the Discontogesellschaft, show the way in which the net profit is distributed.

The balance sheets in this form were a great improvement on those available before 1912, and compare quite favourably with those published by the banks of other countries. Even so, however, the statistics they afford can only be used with a certain amount of caution. Like all balance sheets they only give information with regard to the position at a particular point of time; and this is not likely to be perfectly representative of the year as a whole, because of periodic variations within the year and because of possible ' window dressing.' To some extent these deficiencies can be corrected by comparing the annual (December) balance sheets with those published at two-monthly intervals throughout the year; but the latter also may reflect artificial conditions, and in any case relate to end-of-the-month conditions.[1] Apart from these common limitations, these particular balance sheets have defects of their own in that the distinctions

---

[1] These interim statements, it must be remembered, do not give averages for the month.

between the various items are not drawn with sufficient clearness or in such a way as to give all the information which might be desired. There were also certain regrettable omissions with regard to contingent liabilities and commitments (e.g. liability on re-discounted bills, commitments on syndicate operations and time dealings. Further, it was not shown how far securities had been pledged—whether the bank's own securities or those held ' *auf Stückekonto* ' on behalf of customers or those ' reported '). When all this has been said, however, the balance sheets remain the most important source of banking statistics available; and, used with discretion, they yield broad results with sufficient accuracy.

The 1913 balance sheet figures for the other eight Grossbanken will be found summarized in Appendix III. In order to make their meaning plainer, the figures under the main headings, together with those for 1912, are expressed in the accompanying table (pp. 160-161) as percentages of the balance sheet totals. The figures not being available in similar detail before 1912, it is not possible to continue this table back further. Under broader headings, however, the assets —which here are of most interest—are similarly reduced to percentages for the years 1907-13.

COMPOSITION OF ASSETS, 1907-13

CASH, ETC. AS PERCENTAGE OF TOTAL ASSETS

	1907.	1908.	1909.	1910.	1911.	1912.	1913.
Deutsche Bank - - -	6·0	5·6	6·3	6·4	6·2	5·3	5·7
Dresdner Bank - - -	4·9	4·2	4·2	4·5	3·9	4·0	4·5
Discontogesellschaft - -	4·1	4·3	4·3	4·8	3·9	3·9	4·0
Darmstädter Bank - - -	5·1	5·4	5·0	5·1	5·3	5·2	4·9
A. Schaaffhausen'scher Bank- verein - - - -	2·1	2·4	3·2	3·1	2·4	3·2	3·9
Berliner Handelsgesellschaft -	5·2	5·4	5·2	5·3	5·3	4·6	3·6
Commerz- u. Discontobank -	2·4	3·8	3·0	3·4	2·9	4·6	3·4
Nationalbank - - -	3·5	3·5	2·9	2·8	3·1	3·9	3·4
Mitteldeutsche Creditbank -	3·5	3·9	3·9	4·1	3·9	3·5	3·5
Nine Berlin Banks - - -	4·7	4·6	4·8	4·8	4·5	4·5	4·5

BILLS AS PERCENTAGE OF TOTAL ASSETS

	1907.	1908.	1909.	1910.	1911.	1912.	1913.
Deutsche Bank - - -	33·7	29·3	27·9	28·8	27·4	28·7	28·5
Dresdner Bank - - -	21·5	23·8	21·8	23·1	22·7	19·7	24·4
Discontogesellschaft - -	18·1	18·0	20·4	18·4	17·0	20·0	20·7
Darmstädter Bank - - -	19·0	21·7	18·8	17·7	17·6	13·4	18·9
A. Schaaffhausen'scher Bank-verein - - - -	8·9	13·0	15·0	14·2	14·6	13·8	17·6
Berliner Handelsgesellschaft -	20·8	20·8	20·1	18·4	19·6	18·4	18·8
Commerz- u. Discontobank -	18·5	18·6	18·0	14·5	14·7	11·3	14·9
Nationalbank - - -	20·5	17·9	13·8	16·6	16·5	17·1	20·6
Mitteldeutsche Creditbank -	17·1	17·4	12·6	12·6	13·1	12·5	15·8
Nine Berlin Banks - - -	23·0	22·4	20·0	21·2	20·6	20·2	22·4

LOANS AGAINST PLEDGES (LOMBARDS) AS PERCENTAGE OF TOTAL ASSETS

	1907.	1908.	1909.	1910.	1911.	1912.	1913.
Deutsche Bank - - -	12·0	12·0	14·7	24·1	22·7	20·9 / 10·6	20·0 / 10·4
Dresdner Bank - - -	10·1	10·9	15·7	21·3	16·4	17·3 / 10·2	15·3 / 7·7
Discontogesellschaft - -	5·8	6·5	11·3	17·9	21·1	19·7 / 9·5	19·2 / 8·5
Darmstädter Bank - - -	7·9	9·6	17·5	17·8	14·8	14·9 / 14·0	13·1 / 11·8
A. Schaaffhausen'scher Bank-verein - - - -	4·1	6·0	9·6	10·5	8·4	8·8	4·9
Berliner Handelsgesellschaft -	11·8	12·0	13·5	14·4	13·7	13·4	12·0
Commerz- u. Discontobank -	10·8	11·9	19·2	26·2	25·6	23·8 / 18·1	21·2 / 17·0
Nationalbank - - -	11·9	16·1	27·3	23·0	24·9	16·9	11·6
Mitteldeutsche Creditbank -	4·4	8·7	13·7	12·5	14·0	9·6 / 7·9	10·9 / 9·6
Nine Berlin Banks - - -	9·4	10·4	15·2	20·0 / 15·3	18·8 / 13·6	17·7 / 11·5	15·9 / 9·8

NOTE.—For the years 1907-1909 these percentages relate to loans on securities only : from 1910-1913 the main row covers both loans against securities and loans against commodities : the italicised figures in lower row relate to security loans only. See text.

SECURITIES AS PERCENTAGE OF TOTAL ASSETS

	1907.	1908.	1909.	1910.	1911.	1912.	1913.
Deutsche Bank - - -	6·7	7·0	5·9	9·1	9·3	10·7	13·2
Dresdner Bank - - -	10·3	10·2	8·2	10·3	9·1	10·2	8·7
Discontogesellschaft - -	11·6	11·2	7·3	16·0	15·5	16·2	16·6
Darmstädter Bank - - -	8·2	13·9	11·4	12·3	13·0	12·4	10·9
A. Schaaffhausen'scher Bankverein - - - -	14·2	14·5	13·9	17·8	16·0	16·9	15·3
Berliner Handelsgesellschaft -	19·0	16·4	17·2	17·4	19·0	18·2	19·1
Commerz- u. Discontobank -	13·5	12·2	10·8	12·5	16·3	13·1	11·6
Nationalbank - - -	18·4	16·3	13·2	14·2	12·6	15·7	17·3
Mitteldeutsche Creditbank -	10·1	7·7	8·1	8·6	9·8	11·1	10·6
Nine Berlin Banks - - -	10·8	11·0	9·3	12·4	12·0	13·1	13·2

NOTE.—Securities include syndicate participations and bank participations.

ADVANCES ETC. AS PERCENTAGE OF TOTAL ASSETS

	1907.	1908.	1909.	1910.	1911.	1912.	1913.
Deutsche Bank - - -	40·5	44·7	42·3	30·3	33·1	{32·5 / 42·8}	{31·2 / 40·8}
Dresdner Bank - - -	51·1	48·6	48·0	41·9	45·9	{46·0 / 53·4}	{44·6 / 52·2}
Discontogesellschaft - -	59·0	58·5	55·0	41·0	40·0	{37·7 / 47·9}	{37·3 / 48·0}
Darmstädter Bank - - -	57·8	47·5	45·8	45·2	48·4	{51·8 / 52·8}	{50·2 / 52·0}
A. Schaaffhausen'scher Bankverein - - - -	69·2	62·4	57·7	52·3	56·9	53·8	55·2
Berliner Handelsgesellschaft -	41·7	43·5	42·3	42·2	40·1	43·3	44·2
Commerz- u. Discontobank -	52·3	50·8	46·4	41·2	43·3	{44·9 / 50·5}	{46·8 / 51·0}
Nationalbank - - -	44·5	45·0	38·8	42·0	41·8	45·3	45·7
Mitteldeutsche Creditbank -	62·5	59·5	58·6	59·2	56·5	{59·5 / 61·2}	{55·7 / 57·0}
Nine Berlin Banks - - -	50·9	49·8	47·7	{40·3 / 45·0}	{42·3 / 47·5}	{42·5 / 48·6}	{41·9 / 48·0}

NOTE.—Balances with correspondent banks are included with Advances throughout: for years 1907-1909 Advances include advances against commodities, and in later years these are covered by the italicised figures: the main row from 1910-1913 relates to Advances exclusive of commodity advances. See text.

It is perhaps advisable to refer to the longer series first in order to put the 1912-13 figures in their proper setting. This series is compiled from the *Deutsch-Oekonomist* banking annuals, and a difficulty arises owing to changes in the scope of the figures relating to Lombards and Advances in 1910. Prior to that year Advances against Commodities were not returned separately by the banks, but were included in Advances in general: when in 1910 and later years the separation was made by most of the Berlin banks, the *Deutsch-Oekonomist* analyses of assets grouped these commodity advances with the bourse loans under the heading Lombards. This obviously impairs the comparability of the percentages under the two headings before and after 1910. For the years 1912 and 1913 the amount of these commodity advances is known, and they can therefore be eliminated from the Lombards and included with Advances, for the sake of comparisons with earlier years: this is done in the percentages given in a lower row. Unfortunately similar information is not available with regard to the individual banks in 1910 and 1911; here we can only correct the average percentages for all the Berlin banks, with the aid of data given in a publication of the Statistisches Reichsamt *Die deutschen Banken, 1924-1926* (pp. 104-5).

These corrections, however, together with the percentages for three banks which were not affected by the change (Berliner Handelsgesellschaft, Schaaff-hausen'scher Bankverein, and Nationalbank), suffice to show that the bourse loans increased in importance from 1907 to 1910, and then declined from 1910 to 1913. According to the statistical review just cited, this is a typical movement, these loans expanding most during a period of depression, particularly during its last phases, and falling off (relatively) as trade improves.[1] The movement in the percentages for Advances is the

---

[1] *Op. cit.* pp. 9-10.

		Deutsche.	Dresdner.	Disconto.	Darm-städter.
Cash	1912	5·3	4·0	3·9	5·2
	1913	5·7	4·5	4·0	4·9
Bills.	1912	28·7	19·7	20·0	13·4
	1913	28·5	24·4	20·7	18·9
Balances with Correspondents.	1912	3·2	2·8	4·5	6·3
	1913	2·8	4·0	5·7	5·3
Advances against Commodities.	1912	10·3	7·4	10·2	1·0
	1913	9·6	7·6	10·7	1·8
Bourse Loans.	1912	10·6	10·2	9·5	14·0
	1913	10·4	7·7	8·5	11·8
Securities.	1912	5·0	4·2	3·2	5·3
	1913	7·2	2·8	2·4	5·6
Syndicate Participations.	1912	2·2	3·5	4·0	5·1
	1913	2·4	3·6	4·9	4·5
Bank Participations.	1912	3·5	2·5	9·2	2·1
	1913	3·7	2·4	9·3	0·8
Advances.	1912	29·6	43·1	33·2	45·7
	1913	28·4	40·6	31·6	44·9

PERCENTAGE COMPOSITION OF

		Deutsche.	Dresdner.	Disconto.	Darm-städter.
Capital and Reserves	1912	13·8	18·1	24·5	21·6
	1913	13·9	17·0	22·7	19·7
Deposits and Current Account Balances	1912	69·6	61·4	52·1	61·2
	1913	70·4	62·3	54·4	62·1
Acceptances.	1912	13·8	18·1	20·1	15·5
	1913	13·4	18·7	20·2	17·0

[1] Eight banks, omitting

ASSETS. BERLIN BANKS, 1912-13

Schaaffhausen.	Berliner Handelsgesellschaft.	Commerz.	National.	Mitteldeutsche.	Nine Berlin Banks.
3·2	4·6	4·6	3·9	3·5	4·5
3·9	3·6	3·4	3·4	3·5	4·5
13·8	18·4	11·3	17·1	12·5	20·2
17·6	18·8	14·9	20·6	15·8	22·4
2·4	1·8	3·3	4·8	2·0	3·6
2·7	2·0	8·0	3·5	2·6	4·0
—	—	5·6	—	1·7	6·6 [1]
—	—	4·2	—	1·3	6·5 [1]
8·8	13·4	18·1	16·9	7·9	11·5
4·9	12·0	17·0	11·6	9·6	9·8
7·0	7·3	7·3	5·8	5·5	5·1
5·7	7·8	5·5	6·9	5·2	5·2
5·9	9·0	3·5	8·5	4·6	4·2
5·6	9·5	3·7	9·2	4·4	4·4
3·9	1·9	2·3	1·3	0·9	3·6
3·9	1·8	2·4	1·2	1·0	3·5
51·4	41·4	41·6	40·4	57·3	39·0
52·5	42·2	38·8	42·2	53·1	37·9

LIABILITIES. BERLIN BANKS, 1912-13.

Schaaffhausen.	Berliner Handelsgesellschaft.	Commerz.	National.	Mitteldeutsche.	Nine Berlin Banks.
28·1	25·3	21·2	23·3	30·9	20·3
26·3	26·3	19·5	24·9	26·8	19·5
52·6	55·4	60·4	59·2	44·4	60·5
53·3	53·9	62·2	56·5	50·6	61·4
16·6	16·9	16·3	15·0	22·4	16·5
18·2	17·6	16·4	16·3	20·9	17·0

Berliner Handelsgesellschaft.

reverse of that of the Lombard percentages, but less uniform and regular. In the remaining figures the only discernible tendency is for the proportion of Securities also to move in opposition to that of Lombards, possibly with an earlier turning point. The Cash percentages are more or less constant, while the variations in the figures for Bills are too erratic to yield any general impression.

Returning to the 1912-13 table (pp. 160 and 161) and still looking at the asset percentages, certain differences will be observed between the several banks. So far as these can be summarized, one may say that the D-banks had generally higher percentages for the more liquid assets and (excepting the Darmstädter) lower percentages for the less liquid assets—Securities and Advances—than the other banks. Other points to be noticed are: the predominance of the first three D-banks in foreign trade finance, as shown by Advances against Commodity Shipments and Commodities; the exceptionally high percentage of Securities and Syndicate Participations for the Berliner Handelsgesellschaft; the high percentage of Advances in the case of the Schaaffhausen'scher Bankverein and Mitteldeutsche Creditbank, and of *Reports und Lombards* (stock exchange loans) in the case of the Commerz- u. Discontobank and Nationalbank für Deutschland.

The divergences shown are not so great, however, as to make it impossible to form a general idea of the type of business conducted by the greater German creditbanks before the War. And the idea which emerges from the study of the figures agrees with the description already given in Chapter I (p. 25) of a business composed of many kinds of credit relations in a balanced combination.

In particular it must be emphasized that the balance sheets give no support to the conception of these

German banks as essentially investment or holding companies. In this connexion it is interesting to set the investment percentages (i.e. percentages for securities and syndicate participations together) for the nine German banks against those for three leading English banks at the same time.

INVESTMENTS AS % OF ASSETS 1913

Deutsche Bank -	9·5	London City and Mid-	
Dresdner Bank -	6·3	land Bank -	7·2
Discontogesellschaft -	7·3	Lloyds Bank -	9·8
Darmstädter Bank -	10·1	Barclay & Co. Ltd. -	16·8
Schaaffhausen Bank-verein -	11·4		
Berliner Handels-gesellschaft -	17·3		
Commerz- u. Discon-tobank -	9·2		
Nationalbank -	16·1		
Mitteldeutsche Credit-bank -	9·7		
Average -	9·7		

More must not be read into this comparison than is intended. While the investments of the English joint stock banks are supposed to consist almost entirely of gilt-edged securities, this description could hardly be applied at all to the Syndicate Participations of the German banks and to not more than half of their Securities. Again the German banks may be assumed to have been more intimately involved in industrial and commercial undertakings than the English through the granting of long term current account advances. But the comparison does show that the mere holding of securities did not play so large a part in the business of the German banks as has sometimes been supposed.

The one other matter to excite comment so far as

the assets are concerned is the low percentage of Cash
and Balances at Clearing-banks.   These reserves will
be considered again presently in relation to external
liabilities.   It may be remarked here that the reserve
percentages were higher in the December 31st balance
sheets than in the interim balance sheets.   Thus in
1913 the averages for eight Berlin banks were as
follows:

End of Feb.	April	June	Aug.	Oct.	Dec.
2·4	2·9	3·9	2·7	2·9	4·6%

Whether these reserves were higher or lower at balance sheet days than during the intervening period,
it is not possible to say.   On the one hand cash
had to be parted with to meet end-of-quarter or
end-of-month demands; on the other hand this
might be more than made good by borrowing for
the critical few days at the Reichsbank—at the end
of the year this seems fairly certain to have been
the case.

Turning to the liability percentages, we again
observe differences between the individual banks.   On
examination we find that these differences bear a certain
relation to those on the assets side: the four banks
which had the most liquid assets, had also relatively
large deposit liabilities and small own resources.   The
Commerz- u. Discontobank falls with the D-banks
in respect to the composition of its liabilities; but it
will be remembered that the exceptional proportion of
its assets in *Reports und Lombards* also made its position
more liquid than that of some of the other banks.   The
variations in the importance of the acceptance liabilities
allow of no generalization.

In general the German banks relied on their own
resources for their working funds to a greater extent
than the English.   This may be shown by again

comparing the German percentages with the corresponding ones for three English banks.

1913.	Capital and Reserves.	Deposits.	Acceptances.
	%	%	%
Barclay & Co. Ltd.	7·8	91·5	0·7
Lloyds Bank -	6·8	85·8	7·0
London City and			
Midland Bank -	7·4	86·4	5·7

For this purpose it is perhaps necessary to correct the German Capital and Reserves percentages in order to allow for the fact that part of the capital was invested in other banks and had to serve as a guarantee for other external liabilities. This can be done by deducting the amount of such participations from the capital and from the balance sheet total in each case, with the following results for 1913:

Deutsche Bank - - - -	10·6%
Dresdner Bank - - - ··	14·9
Discontogesellschaft - - -	14·8
Darmstädter Bank - - -	19·0
Berliner Handelsgesellschaft - -	24·9
Schaaffhausen Bankverein ·· -	23·3
Commerz- u. Discontobank - -	17·5
Nationalbank - - - -	24·0
Mitteldeutsche Creditbank - -	26·0

The modifications here made do not seriously alter the results of the comparison with the English figures. It has to be remembered, of course, that the English banks had considerable uncalled or reserve capital, which provided a kind of guarantee for the creditors which was absent in the case of the German banks; but, even so, the relatively large capitals in the actual employment of the latter afforded at least some offset for the less liquid character of their current account advances.

It has been noticed that the banks with the relatively large outside obligations had also the most liquid

assets, but no measurements have been given of the
relations of liquid assets to such obligations.   Here
the difficulty arises that there is no general agreement
as to what precisely should be included under the
heading ' liquid assets,' nor even as to whether certain
classes of assets are more or less liquid than others.
But the view of the *Deutsch-Oekonomist* that the heading
should cover cash, bank balances (including those with
correspondent banks), bills, stock exchange loans, and
such securities as are pledgeable at the Reichsbank,
seems as plausible as any, and by adopting this we are
able to borrow also the following table:

Liquid assets as % of external liabilities (Kreditoren, Depositen, Akzepte, Schecks, Reingewinn, Sonstige Passiva), 1913.[1]

Deutsche Bank - - - -	62·2%
Dresdner Bank - - - -	50·8
Discontogesellschaft - - -	52·2
Darmstädter Bank - - -	53·8
Schaaffhausen Bankverein - -	51·1
Berliner Handelsgesellschaft - -	42·4
Nationalbank - - - -	54·1
Commerz- u. Discontobank - -	55·2
Mitteldeutsche Creditbank - -	46·2
Average - - - -	54·3

Differences in the way in which transactions are booked
and also in the forms of transactions themselves, make
reliable comparisons with English banks in this respect
impossible.   Perhaps, however, this need not be much
regretted, since the importance of the relation which
it is here attempted to measure can be easily over-rated.
What importance it has is chiefly in connexion with the
question of the stability of individual banks.   Any one
of these, pressed for payment by its creditors, should
be able to realize money fairly readily on assets of the

[1] Franz. *Deutsch-Oekonomist* Annual, *Die deutschen Banken im Jahre,*
1913, p. 20.

kind classed above as liquid: and for this reason it is desirable that each should maintain a favourable relation between these assets and its outside liabilities. But even with regard to this matter no reliable judgment can be formed without some knowledge of the quality of the assets held, particularly of the bills, for some of the worst bank failures have followed close upon the publication of a most liquid balance sheet. And with regard to the stability of the banking system as a whole, all calculations of realizable assets are apt to be misleading. For no general liquidation of credit would be possible without special assistance from the central bank; and the extent to which this can be available depends on several things besides the assets of the ordinary banks.

Of more importance is the relation of cash—including balances with ' note-issuing and clearing banks '—to outside liabilities. The table on p. 168 shows the cash reserves as percentages (a) of all external liabilities, including acceptance liabilities against which the banks had offsetting claims on their customers; (b) of deposits (in widest sense) alone. For purposes of comparison the corresponding percentages for three leading English banks have been inserted.

The comparison with the English banks is strikingly unfavourable to the German, even if the acceptance liabilities (relatively larger in the case of the German banks) are left out of account. How far the conclusion suggested by this comparison requires to be modified by allowance for differences in circumstances is a question which cannot be answered with precision. On behalf of the German banks it might be claimed that they required less ' till ' money than the English, because they had fewer offices and their transactions were more concentrated. But one may suppose that the effect of this circumstance was at least offset by the less developed use of the cheque in Germany, which

CASH RESERVES, 31.12.13

(a) As percentage of deposits, current account balances, and acceptances (external liabilities).

Deutsche Bank -	-	6·8	London City and Mid-	
Dresdner Bank -	-	5·5	land Bank -	- 17·2
Discontogesellschaft	-	5·4	Lloyds Bank -	- 16·3
Darmstädter Bank	-	6·3	Barclay & Co. Ltd. -	15·0
Schaaffhausen'scher				
Bankverein -	-	5·4		
Berliner Handelsgesell-				
schaft [1] -	- -	5·1		
Nationalbank -	-	4·7		
Commerz- u. Disconto-				
bánk -	- -	4·4		
Mitteldeutsche Credit-				
bank -	- -	4·9		
Average (weighted)	-	5·8		

(b) As percentage of deposits and current account balances.

Deutsche Bank -	-	8·0	London City and Mid-	
Dresdner Bank -	-	7·2	land Bank -	- 18·4
Discontogesellschaft	-	7·4	Lloyds Bank -	- 17·6
Darmstädter Bank	-	8·0	Barclay & Co. Ltd. -	15·1
Schaaffhausen'scher				
Bankverein -	-	7·2		
Berliner Handelsgesell-				
schaft [1] -	- -	6·8		
Nationalbank -	-	6·1		
Commerz- u. Disconto-				
bank -	- -	5·5		
Mitteldeutsche Credit-				
bank -	- -	6·9		
Average (weighted)	-	7·4		

[1] Balances at note issuing and clearing banks not shown; hence percentage relates only to cash actually held.

must have led to more frequent withdrawals of cash.
(Other things being equal, the cash holding of a bank
should bear a certain relation to the normal cash turnover. The greater the latter in relation to balances
held, the greater should be the reserve ratio.) A
better excuse for the German banks is to be found in
the relatively large proportion of their deposits (using
this term again in the widest sense), which were subject
to notice of withdrawal.

According to the calculation of the *Statistisches
Reichsamt*[1] relating to eight Berlin banks at end of 1913,
the deposits and current account balances were distributed according to terms of withdrawal as follows:

Withdrawal within 7 days - -	56·8%
„ at notice of from 7 days	
to 3 months - -	29·8
„ with longer notice only -	13·4

No information is available, unfortunately, with regard
to the position of the English banks in this respect;
but it is probable that their liabilities as well as their
assets were more liquid. When all is said, however,
the comparative weakness of the German banks in
respect of cash reserves may be considered to be sufficiently well established.

So far we have concerned ourselves exclusively with
the balance sheets of the nine great Berlin banks, and
it must be emphasized that these relate solely to the
business carried on by each bank directly and in its own
name. They do not cover the business of the subsidiary or affiliated banks (*Konzernbanken*) and fail
therefore to show the position of the groups (*Konzerne*)
as a whole. Unfortunately, it is impossible to con-
struct composite balance sheets which would do this
correctly. The balance sheets of the individual banks
are available for the purpose, but it is impossible to

[1] *Die deutschen Banken, 1924-1926*, p. 15.

PROVINCIAL BANKS: PERCENTAGE COMPOSITION OF ASSETS, 1913

	Cash Reserve.	Bills.	Balances with Correspondents.	Bourse Loans.	Advances against Goods.	Securities.	Syndicate Participations.	Bank Participations.	Advances.
Rheinische Creditbank - -	1·7	15·5	3·8	11·3	1·2	4·0	6·0	2·9	51·1
Rhein-Westfälische Discontogesellschaft - -	2·4	11·9	2·3	17·3	2·9	4·1	2·0	12·1	41·6
Barmer Bankverein - -	3·0	16·9	3·0	8·3	4·2	4·8	0·6	3·2	52·6
Essener Creditanstalt - -	6·3	21·7	4·3	10·1	—	6·3	1·6	1·1	46·3
Bergisch-Märkische Bank -	3·1	18·9	5·7	19·7	0·1	3·3	1·1	0·2	44·0
Mitteldeutsche Privatbank-	3·3	12·0	2·2	18·1	13·3	4·5	2·3	4·1	37·7
Norddeutsche Bank - -	1·7 [1]	25·6	4·9	11·1	3·1	2·3	2·9	3·6	43·3
Pfälzische Bank - - -	2·6	14·4	3·6	9·8	1·1	5·0	1·9	—	57·4
Schlesische Bankverein - -	3·1	22·7	1·1	10·5	—	10·0	2·5	2·5	45·8

[1] Balances at Clearing Banks not included.

PROVINCIAL BANKS: PERCENTAGE COMPOSITION OF LIABILITIES, 1913

	Capital and Reserves.	Deposits and Current Account Balances.	Acceptances.
Rheinische Creditbank - -	27·1	44·9	24·8
Rhein-Westfälische Discontogesellschaft - -	36·5	38·6	22·8
Barmer Bankverein - -	35·0	39·0	23·9
Essener Creditanstalt - -	36·5	52·3	7·6
Bergisch-Märkische Bank -	26·7	59·1	11·3
Mitteldeutsche Privatbank -	23·3	58·5	16·5

eliminate in them the items which offset one another for the group as a whole; and to include them would not merely inflate the group balance sheets (no great matter perhaps), but would also distort the composition of the assets by overstating the more liquid items, such as bank balances, 'lombards,' and bills other than own acceptances and own drafts. We shall, therefore, content ourselves with adding a table (p. 170) showing the composition of the assets and liabilities of the nine largest provincial banks at the end of 1913, treating these banks as individual concerns without reference to their adherence to groups.

Comparing this table with the corresponding one relating to the Berlin banks, it will be noticed that the provincial banks show low percentages in the case of the most liquid assets and also in security holdings and syndicate participations; higher percentages in advances (*Debitoren*) and—rather surprisingly—bourse loans. On the liability side their own resources are seen to be relatively greater, their deposits, etc., relatively smaller.

In conjunction with its annual balance sheet each bank has to publish a profit and loss account. No such standard form having been adopted as in the case of the balance sheet, there is some variety in the headings employed in the division of receipts and expenditures. The scheme on p. 172 may be given as typical of the more detailed accounts. In less detailed statements 'charges and commissions' may be thrown together with 'interest and discounts,' the last three items on the receipts side may be amalgamated, whilst on the other side (expenditure) expenses of management and taxes may be combined. There is also a diversity of practice in the deductions made before the net profit is arrived at: thus some banks treat contributions to pension reserves and directors' fees as expenses rather than as part of the net profit.

PROFIT AND LOSS ACCOUNT OF *X* BANK

Expenditure.	Receipts.
To expenses of management.	Brought forward.
To taxes.	By interest and discounts.
To depreciation	By charges and commissions.
(*a*) of real property.	By security holdings and deal-
(*b*) of debts and securities.	ings.
To net profit divided into:	By syndicate transactions.
(*a*) addition to general re-	By participations in other
serves.	banks.
(*b*) contribution to pension	
funds.	
(*c*) directors' fees.	
(*d*) carry over to next year.	
(*e*) dividends.	

In principle the profit and loss accounts should be a most valuable supplement to the balance sheets, because they relate to the business of the whole year, and again because they cover the business done by the banks on commission or as intermediaries. Actually, however, their use is very limited. As will be seen from our example above, even in the fullest form of account commonly to be met with, the information given is very scanty. No light is thrown, for example, upon the contribution of the various branches of credit business to the interest account, nor upon relative importance of the many sources of commissions. One can do little more than take the earnings by way of interest (with discounts) and charges together as representing what the banks made in the so-called regular banking (i.e. in transactions which do not lock-up considerable sums), and the earnings from securities and syndicate transactions together as representing what they made in the financing branch of their business. Yet in making only this broad division of receipts we encounter a certain difficulty, namely, that while many banks debited the security account and credited the interest account with 4% interest on their investments—a course which seems legitimate in itself —this practice was not universal; in particular cases it may be impossible to tell whether it has been done or not.   These are shortcomings in the description of the receipts; not less serious is the fact that the amounts shown under the various descriptions are seldom precisely the amounts which were actually earned.   To a greater or less degree the real earnings were commonly written down, either to meet undisclosed losses or to form secret reserves—this, it must be understood, quite apart from sums openly put to depreciation or reserves out of the gross profit.   This obviously introduces a certain artificiality into the figure for gross profit, and may also affect the proportionate contribution from various sources.   Incidentally, it means that losses, covered by undisclosed earnings or by drawing upon secret reserves, may be entirely concealed from the public.

Such use as the published profit and loss accounts have lies chiefly in affording a basis for comparisons between different years, in which it may be assumed that the errors more or less cancel out.   Thus, on the side of receipts, one can trace the changes in the relative contributions made under the different headings and particularly under the two groups of headings which represent regular and irregular banking respectively; and on the other side one can observe the changes in the proportions of gross profit absorbed by expenses. A selection from the statistics relating to the former matter has already been given in Chapter I (p. 26), and we here insert two tables (p. 174) relating to the latter.

The first table relating to the eight years immediately before the War is based on figures given in the *Deutsch-Oekonomist* annual reviews, and shows the relation between gross profits and business expenses,

taking the latter to include taxes but to exclude allocations to pension and other special funds and also
directors' fees. The second table, giving five year
averages for a longer period, is taken from Bosenick,[1]

EXPENSES AS % OF GROSS PROFITS

(a) Yearly percentages from the DEUTSCH-OEKONOMIST.

	1906.	1907.	1908.	1909.	1910.	1911.	1912.	1913.
Deutsche Bank - - -	36·0	37·5	38·0	40·8	42·5	43·9	36·7	35·4
Dresdner Bank - - -	28·0	30·7	33·0	33·9	34·4	36·6	38·3	38·2
Discontogesellschaft - -	29·0	30·5	30·0	30·6	33·1	34·2	35·6	36·4
Darmstädter Bank - -	37·0	42·7	42·0	43·0	47·9	49·3	42·8	46·0
Schaaffhausen Bankverein -	16·0	18·4	21·0	23·7	25·0	25·6	31·8	35·4
Berliner Handelsgesellschaft	15·0	18·1	20·0	17·3	19·5	19·0	21·1	23·3
Commerz- u. Discontobank -	36·0	41·8	46·0	45·4	47·1	48·1	47·1	46·9
Nationalbank - - -	22·0	27·9	28·0	28·8	28·0	46·2	30·9	33·8
Mitteldeutsche Creditbank -	30·0	33·3	35·0	39·0	39·8	39·5	33·6	36·6
Average - - -	30·0	33·0	34·0	34·5	36·5	37·5	36·3	37·1

(b) Quinquennial averages from Bosenick.

	1886-90.	1891-95.	1896-1900.	1901-05.	1906-10.
Deutsche Bank - - - -	40·7	45·5	40·5	46·3	51·9
Dresdner Bank - - - -	34·4	36·1	43·3	54·4	55·1
Discontogesellschaft - - -	31·3	45·1	31·4	38·4	41·2
Darmstädter Bank - - -	24·4	27·3	27·8	37·7	47·2
Schaaffhausen Bankverein - -	42·1	25·9	24·4	30·9	35·7
Berliner Handelsgesellschaft - -	34·0	35·1	30·8	36·3	32·5
Commerz- u Discontobank - -	16·5	27·1	35·7	43·0	53·3
Nationalbank - - - -	30·8	38·2	36·9	52·4	47·2
Mitteldeutsche Creditbank - -	34·4	39·7	38·8	42·1	46·7

and while also showing the proportion of gross profits
absorbed by costs construes the last term more widely
to include pension fund contributions and a proportion
of the directors' fees. In both tables year to year
variations are to be seen, due very largely to changing

[1] *Neudeutsche gemischte Bankwirtschaft.* Anlage VI, p. 244.

conditions of trade; but in both there is discernible a general tendency for the costs to become relatively higher.

This tendency attracted considerable attention just before the War and was the subject of discussion both amongst practical bankers and theoretical writers—of whom Bosenick may be mentioned in particular. For the former it pointed to the conclusion that the charges must be increased; for the latter that the development of banking organization had been accompanied by a loss of efficiency. As a question relating to the development of the banks it does not perhaps directly concern us in this chapter; but on the other hand the importance which it attained just at this time gives us some justification for examining it further.

It may be suggested, then, that the figures seem hardly to warrant the misgivings which they excited, either from a public or a private point of view. To begin with, it may be doubted whether the errors acknowledged to exist in the figures for each year do actually cancel out in the comparisons between different years or series of years. On the contrary there is some reason to think that the under-statement of gross profits became greater year by year, owing to an extension of the practice of building up secret reserves out of undisclosed profits. But taking the figures as they stand, they do not necessarily lead to unfavourable conclusions. Looking at the matter from the point of view of the public, there would be no reason for complaint if the increase in costs in relation to earnings was due to lower charges or to an increase in gratuitous services— and this was precisely the explanation which the banks put forward. But this, if true, need not mean that the development was prejudicial to the private interests of the banks. The smaller margin of profit per transaction might have been offset so far as profits as a whole were concerned by the larger number of transactions performed. And when one looks at the further evidence, this does appear to have been the case. From the table below it will be seen that the dividends tended on the whole rather to increase than decrease,

DIVIDENDS

(a) Yearly.

	1906.	1907.	1908.	1909.	1910.	1911.	1912.	1913.
Deutsche Bank - - -	12·0	12·0	12·0	12·5	12·5	12·5	12·5	12·5
Dresdner Bank - - -	8·5	7·0	7·5	8·5	8·5	8·5	8·5	8·5
Discontogesellschaft - -	9·0	9·0	9·0	9·5	10·0	10·0	10·0	10·0
Darmstädter Bank - -	8·0	6·0	6·0	6·5	6·5	6·5	6·5	6·5
Schaaffhausen Bankverein -	8·5	7·0	7·0	7·5	7·5	7·5	5·0	3·0
Berliner Handelsgesellschaft	9·0	9·0	9·0	9·0	9·0	9·5	9·5	8·5
Commerz- u. Discontobank -	6·5	5·5	5·5	6·0	6·0	6·0	7·0	6·0
Nationalbank - - -	7·5	6·0	6·0	6·5	7·0	7·0	7·0	6·0
Mitteldeutsche Creditbank -	6·5	6·5	6·5	6·0	6·5	6·5	6·5	6·5
Average - - -	8·8	7·9	8·0	8·5	8·7	8·7	8·5	8·0

(b) Quinquennial averages.

	1871-75.	1876-80.	1881-86.	1886-90.	1891-95.	1896-1900.	1901-05.	1906 10.
Deutsche Bank - - -	5·5	7·5	9·5	9·4	8·8	10·5	11·4	12·2
Dresdner Bank - - -	4·7	7·4	8·0	8·8	7·1	8·6	6·6	8·0
Discontogesellschaft - -	16·8	7·1	10·9	11·4	7·6	9·8	8·5	9·3
Darmstädter Bank - -	11·2	7·7	8·0	8·5	6·2	7·4	6·2	6·6
Schaaffhausen Bankverein -	8·0	2·3	3·9	4·6	6·3	7·8	6·3	7·5
Berliner Handelsgesellschaft	8·7	2·1	6·0	9·9	6·7	8·9	7·9	9·0
Commerz- u. Discontobank -	4·8	6·5	7·1	6·4	5·1	6·0	6·1	5·9
Nationalbank - - -	—	—	5·5	7·2	6·2	8·1	5·2	6·6
Mitteldeutsche Creditbank -	7·2	2·3	4·6	5·7	4·9	6·0	5·8	6·4

and certainly became steadier from year to year. Also it is particularly worth noticing that the newer banks which extended their organization most, such as the Deutsche and Dresdner, showed the most marked increase in dividends. It must be admitted against this that the proportion of net profit set to reserves tended rather (but not very distinctly) to decline;[1] but this was probably offset by additions to secret reserves.

But whilst we need not agree that the statistics show a development which had been really unfavourable to the banks up to this point, it can be understood that the banks adopted the view that their costs left them

[1]   PERCENTAGE OF NET PROFITS ASSIGNED TO
                                DIVIDENDS

	1886-90.	1891-95.	1896-1900.	1901-05.	1906-10.
Deutsche Bank - - - -	87·8	90·8	90·4	90·2	90·6
Dresdner Bank - - -	88·8	75·0	100·0	94·5	96·5
Discontogesellschaft - -	88·1	99·1	95·7	100·0	91·2
Darmstädter Bank - - -	95·9	100·4	99·7	90·4	94·5
Schaaffhausen'scher Bankverein -	88·0	89·5	91·1	91·2	88·7
Berliner Handelsgesellschaft - -	88·5	90·3	99·9	99·4	94·3
Commerz- u. Discontobank - -	98·3	97·6	83·4	94·7	92·1
Nationalbank - - - -	70·3	94·1	96·5	94·3	91·4
Mitteldeutsche Creditbank - -	92·2	93·2	91·2	90·8	91·5

Bosenick, *op. cit.* p. 245. Bosenick is also able to argue that the sums dispensed as dividends represented a declining percentage of share capital and reserves together, or as he calls it the capital permanently employed in the undertaking. The facts are as follows :

	1871-75.	1876-80.	1881-85.	1886-90.	1891-95.	1896-1900.	1901-05.	1906-10.
Deutsche Bank - - -	4·6	6·6	7·6	7·2	6·4	7·8	8·2	8·0
Dresdner Bank - - -	4·9	7·2	7·0	7·8	5·9	6·8	5·3	6·2
Discontogesellschaft - -	13·9	6·3	9·0	9·1	6·0	7·7	6·4	6·9
Darmstädter Bank - -	8·2	6·7	6·9	7·1	5·1	6·0	5·4	5·5
Schaaffhausen'scher Bank-verein - - - -	7·2	2·3	3·8	4·5	5·9	6·6	5·3	6·0
Berliner Handelsgesellschaft	7·3	1·8	7·1	7·6	5·1	6·9	6·2	6·8
Commerz- u. Discontobank -	4·0	6·1	6·3	5·8	4·6	5·1	5·4	5·1
Nationalbank - - -	—	—	4·8	6·6	5·3	6·8	4·5	5·7
Mitteldeutsche Creditbank -	5·6	2·1	4·5	5·5	4·6	5·5	5·2	5·6

It will be seen that if there is in general a downward tendency (?), it is not uniform or marked. In any case it is questionable whether companies should expect or be expected to maintain a uniform dividend on capital plus reserves. Reserves are formed to increase the security of the concern and perhaps to add to the stability of its dividends, not to increase the dividends proportionately.

no margin to allow of a reduction of their future earnings.   We shall not be surprised to find then that they were unwilling to accede to the demands of the Reichsbank for the maintenance of larger reserves, without first providing themselves with compensation for the loss of interest which this would involve by reducing the rates of interest which they paid to their customers or increasing their charges.   In both directions it appears that there was room for a tightening up of terms without undue harshness towards the customers; for under the stress of competition between the banks, to some extent also between banks proper and savings banks, the terms granted had become exceedingly favourable.   Interest was paid at relatively high rates upon deposits, particularly upon *Ultimogeld* or month-to-month monies, for which the banks competed very strongly; interest was very generally paid upon merely temporary balances, including those subject to withdrawal by cheque; on the other side customers were provided with extremely cheap acceptance credit.   It is interesting to notice that a less accommodating attitude in these matters was urged upon the banks by Havenstein.   In this the President of the Reichsbank was not merely concerned with securing an improvement in the banks' revenue, but also with checking undesirable extensions of credit.

The terms could not be changed, however, without restricting the competition of which they were the result, and this required organized co-operation. Efforts to establish general agreements were at first thwarted by the differences of interest between the large and the small banking firms, and between those of Berlin and those of the provinces; although these obstacles tended to become less serious as the large Berlin banks won their way to predominance.   In Berlin itself a fairly effective organization of the larger banks and bankers had grown up since the eighties in the so-called *Stempelvereinigung*, and local associations were also established in Cologne, Munich, and Mannheim in the years 1908-1909. These organizations were able to do something to regulate terms in their own localities, but were handicapped by competition from other centres. A national association of banks and bankers—the *Zentralverband des deutschen Bank- u. Bankiergewerbes*—had been formed in 1901, and several conferences were held which awakened opinion to the advantages of common action. Tangible results on a national scale were only achieved, however, after the energetic intervention of Havenstein in 1913.

In this year local associations were formed under the guidance of the Berlin Stempelvereinigung at ten further provincial centres—Bremen, Breslau, Dresden, Frankfurt a. M., Hamburg, Leipzig, Stettin, Augsburg, Nuremburg, and Stuttgart; and representatives of these and the three earlier provincial associations came to Berlin to work out a scheme for the common regulation of terms. The result of this so-called *Konditionen-Kartell* was the first *Allgemeine Abmachung* or General Agreement.

The provisions of this agreement may be briefly summarized as follows:

1. Credit and debit interest rates in general. It was found impossible to fix uniform rates throughout Germany. In each locality rates were to be fixed as near as possible to the Berlin rates. The one fixed rule was that current account advances were to cost at least 1% over Bank rate and not less than 5%. Provincial banks dealing with customers outside their own towns, however, were to charge and allow the Berlin rates.

2. *Ultimo* loans, i.e. money taken up by the banks, ostensibly to be re-lent for a month on the Stock Exchange. Rates here were regulated uniformly in

relation to the market *Ultimo* rate, with a concession in favour of bank lenders as against others. Further, in connexion with these loans minimum amounts were fixed for loans received from others than banks or bankers. Canvassing for such loans and giving security in return was generally deprecated.

3. Minimum rates of commission were fixed for acceptances. ($\frac{1}{4}\%$ for domestic acceptances, $\frac{1}{8}\%$—in some cases $\frac{1}{8}\%$—for foreign acceptances.)

It will be noticed that what was probably the most important matter, the interest to be paid upon deposits and credit balances, was only imperfectly controlled; and in other respects the agreement seems to have been more important in checking undercutting than in bringing about a general increase of charges. But whatever its immediate effects—and, of course, the outbreak of the War changed the whole situation a year later—it must be regarded as of considerable importance as a first step in the direction of replacing competition by general agreements.

In concluding this chapter it may be mentioned that the decade before the War was free from serious bank catastrophes: indeed since the eighties these have been very rare. The economic crisis of 1901 produced a certain number of bank failures, including those of the *Leipziger Bank* and the *Dresdner Kreditanstalt*; but neither of these banks was typical of the German banking system, although of considerable local importance. Both were independent provincial banks and each became involved in the fate of one particular industrial concern—respectively the Trebertrocknung Company and the Kummer electrical group. It was this failure to distribute their risks which was responsible for their downfall.[1] With the exception of the Dresdner Bank,

---

[1] In the case of the Leipziger Bank, at least, the disaster was aggravated by the adoption of various improper means in the hope of saving the situation. For particulars of both cases, see Schulze, *Die Bankkatastrophen in Sachsen.*

which was affected by a local panic, following the
failures just mentioned, the big Berlin banks came
through the period of stress without difficulty, and the
Deutsche Bank was able to take advantage of the
situation in Saxony by acquiring the connexions of the
Leipziger Bank. After 1901, the only failures to
mention are those of the *Vereinsbank*, Frankfort am
Oder, and the *Niederdeutsche Bank*, Dortmund, both
in 1910; but neither bank had ever been really
important. Small local banks continued to get into
difficulties from time to time, and had then either to
liquidate or obtain support from a Berlin bank; but
one can say in general of all these casualities that they
resulted from attempts to resist the main tendency
towards concentration in banking and a distribution of
risks. The larger banks had, of course, their losses,
and sometimes serious ones. In particular we may
refer to those incurred in connexion with real estate
development companies just before the War: the
Deutsche Bank and the Bergisch-Märkische Bank lost
some 12 million marks in 1911 through the difficulties
of the Berlin *Terrain- und Baugesellschaft;* the A.
Schaaffhausen'scher Bankverein lost several millions in
Berlin real estate projects in 1913—hence the reduction
in dividends; the Nationalbank für Deutschland lost
some seven millions in the same way in the first part of
1914. But these losses did not imperil the solvency
of the banks; those of the Schaaffhausen'scher Bankverein contributed something to bring about its surrender to the Discontogesellschaft, but those of the
Deutsche Bank did not even appear in its published
accounts.

PART II

THE CREDITBANKS SINCE 1914

CHAPTER VI

THE CREDITBANKS DURING THE WAR

I

THE outbreak of the War occasioned a financial crisis in each of the countries concerned and thereby necessitated the adoption of various emergency measures. Some of these, designed purely to meet the panic and dislocation of the first weeks, could be gradually withdrawn as adjustment was made to war conditions. Others, however, which can be regarded rather as measures of financial mobilization, were continued throughout the War and longer.

In Germany the question of the best means of dealing with such a crisis had been much discussed amongst bankers and economists after the war scare in 1911, and fairly general agreement had been reached as to the chief steps to be taken. As a preparation, the Reichsbank had printed a number of small notes considerably in excess of the amount likely to be called for in ordinary times. At the same time, as we have seen, additional emphasis had been given to the demand that the banks should increase their reserves.

With respect to this last matter, some improvement is to be recorded during the first half of 1914. This is not at once evident from a comparison of the June 30th 1914 balance sheets with those for the end of 1913, because, as has been mentioned, the cash reserves were normally higher on December 31st than on other balance sheet dates. But comparing the position in June 1914 with that existing a year earlier, we find that the cash reserves of eight Berliner Grossbanken increased from an average of 3·9% of total liabilities to 4·5%, and from an average of 5·4% of their deposit liabilities to 6·3%.[1] The position of the Reichsbank also improved during the first half of 1914, the metallic reserve increasing from 1,446·8 million marks to 1,630·6 million marks, and the ratio of cash to note issue from about 58% to about 70%. How far these improvements were due to deliberate effort, how far to the influence of advancing trade depression, it would be difficult to say. In any case, they left the reserves of the banks very much below the proportion called for by Havenstein; and they cannot have materially modified the need for special measures in the situation which arose at the beginning of the War.

As in other countries, the Stock Exchange was the first section of business to be affected, and prices of securities fell heavily from July 25th onwards. In order to check the collapse the banks formed a syndicate, which made extensive purchases, at any rate on the time market.[2] But the resources which they could spare were not equal to the task, and the intervention of the bourse authorities became necessary in the interest of security owners. In Berlin the July settlement for time dealings was put forward to the 27th and carried out on the arbitrary basis of the opening price of the 25th; on the 29th quotations of dealings for the next settlement were suspended; and this was followed by the suspension of all official dealings and

---

[1] *Die deutschen Banken 1924-26*, p. 11, also pp. 108-9.

[2] Klebba, *Börse und Effektenhandel im Kriege*, p. 4, quotes an estimate which puts the purchases of this syndicate at twenty million marks.

all quotations on 31st.[1] This meant that the Bourse was closed, although the rooms remained open for the use of members. Later, in the middle of August, it was decided to prolong the transactions due for settlement at the end of that month until the end of September. The moratorium thus introduced was subsequently extended repeatedly, and it may be noted that it was applied not only to bourse transactions in the strictest sense, but also to *Ultimo* loans in connexion therewith, and here to *Ultimo* money taken up by the banks as well as to such money lent by them.[2]

Moratoria were also provided in certain other cases, but the general plan adopted to relieve the crisis was that of assisting debtors—including the banks—to meet their obligations by means of extensive credits. For this purpose the existing credit system was modified in two ways. In the first place new organs were established, the *Darlehnskassen* or loan offices, administered by the Reichsbank through its various offices but legally distinct from the Reichsbank. These lent money upon a wide variety of pledges, obtaining the funds by issuing a new kind of paper money, the *Darlehnskassenscheine*, which were not legal tender but were accepted in payment at all government offices. In the second place, the notes of the Reichsbank (already legal tender) were made inconvertible and the restrictions on their issue relaxed. The limitation on the absolute amount of the fiduciary issue was at once entirely abandoned; the principle that the outstanding notes should be covered to at least one-third by cash was nominally retained, but was rendered nugatory by

---

[1] Klebba, *op. cit.*, p. 46.

[2] The legal validity of this application of the moratorium was questionable. The moratorium was decreed by the Bourse authorities exercising their general powers of controlling bourse transactions. *Prima facie* this did not extend to regulating, say, a loan from a provincial bank to a Berlin bank.

an extension of the term cash to include the new *Darlehnskassenscheine*. (In practice, it appears, the *Darlehnskassen* mostly paid out Reichsbank notes and the *Darlehnskassenscheine* passed into the Reichsbank reserve.) These changes provided ample credit facilities for the general public. To enable the Reich Government to borrow more freely, the Bank Act was further amended to permit *Schatzanweisungen* (or short-term treasury bonds) to be held as cover other than cash for the Reichsbank note circulation.

The publication of two-monthly balance sheets being suspended with the outbreak of the War, no statistics are available with respect to the creditbanks between the end of June and the end of December. For an idea of the amount of cash withdrawals during the critical period we are obliged to rely, therefore, entirely upon estimates; these usually set them at from 15% to 20% of the deposit and current account balances, i.e. in absolute numbers, roughly one milliard for the eight Berlin banks and two milliards for all the banks.[1] During the same time, between July 25th and August 15th, the Reichsbank increased its discounts of commercial bills by about 2·2 milliard.[2] It is supposed that this sum represented for the most part re-discounts on behalf of the banks; on the other hand, that the banks made little use of the *Darlehnskassen*.

Opinions differ as to the way in which the banks acquitted themselves in the emergency: against their own self-congratulatory declarations has to be set a certain amount of criticism on the part of the public.

---

[1] Prion quotes with approval statements that the withdrawals were equal to about 20% of the *fremde Gelder* (*Die deutschen Banken im Kriege*, p. 21-22), but later he computes them as 20% of the deposits, etc., due within seven days (p. 32). I assume that he has made a slip in the latter place.

[2] Prion, *op. cit.* p. 24.

The charges involved in the latter were that the banks refused to pay out more than a certain proportion of their customers' deposits, and that they not only withheld new credits but drastically recalled those previously granted. With regard to the first point, it is not clear whether the deposits in question were deposits repayable on demand or deposits with respect to which the banks were entitled to previous notice of withdrawal; in any case, it is impossible to determine how far either charge would be true of the banks generally. In certain parts of the country—particularly the western margin—the panic was more acute than in others, and here it is likely enough that the banks felt obliged to put their own safety first; elsewhere they may have acted more in accordance with their own account. For the rest, the charge of credit restriction has been more generally endorsed than that of withholding payment of deposits.

Of the banking system as a whole it can be said that it withstood the crisis better than might have been expected in view of the experiences of 1907 and 1911. Paradoxical as it seems at first, the explanation is to be found in a sense in the very seriousness of the situation in 1914. In such a situation the adoption of emergency measures is inevitable; this being so, the outcome depends far more upon the adequacy of those measures and the readiness and certainty with which they are applied than upon the conditions by which the strength of a financial system is measured in ordinary circumstances. On the whole the situation was handled well; if there were difficulties which might have been avoided, it was chiefly because for a while there was some uncertainty as to the intentions of the Government.

The critical period did not last beyond the middle of August and was followed by steady recovery during the autumn. By the end of the year deposits had reached and passed the figure for June 30th, while the Bank rate, which had been raised from 5% to 6% at the beginning of August, was put back to 5% on December 23rd.

The transition from peace to war, the interruption of foreign trade, and the change in the course of domestic demand, were naturally accompanied by losses in which the banks shared.   In the balance sheets published by the eight Berlin banks at the end of 1914, the aggregate sum set aside for bad debts and depreciated assets amounted to 30·9 million marks. This figure includes losses incurred in the first part of the year—notably the heavy losses of the Nationalbank in connexion with its real estate interests—but, on the other hand, it does not include the undisclosed losses met by understating profits or by drawing upon secret reserves, nor losses arising from the disturbance of pre-war business which were only brought into account in later years.[1]   When all allowances are made on either side, one may suppose that the losses due to the War were in the neighbourhood of 0·5% of the banks' loans and investments.[2]   The general effect was to reduce the banks' dividends for 1914 by about 2% or 3%. (The Nationalbank passed its dividend altogether, but, as said above, this bank had incurred very heavy losses quite unconnected with the War.)

II

German opinion appears to be unanimous in finding the dominant characteristic of the money market during the War in *Geldflüssigkeit* or the abundance of funds.   For an indication of this, reference is made

---

[1] It should also be said that it does not include the loss of assets embodied in the London branches.

[2] Cf. Prion, *op. cit.* pp. 113, 121

to the remarkable growth of the deposits with the banks, as shown in the following table:

DEPOSITS AND CURRENT ACCOUNT BALANCES
1913-18

(*a*) For 8 Berliner Grossbanken together.
(*b*) For all banks having more than a million marks capital together.

Dec. 31st.				(*a*)	(*b*)
1913	-	-	-	5,149	9,641
1914	-	-	-	5,321	9,645
1915	-	-	-	6,856	11,769
1916	-	-	-	9,396	15,378
1917	-	-	-	15,210	23,181
1918	-	-	-	19,696	29,981

The idea of abundance involves more, however, than the mere size of the supply, considered absolutely; it implies that the supply is large in relation to the requirements. And in this stricter sense it is by no means certain that loanable money was especially abundant in Germany during the War. The obvious test to apply here, the determination of the general trend of interest rates, is made difficult by the fact that the War introduced new types of loan transactions and altered the relative importance of the old ones. On the whole, it seems safe to say, however, that the interest rates were not far from those prevailing on the average in pre-war times, but not so low as in a pre-war year of abundant money. The Bank rate of discount remained throughout at 5%; the interest allowed by the banks to their customers seems to have been about the same as was usual before the War; the banks lent less at the highest rates (current account loans), practically nothing at the lowest rates (day to day money), applied before the War, but lent chiefly at rates from 4% to 5%, which must be something like the average of the pre-war rates. The nine war loans floated by the Government, it may be added, all bore interest at 5%. However, whether the term abundance is strictly applicable or not, it may be agreed that it is remarkable that there was not a definite scarcity of loanable money, in view of the large sums borrowed by the Imperial Government; and this, in conjunction with the striking increase in deposits, calls for explanation.

Contributions towards an explanation can be found in several directions. In the first place, the War brought a considerable curtailment of the field for the employment of capital: there was little foreign trade to be financed; there was no export of capital; and investment in home undertakings was restricted, at first by the force of circumstances, and later by Government control. At the same time, until the later stages when the profiteers began to spend lavishly, the amount of saving probably increased rather than diminished. As the War progressed, however, these influences must have been far outweighed by the increasing demand for loans on the part of the Government. Since deposits continued to grow, and even grew faster in the later war years, since again the market continued to be tolerably easy, further explanation must be sought elsewhere.

Another circumstance often referred to in explanation of the condition of the money market is the fact that the Government, which provided an ever growing part of the demand for goods and services, paid at once in cash instead of taking credit for the period usual in private commerce. This meant that the traders' requirements in circulating capital were very much reduced, so that in place of borrowing from the banks they were able to build up substantial credit balances. Much the same result was also produced by another practice of the Government, that of buying up existing stocks of goods in advance of its requirements. But clearly no final explanation can be found here. We have to enquire how the Government obtained the money with which to make its payments.

The answer is that war expenditure was met entirely by borrowing, in the first instance by the sale of treasury bills (*Schatzanweisungen*). The policy was to raise money on these as required, and then to convert them at intervals into War Loan. Actually, however, it was found impossible to fund the whole of the floating debt, and the unfunded residue increased, both absolutely and relatively, as the War went on. Thus, according to Lansburgh,[1] the fifth War Loan in the autumn of 1916 brought the funded war debt to just under 46 milliards out of total war costs of 52 milliards, leaving rather more than 6 milliards as unconverted floating debt. At the end of the War of total war costs of 145 milliards, 50 milliards were still unfunded.[2]

The question becomes then: with what money were the treasury bills bought? So far as it was with money already in the short loan market, the Government's practice of prompt payment only returned to that market what it first took away. The position might perhaps be considered different if they were bought with money normally destined to permanent investment; but in any case, the diversion of this money to the short loan market has already been taken into account above, and our further analysis only suggests in more detail how it came about. We are seeking here an additional factor contributing to the ease of the market. Such is in fact to be found in the purchase of treasury bills with money created for the purpose.

The possibility of doing this was provided, as we have seen, by the amendment of the Bank Act at the beginning of the War. The returns of the Reichsbank

[1] *Die Politik der Reichsbank*, p. 14.
[2] *Ibid*. p. 16.

do not show separately the holdings of *Schatzanwei-sungen* but include them under the heading Securities (*Effekten*). Since it is officially stated, however, that during the War Securities consisted mainly of *Schatzanweisungen*, almost the whole of the increase under this heading can be attributed to the latter. The next table shows this increase, also that in the note circulation not covered by metal.

REICHSBANK, 1913-1918

Dec. 31st.	Million Marks.			
	Securities.		Uncovered Note Circulation.	
	Average.	Maximum.	Average.	Maximum.
1913 -	95·8	403·4	607·5	1,155·7
1914 -	860·4	2,772·1	1,201·1	2,916·2
1915 -	3,880·1	6,867·9	3,004·8	4,440·7
1916 -	5,941·3	10,032·4	4,365·2	5,517·9
1917 -	10,170·3	15,394·1	6,477·7	8,879·8
1918 -	16,360·2	27,313·1	11,194·0	19,905·6

It will be noticed that except for the last year—which extends beyond the War and was affected by the Revolution—the holdings of securities (treasury bills) increased faster than the fiduciary note circulation. This is to be explained by the fact that the Bank's other investments, especially commercial bills, declined very greatly. None the less, the table shows clearly that the treasury bills were very largely purchased by issues of new paper money.

The effects of this course upon the money market would seem to be three.

1. In correspondence with the general rise in prices and incomes resulting from this inflation, the nominal value of bank deposits would increase. But so far as

this result was simply due to inflation it would not produce easier conditions in the money market, because the nominal value of the loans required would increase *pari passu*.

2. But because the new notes were put into circulation in making loans, at the time of issue they relieved the strain on the existing supply of funds. As they were continually being issued in this way on an increasing scale, the relief was continuous.

3. Lastly, this borrowing of new money from the Reichsbank, in conjunction with the Government's practice of prompt payment, increased the supply of real funds *passing through* the market, in the sense that the growth of funds in nominal value was greater than the depreciation in the purchasing power of each nominal unit. The earlier receipts of the traders increased their funds and through them those of the banks; the incursion of the new money by which they were paid added to the depreciation of the currency, but this effect was spread over the whole stock of money. But the method of payment adopted by the Government ought only to be cited in explanation of how it was that the market could lend as much as it did; it is not an explanation of such conditions of ease as existed in the market, since it correspondingly increased the demand for loans. In other words, it affected the quantity of business done at the rates, not the rates themselves.

To inflation by Reichsbank issues was added inflation by those of the *Darlehnskassen*. These, too, contributed to the supply of loans and also helped to finance the Reich Government in so far as they originated in advances in connexion with War Loan subscriptions. The following table shows the outstanding loans and the computed note circulation of the *Darlehnskassen* at the end of each year. The latter figure is in each case equivalent to the loans less the notes (*Kassenscheine*) estimated to be held by the Reichsbank.[1]

DARLEHNSKASSEN

	Million Marks.	
Dec. 31st.	Outstanding Loans.	Net Circulation.
1914 -	1,317·2	?
1915 -	2,347·8	1,300
1916 -	3,407·9	3,000
1917 -	7,689·3	6,500
1918 -	15,625·6	10,400

A further question which ought to be considered here is whether inflation by note issues was supplemented by inflation of bank deposit credit. This question it is extremely difficult to answer satisfactorily; but the fact that the increase in deposits was small in comparison with that in the note circulation seems to make it superfluous to assume that the former were increased by the banks' lending policy.

III

In the business of the creditbanks the War period was distinguished by three features: firstly, the increase—partly real and partly nominal—in deposits; secondly, the preponderance of public borrowing as against that of private business; and thirdly, the comparative insignificance of transactions in connexion with the Stock Exchange. Together these gave·the banks the character of deposit banks lending chiefly to public authorities.

[1] The small amount of *Pfandscheine* outstanding ought really to have been subtracted also from the total loans, since they represented borrowing by the *Kassen*, and so far as these borrowed they could lend without creating new money. But the amount involved is too small to matter.

Of the first feature enough has been said above. The chief causes of the decline in the business demand for credit—the curtailment of foreign trade, the method by which war deliveries were financed—have also been dealt with, while no explanation is needed for the increase in public demand. As to the ways in which the banks satisfied the latter, however, there remains something to be said.

Direct lending to the Government of the Reich was for the most part in the form of the purchase of *Schatzanweisungen*, only to a comparatively small extent in the form of subscriptions to War Loan. There was also, however, a considerable amount of indirect lending to the Reich in the form of advances to enable customers to subscribe to War Loan. Apart from this, the banks lent large sums to the *Kriegsgesellschaften*—or associations formed by the Government for special war purposes, such as the purchase and distribution of supplies—and to the municipal governments, which were precluded from raising loans in the ordinary way, lest they should compete with the Government of the Reich. In the former case the loans were chiefly given in the form of current account advances; in the latter most commonly on the pledge of securities (*Lombarddarlehen*),[1] but also in the form of discount or current account credit.

Turning now to the third feature, the opportunities both for dealing in securities—on commission or otherwise—and for the creation of new securities were limited by the war-time regulation of the stock market. At first, while the Bourse was entirely closed, there was naturally no such business to be done. In the course of 1915, however, there was a revival of the free or unofficial market; and although the banks did not at

---

[1] Municipalities often had remainders of previous issues of their own on their hands, which they could use in this way ; in other cases the creation of new stock for the purpose was allowed. See Prion, *op. cit.* p. 96.

once participate—restrained by uncertainty as to the official attitude towards the development—they began to do so, with the approval of the Reichsbank, towards the close of the year.[1]   About two years later, in December 1917, the official market was re-opened for cash dealings in dividend papers.   In order to protect the market for War Loan, the Bourse remained closed for all other fixed interest obligations and also for preference shares; while to prevent incitement to speculation all publication of prices was prohibited throughout the War.   Despite these limitations it would appear from the clearing statistics of the *Bank des Berliner Kassenvereins*[2] that the volume of stock exchange transactions in 1917 and 1918 exceeded in money value those in 1913.   So far as can be ascertained the banks gave no credit in connexion with these transactions, but of course they drew profit from them. The re-opening of the Bourse also gave the banks an opportunity of reducing their own holdings of securities, particularly by the sale of those taken up at the beginning of the War.

Side by side with the relaxation of the restrictions on the market went an increase in capital issues.   The companies concerned were mostly those engaged on war work, and the development was so far countenanced officially that, in anticipation of the re-opening of the Bourse, the admission (*Zulassung*) of new shares of companies already listed was resumed in October 1917.   It was not, however, allowed to proceed unchecked.   The issue of obligations and preference shares and the formation of new companies required

---

[1] A technical peculiarity of the business thus commenced was that the banks, although acting in effect as intermediaries in these unofficial dealings, refused to accept the full obligation of commission agents.   In legal form the bank assumed the position of a principal in each transaction, as against both the buyer and seller.   This practice was dropped in 1917 with the resumption of official transactions.

[2] Quoted Klebba, *op. cit.* p. 70.

official sanction in every instance (Orders of March and November 1917); and even the raising of additional share capital was indirectly controlled through the Bourse authorities. According to the figures given by Klebba,[1] the admissions of new securities to the Berlin Exchange were in 1917 about one-tenth of the pre-war average, and in 1918 about one-quarter. The banks, of course, had an interest in this business, but it is unlikely that they played a leading part in it, and certain that they did not carry the new shares for any time themselves.

It will be seen that the Stock Exchange recovered some of its importance for the banks towards the close of the War. The extent of this recovery, however, was less than may appear at first sight, because some allowance has to be made for inflated values; or, arriving at the same conclusion by a somewhat different road, because if the stock exchange transactions tended to return to the pre-war amount, other transactions far exceeded their pre-war amounts. And, of course, the fact that no loans were made on the Stock Exchange meant a considerable diminution of its importance, as well as another curtailment of the field for private credit operations.

Some compensation for the decline in normal business was found in handling customers' applications for War Loan. Here the banks took no responsibility, but earned a small commission of 30 to 35 pfennige per thousand marks. Apparently from 50% to 60% of the total War Loan subscriptions were made through the banks.

The accompanying tables, continuing those of the previous chapter, show the main balance sheet items as percentages of the balance sheet totals.

[1] *Op. cit.* p. 96.

CASH, ETC. AS PERCENTAGE OF TOTAL ASSETS

	1913.	1914.	1915.	1916.	1917.	1918.
Deutsche Bank - - -	5·7	10·5	9·3	7·3	7·9	6·0
Dresdner Bank - - -	4·5	7·1	8·8	9·7	8·9	8·5
Discontogesellschaft - -	4·0	3·7	7·4	8·0	6·4	4·7
Darmstädter Bank - - -	4·9	6·4	8·8	8·4	7·3	9·2
Berliner Handelsgesellschaft -	3·6	2·0	2·0	2·7	2·2	2·4
Commerz- u. Discontobank -	3·4	4·6	3·0	2·4	2·2	1·8
Nationalbank - - -	3·4	5·2	5·2	6·8	9·1	6·8
Mitteldeutsche Creditbank -	3·5	8·0	6·9	5·3	5·8	7·2
Eight Berlin Banks - -	4·6	7·0	7·9	7·4	7·1	6·3

BILLS AS PERCENTAGE OF TOTAL ASSETS

	1913.	1914.	1915.	1916.	1917.	1918.
Deutsche Bank - - -	28·5	25·1	32·2	40·7	48·4	58·9
Dresdner Bank - - -	24·4	23·8	22·4	33·2	35·3	51·6
Discontogesellschaft - -	20·7	25·7	34·5	38·7	47·2	45·7
Darmstädter Bank - - -	18·9	17·6	18·4	17·1	22·3	37·4
Berliner Handelsgesellschaft -	18·8	18·5	19·5	18·5	21·6	19·6
Commerz- u. Discontobank -	14·9	11·7	15·7	35·6	41·3	50·2
Nationalbank - - -	20·6	16·4	19·2	23·1	26·8	32·3
Mitteldeutsche Creditbank -	15·8	15·5	13·1	21·0	27·6	45·3
Eight Berlin Banks - -	22·8	22·1	26·6	33·8	40·4	49·6

BALANCES WITH CORRESPONDENTS AS PERCENTAGE OF TOTAL ASSETS

	1913.	1914.	1915.	1916.	1917.	1918.
Deutsche Bank - - -	2·8	2·7	3·3	4·9	8·1	3·6
Dresdner Bank - - -	4·0	4·5	4·2	4·1	6·8	2·3
Discontogesellschaft - -	5·7	6·4	5·0	5·3	6·7	9·4
Darmstädter Bank - - -	5·3	5·4	7·8	10·7	10·8	5·9
Berliner Handelsgesellschaft -	2·0	2·4	2·6	4·4	2·5	3·0
Commerz- u. Discontobank -	8·0	6·5	6·6	6·9	7·4	4·3
Nationalbank - - -	3·5	3·5	3·7	3·0	2·6	2·4
Mitteldeutsche Creditbank -	2·6	3·7	4·9	10·8	17·4	8·6
Eight Berlin Banks - -	4·1	4·3	4·5	5·6	7·7	4·8

BOURSE LOANS AS PERCENTAGE OF TOTAL ASSETS

	1913.	1914.	1915.	1916.	1917.	1918.
Deutsche Bank - - -	10·4	9·5	10·4	12·8	9·5	8·0
Dresdner Bank - - -	7·7	6·9	9·5	8·3	6·2	7·0
Discontogesellschaft - -	8·5	7·8	6·5	6·1	8·4	6·9
Darmstädter Bank - - -	11·8	9·8	11·4	21·0	21·2	16·4
Berliner Handelsgesellschaft -	12·0	11·7	3·1	1·3	0·8	0·5
Commerz- u. Discontobank -	17·0	13·6	19·7	16·8	16·8	10·8
Nationalbank - - -	11·6	10·3	12·0	16·0	20·3	20·7
Mitteldeutsche Creditbank -	9·6	5·3	2·1	11·8	10·3	7·2
Eight Berlin Banks - -	10·3	9·0	9·5	11·4	10·3	8·7

ADVANCES AGAINST COMMODITIES AS PERCENTAGE OF TOTAL ASSETS

	1913.	1914.	1915.	1916.	1917.	1918.
Deutsche Bank - - -	9·6	3·7	5·3	5·1	1·9	0·7
Dresdner Bank - - -	7·6	1·6	0·5	0·8	0·5	0·3
Discontogesellschaft - -	10·7	0·6	1·0	0·7	0·9	0·4
Darmstädter Bank - - -	1·8	1·8	0·8	1·8	2·4	0·9
Berliner Handelsgesellschaft [1] -	—	—	—	—	—	—
Commerz- u. Discontobank -	4·2	3·1	0·4	0·6	0·3	0·2
Nationalbank - - -	—	1·2	0·8	0·9	0·7	0·5
Mitteldeutsche Creditbank -	1·3	1·3	1·0	0·3	0·01	0·05
Seven Berlin Banks - -	7·1	2·3	2·4	2·3	1·2	0·5

[1] The Berliner Handelsgesellschaft did not return these advances separately.

ADVANCES AS PERCENTAGE OF TOTAL ASSETS

	1913.	1914.	1915.	1916.	1917.	1918.
Deutsche Bank - - -	28·8	36·2	28·8	21·5	18·4	12·9
Dresdner Bank - - -	40·6	41·4	41·1	34·6	34·6	22·8
Discontogesellschaft - -	31·6	30·4	26·2	24·8	19·4	20·5
Darmstädter Bank - - -	44·9	45·9	40·4	31·5	28·8	23·5
Berliner Handelsgesellschaft -	42·2	40·0	51·5	52·2	56·0	54·9
Commerz- u. Discontobank -	38·8	44·2	40·3	29·3	26·9	24·8
Nationalbank - - -	42·2	45·5	43·1	38·4	31·7	28·6
Mitteldeutsche Creditbank -	53·1	55·2	61·2	41·7	33·5	26·1
Eight Berlin Banks - -	36·8	39·1	35·3	28·8	25·5	20·5

SECURITIES AS PERCENTAGE OF TOTAL ASSETS

(a) Own Securities.   (b) Syndicate Participations
(c) Bank Participations.

		1913.	1914.	1519.	1916.	1917.	1918.
Deutsche Bank	a.	7·2	6·4	5·3	4·0	4·0	3·1
	b.	2·4	2·0	1·6	1·0	0·4	0·3
	c.	3·7	2·2	2·0	1·5	0·6	0·5
Dresdner Bank	a.	2·8	3·8	4·1	2·6	2·4	3·2
	b.	3·6	4·6	3·8	2·6	1·6	1·2
	c.	2·4	2·7	2·4	1·7	1·9	1·5
Discontogesellschaft	a.	2.4	2.8	2.4	2·8	2·3	2·2
	b.	4·9	4·3	2·8	2·1	1·3	1·1
	c.	9·3	15·8	12·0	10·1	6·2	5·1
Darmstädter Bank	a.	5·6	6·0	5·5	4·1	3·3	3·7
	b.	4·5	4·1	3·9	3·1	1·9	1·4
	c.	0·8	0·9	0·9	0·7	0·5	0·5
Berliner Handelsgesellschaft	a.	7·8	8·8	6·8	9·0	8·5	12·7
	b.	9·5	10·1	10·5	7·7	5·1	4·2
	c.	1·8	1·9	1·9	1·6	1·3	1·1
Commerz- u. Discontobank	a.	5·5	7·1	7·4	3·6	2·3	5·0
	b.	3·7	4·6	3·1	2·2	1·4	1·4
	c.	2·4	2·5	2·2	1·6	1·1	0·8
Nationalbank	a.	6·9	6·8	4·9	4·2	3·2	3·8
	b.	9·2	8·3	7·7	5·2	3·8	3·0
	c.	1·2	1·2	1·3	0·8	0·6	0·9
Mitteldeutsche Creditbank	a.	5·2	4·7	4·5	4·0	1·8	2·6
	b.	4·4	2·5	2·5	1·9	1·2	1·4
	c.	1·0	0·6	0·9	0·8	0·3	0·2
Eight Berlin Banks	a.	5·2	5·5	4·7	3·8	3·3	3·5
	b.	4·3	4·1	3·3	2·3	1·3	1·1
	c.	3·5	4·3	3·8	3·0	2·0	1·6

CAPITAL AND RESERVES AS PERCENTAGE OF TOTAL LIABILITIES

	1913.	1914.	1915.	1916.	1917.	1918.
Deutsche Bank	13·9	16·0	13·5	10·5	8·0	6·4
Dresdner Bank	17·0	18·8	16·6	12·3	10·0	7·4
Discontogesellschaft	22·7	29·8	23·0	19·5	12·9	10·3
Darmstädter Bank	19·7	19·4	18·4	15·6	11·3	8·5
Berliner Handelsgesellschaft	26·3	27·2	28·1	25·8	22·3	18·7
Commerz- u. Discontobank	19·5	20·5	18·1	13·3	9·1	6·9
Nationalbank	24·9	24·7	26·5	23·2	16·9	13·6
Mitteldeutsche Creditbank	26·8	22·5	21·4	18·9	12·8	9·3
Eight Berlin Banks	19·0	20·9	18·3	14·7	10·7	8·3

DEPOSITS AND CURRENT ACCOUNT BALANCES AS PERCENTAGE OF TOTAL LIABILITIES

	1913.	1914.	1915.	1916.	1917.	1918.
Deutsche Bank - - -	70·4	76·0	80·4	85·9	90·0	86·0
Dresdner Bank - - -	62·3	68·4	75·6	82·6	86·7	90·2
Discontogesellschaft - -	54·4	57·3	69·4	76·5	83·7	84·5
Darmstädter Bank - - -	62·1	59·7	72·2	78·6	84·4	88·3
Berliner Handelsgesellschaft -	53·9	49·4	55·0	62·3	68·0	73·7
Commerz- u. Discontobank -	62·2	61·7	73·7	81·7	86·0	89·0
Nationalbank - - -	56·5	53·0	57·4	66·2	76·7	82·6
Mitteldeutsche Creditbank -	50·6	52·3	64·4	73·5	83·1	88·6
Eight Berlin Banks - -	62·1	65·0	73·3	80·3	83·9	86·6

ACCEPTANCES AS PERCENTAGE OF TOTAL LIABILITIES

	1913.	1914.	1915.	1916.	1917.	1918.
Deutsche Bank - - -	13·4	6·0	4·0	1·7	1·0	0·9
Dresdner Bank - - -	18·7	10·6	5·9	3·2	2·2	1·4
Discontogesellschaft - -	20·2	10·8	5·5	2·1	2·0	1·6
Darmstädter Bank - - -	17·0	20·0	8·6	5·0	3·0	2·1
Berliner Handelsgesellschaft -	17·6	22·3	15·3	9·8	7·3	5·5
Commerz- u. Discontobank -	16·4	16·0	6·6	3·7	4·1	3·4
Nationalbank - - -	16·3	21·6	13·7	8·5	4·6	2·7
Mitteldeutsche Creditbank -	20·9	23·8	12·8	6·1	3·0	1·3
Eight Berlin Banks - -	16·9	12·4	6·5	3·3	2·2	1·6

On the liability side the changes are clearly defined and free from ambiguity; capital resources diminished in importance (despite a certain absolute increase); deposits constituted a continuously increasing proportion of the liabilities; whilst the acceptances became insignificant. The last change was absolute as well as relative, as the following figures show:

ACCEPTANCES OF BERLINER GROSSBANKEN
(Without Berliner Handelsgesellschaft)

					Million Marks
1913	-	-	-	-	1,179·3
1914	-	-	-	-	881·9
1915	-	-	-	-	512·3
1916	-	-	-	-	306·9
1917	-	-	-	-	309·3
1918	-	-	-	-	259·6

This decline is to be attributed to the contraction of foreign trade, to changed methods of financing the remainder of such trade, and to the disuse of bills in domestic commerce.

The changes in the banks' loans and investments are not shown so clearly on the other side of the balance sheets, because no distinction is made as a rule between loans to private business and loans to public authorities, and because war-time transactions were booked under headings which stood for other kinds of business in peace. Thus it has to be surmised (pretty safely) that the increased importance of Bills was due to holdings of *Schatzanweisungen*, and *Reports und Lombards* must be taken to mean loans against security collateral (particularly to municipal authorities and War Loan subscribers) rather than bourse loans. A further complication is introduced by the fact that the practice of the banks was not uniform in booking the war-time transactions; this no doubt accounts for the difference between the Berliner Handelsgesellschaft and most other banks in respect of the changes in *Reports und Lombards* and Advances. The general tendency for Advances to decline in relative importance reflects, but probably under-estimates, the decline in business advances.

The changes under the remaining heads are plainer and need little comment. The diminished Commodity Advances (*Vorschüsse gegen Warenverschiffungen*) are readily to be explained by diminished exports. Cash and Balances with Correspondents (*Nostroguthaben*) were relatively larger than before the War: the former perhaps because opportunities for the most liquid kinds of investment were limited,[1] the latter because foreign balances were essential for the financing of trade with

---

[1] This point is rather doubtful, because Treasury Bills could be had in plenty, and could, if necessary, be re-discounted at the Reichsbank. Perhaps the banks felt it inadvisable to depend entirely on these.

ASSETS OF SEVEN BERLINER GROSSBANKEN
Taken together (exc. Berliner Handelsgesellschaft)

Dec. 31st.	Millions of Marks.							
	Loans on Securities.	Advances against Commodities.	Balances with Correspondent Banks.	Own Securities.	Of which, Government Securities.	Syndicate Participations.	Bank Participations.	Advances.
1913 -	728	510	308	359	199	283	262	2,609
1914 -	679	175	336	401	239	283	347	2,994
1915 -	877	210	409	408	270	255	350	3,036
1916 -	1,327	262	635	391	281	224	342	3,075
1917 -	1,823	215	1,346	523	394	205	345	4,158
1918 -	1,982	116	1,073	692	542	214	359	4,246

DIVIDENDS DURING THE WAR

	1913.	1914.	1915.	1916.	1917.	1918.
Deutsche Bank - -	$12\frac{1}{2}$	10	$12\frac{1}{2}$	$12\frac{1}{2}$	14	12
Discontogesellschaft -	10	8	$8\frac{1}{2}$	10	11	9
Dresdner Bank - -	$8\frac{1}{2}$	6	6	8	$8\frac{1}{2}$	7
Darmstädter Bank -	$6\frac{1}{4}$	4	5	6	7	6
Nationalbank - -	6	—	4	$4\frac{1}{2}$	6	5
Commerz- u. Discontobank	6	$4\frac{1}{2}$	$4\frac{1}{2}$	6	7	7
Mitteldeutsche Creditbank	$6\frac{1}{2}$	$5\frac{1}{2}$	$5\frac{1}{2}$	$6\frac{1}{2}$	7	7
Berliner Handelsgesellschaft	$8\frac{1}{2}$	5	6	7	8	8

EXPENSES AS % OF GROSS PROFITS
(Seven Berlin banks taken together)

1913 - - - - -	37·1%
1914 - - - - -	39·7
1915 - - - - -	38·6
1916 - - - - -	40·2
1917 - - - - -	44·4
1918 - - - - -	57·3

other countries under war conditions. Finally, the
Security Holdings diminished relatively. Reference
to the table relating to the assets of the seven Berlin
banks collectively shows that, at their mark valuation,
Syndicate Participations also diminished absolutely,
whilst Own Securities only increased by the amount
of Government Securities acquired. Bank Participations were more or less stationary after the increase in
1914, which occurred before the outbreak of the War
(*Disconto-Schaaffhausen* transaction).

Owing to the restrictions imposed by war conditions
on certain profitable branches of business, the gross
profits of the banks did not increase in the same proportion as the funds at their disposal. At the same
time the proportion of the gross profits absorbed by
costs increased, and that more rapidly than in the
previous years. The explanation of this development
is probably to be found in the lower efficiency of substitute labour, payments to those in the field, and higher
wages and salaries. For the shareholders the outcome
was dividends which were tolerably satisfactory, but
hardly more than that. Averaging for the war years
and making some allowance for changes in the value
of money, the real profits distributed were below the
level attained immediately before the War.

IV

Circumstances during the War were favourable to
concentration in banking, and enabled the Berlin banks
to strengthen their position. The organization of the
country for war involved centralization; the Government dealt either with large firms, which would be
closely connected with the capital in any case, or with
more or less official organizations specially formed to
give centralized control; and this naturally gave a new
advantage to the financial institutions located at the

centre. This advantage was reinforced when banking itself came under government control through the *Devisenordnung* (Foreign Exchange Order) of January, 1916, and the exclusive right to deal in foreign bills was conferred on the eight Berliner Grossbanken and the Norddeutsche Bank—the last, it will be remembered, the property of the Discontogesellschaft. It is also to be mentioned that the prohibition of the publication of bourse prices, in its first and stricter form, put the provincial banks and bankers at a disadvantage as compared with the branches of a Berlin bank: the latter could receive daily information from Berlin which they could pass on to their customers in answer to definite questions; the former could only obtain information by themselves making definite inquiries.

In the organization of the banks, the first year or eighteen months of the War saw no expansion, but rather contraction, it being necessary to close a number of offices owing to the shortage of men. In 1916, however, and more distinctly in 1917, the programme of extension was resumed. Especial attention was paid at this time to the eastern margin: in 1916 the *Ostbank für Handel u. Gewerbe* (Darmstädter group) opened nine branches in the occupied Russian territory; in 1917 the Mitteldeutsche Creditbank opened a branch at Königsberg, and the Discontogesellschaft acquired branches there and at Tilsit through the absorption of the *Königsberger Vereinsbank*; in the same year the Berliner Handelsgesellschaft, departing from its traditional policy of centralization and self-sufficiency, entered into close relations with the *Danziger Privatbank*. But the rest of Germany was not neglected, and in 1917 the Discontogesellschaft came to understandings with the *Vereinsbank*, Hamburg, and the *Bayerische Hypotheken und Wechselbank*, Munich.[1] A number of new branches were opened

[1] Extending a pre-war understanding in the latter case.

in the following year by the Dresdner and Darmstädter Banks; presumably the staff problem had by this time been overcome by the employment of women. Abroad the Deutsche Bank opened a branch at Sofia in 1916.

The year 1917 also witnessed changes in the composition of the bank groups through the absorption of provincial members. The most important cases are the fusion of the *Schlesischer Bankverein* (Breslau) and the *Norddeutsche Kreditbank* (Königsberg) by the Deutsche Bank; but we may also mention the absorption of the *Rheinisch-Westfälische Discontogesellschaft* and the *Mulheimer Bank* by the Dresdner Bank, and of the *Rheinische Bank* and the *Magdeburger Bankverein* by the Discontogesellschaft. The *Rheinisch-Westfälische Discontogesellschaft* had previously belonged to the Disconto group, and strangely, the *Rheinische Bank* to the Dresdner group;[1] in the other cases the change simply meant converting affiliated institutions into branches. This may be regarded as the continuation of a pre-war tendency—manifested most strikingly just before the War in the fusion of the *Bergisch-Märkische Bank* by the Deutsche Bank; but it seems likely that a new factor was introduced at this juncture in the desire to escape double taxation at war-time rates.[2]

These developments show their effect in a rise of the share of the great Berlin banks in the total deposits (including current account balances) of all banks having at least a million marks capital from 53·4% in 1913 to 65·6% in 1918—and this notwithstanding the fact

---

[1] There was no direct exchange here. The Rheinische Bank shares belonging to the Dresdner Bank were exchanged with the Schaaffhausen'scher Bankverein for shares in the Deutsch-Südamerikanische Bank and others; the Schaaffhausen'scher Bankverein handed the Rheinische Bank shares over to the Discontogesellschaft, keeping some branches. Prion, *op. cit.* p. 57. No information is available as to why or how the Rheinisch-Westfälische Discontogesellschaft left the Disconto group.

[2] See Prion, *op. cit.*, p. 59.

that the Schaaffhausen'scher Bankverein had ceased to rank as a Berlin bank.

Against the increasing concentration in private banking organization must be set a certain extension of public banking, through a widening of the activities of the communal savings banks. The origin of this development lies strictly in the pre-war period, in the concession to the savings banks of the right to keep cheque accounts for their customers at the time of the passing of the *Scheckgesetz* (1909). It was during the War, however, that the Government, as part of its programme for economizing the use of cash—wrongly conceived as a means of combating inflation—particularly encouraged these institutions to make use of their powers and to build up a higher federal organization of district *Girozentralen* for the purpose of clearing and offsetting transfers (or payments) between one savings bank and another.[1] In 1917 the Prussian Government supported this policy by raising the limit which it had imposed on the total of balances subject to immediate disposition from 10% of the proper savings balances of each institution to 25%. In the spring of 1918 a central clearing institution for the whole Reich was established in Berlin, the *Deutsche Girozentrale*. Alongside of the expansion of the savings banks in this direction, the desire to enlist their support in placing War Loan led to an extension of their powers of dealing in securities. We have here the beginnings of a development which was to become extremely important in the years following the Armistice.

[1] See Appendix II.

CHAPTER VII

THE PERIOD OF INFLATION, 1918-1923

I

As is well known, the inflation begun during the War was continued after the Armistice, and was carried to such lengths that finally the whole currency system broke down in the autumn of 1923. The years from 1919 to 1923 form naturally a distinct period in which all financial relations—and, indeed, economic relations generally—were dominated by inflation and its effects.

The following table shows the increase in the note circulation of the Reichsbank, and also the depreciation of the mark as measured by the dollar exchange:

	Note Issue of Reichsbank.	Dollar Quotation.	Depreciation Factor (roughly).
Dec. 31, 1913 -	2,593·4 million	4·19	—
,, 1918 -	22,187·8 ,,	8·0	2
,, 1919 -	35,698·4 ,,	48·0	12
,, 1920 -	68,805·0 ,,	73·0	17·5
,, 1921 -	113,639·5 ,,	184·0	44
,, 1922 -	1,280,100·0 ,,	7,350·0	1,750
Nov. 18, 1923 -	92,844,720·7 billion	4·2 billion	1 billion

Great as was the expansion of the note circulation, it was less than proportional to the shrinkage in the value of the mark, internally—in domestic purchasing power—and externally—in terms of the foreign ex-

changes.   For this several reasons may be given.   In
the first place, once the tendency for prices to rise had
become marked, people hastened to make their purchases as early as possible, and thus, by keeping money
in hand for shorter periods, increased its velocity of
circulation.   As depreciation advanced, this developed
into a regular ' flight from the mark '; it was preferred
to hold wealth in any other form rather than that of
money, and even to spend money in quite unnecessary
consumption rather than to keep it.   At the same time
various substitutes—foreign coins and notes, foreign
bills of exchange, gold loan script, etc.—were introduced to replace the discredited paper marks.   As the
outcome of these developments the *effective supply of
money* increased much faster than the note circulation;
and the tendency would be for prices to rise at least in
correspondence with the former, and for the real value
of the total note circulation to decline, despite the great
increase in its nominal amount.   Meantime the external value of the mark anticipated to a greater or less
degree the further decline in its internal value.   It is
a matter of dispute how far, if at all, the fall in the
exchange value of the mark reacted on its internal
value during the earlier years of the period, say from
1920 to 1922.   The more general view in Germany
is that the exchange movements tended to produce
corresponding changes in internal prices.[1]   But whatever may be the truth with regard to these years, it is
certain that in the closing stage of inflation the internal
price level almost ceased to have an independent
existence, prices being for the most part automatically
adjusted to the changes in the dollar quotation.   As
the quotation soared upwards without regard to either
the quantity of notes in circulation or even the effective
supply of money in the widest sense, there resulted,
paradoxically enough, an acute shortage of means of

[1] See Helfferich, *Money*, vol. ii. p. 601, for example.

payment; and although the printing press was kept working at full pressure and a large amount of private emergency money was created, with and without authority, the void widened more rapidly than it could be filled.

The condition of the Berlin money market continued to be easy, at least until the summer of 1922. The Reichsbank discount rate remained unchanged until this time at 5%; while market rates for day to day money varied between 4% and $4\frac{1}{2}$%, the private discount rate being rather higher. The underlying conditions, however, were at this time rather different from those prevailing during the War. The expenditure of the Reich continued to be met mainly by borrowing on *Schatzanweisungen*—which were no longer redeemed, even in part, by funding operations—but the proportion of these bills taken up by the banks and the market steadily declined. This meant, of course, that the financing of the Government depended more and more upon the extension of the note issues of the Reichsbank. At the same time, however, as with the cessation of hostilities administrative disbursements came to predominate in Government expenditure over the purchase of supplies, the Government's terms of payment did not have the effect of bringing more money into the market. In the sphere of private finance, the resumption of foreign trade and the increase in ordinary commerce generally must have occasioned an increased demand for credit; but against this commerce began to receive a larger share in the credits of the Reichsbank. In general, then, the ease with which loans were obtainable at the Reichsbank, based on the freedom with which it extended its issues, was more than ever the determining factor.[1]

---

[1] It should perhaps be suggested that money market indices somewhat exaggerated the ease of the short loan market as a whole, because the banks tended to increase the proportion of their funds invested on short terms in

At the end of July, 1922, the Bank rate was raised to 6%; and thereafter it was repeatedly raised at short intervals, until the record figure of 90% was reached in September, 1923.

REICHSBANK DISCOUNT RATE

1915—July 1922 - -	5%
July 28, 1922 - - ..	6
August 28, 1922 - -	7
September 21, 1922 - ..	8
November 13, 1922 - -	10
January 18, 1923 - -	12
April 23, 1923 - - -	18
August 2, 1923 - - -	30
September 15, 1923 - -	90
December 29, 1923 - -	10 (for valorised bills).

The rise in the rates for day to day money was at first roughly commensurate with that of the Bank rate, but was eventually much greater. Taking the charge for loans upon the best securities as our example, this varied between $5\frac{1}{2}\%$ and $6\frac{1}{2}\%$ during August 1922, and between $7\frac{1}{2}\%$ and $8\frac{1}{2}\%$ during the following autumn. During January 1923 it ranged between 9% and 10%, rising to 15% at the beginning of February. After a relapse to the region of 10% at the end of this month—at which level it remained during March—there was another rise in April and the range during the second quarter was from 12% to 18%. Then in July came the great increase which necessitated a change in the quotations from rates per annum to rates per diem. Varying at first between $\frac{1}{2}\%$ and 1% per diem, after the end of July the rate began to fluctuate more violently; up to 3% per diem, and down again to $\frac{1}{2}\%$ in August; up to 20% and down to 1%

the market in their first efforts to escape the effects of depreciation. Loans to customers on current account had become more expensive, the rate being raised to 2% over Bank rate in 1920, in addition to which new charges were levied which were interest in all but name.

in September; between 3% and 20% in October. As a climax a rate of 40% per diem was reached in the second week of November.[1] A private discount rate was not quoted during the second half of 1923.

Allowance being made for the current depreciation of the mark, the successive discount rates of the Reichsbank were not really high, often indeed represented a negative rate of real interest; and this, moreover, was commonly understood and taken advantage of at the time.[2] The interpretation of the free market rates is a matter of greater difficulty; for it is impossible to ascertain how far they reflect the anticipation of depreciation, and how far they reflect a real shortage of loanable money. There being no certainty as to what the rate of depreciation would be from day to day, the allowance to be made on this account was a matter for individual estimate; and these estimates mingled with other individual considerations in determining demand and supply. From the common report that to save their spare money from depreciation people transferred it abroad, or converted it into durable forms of real wealth (*Sachwerte*), or even spent it in unnecessary and abnormal consumption, the inference might be drawn that the prevailing interest rates did not fully cover the depreciation which was generally anticipated; in other words, that loanable money was sufficiently plentiful for the terms to be distinctly in favour of the borrowers. This inference, however, would hardly be correct—except in relation

[1] Figures collected from monthly reports in *Die Bank*.

[2] It may be well to warn the hasty reader that the difference between the Reichsbank rates and those of the market was less than may appear at first sight, since discount rates and interest rates are not directly comparable. A 90% discount rate is equivalent to a 900% rate of interest. A debt of 1,000 marks due in twelve months, for example, when discounted at 90% realizes only 100 marks : for the loan of the 100 marks for a year, the discounter obtains 900 marks in interest. But even so the current rate of depreciation was in the last stages greater than this.

to Reichsbank loans. The amount of depreciation which would occur in any future period being so uncertain, both borrowers and lenders would wish to protect themselves by a certain margin in their own favour. As between a borrower and a lender who took precisely the same view of the future of the mark, then, it would be impossible to find terms satisfactory to both; and quite possibly the prevailing terms would be satisfactory to neither. It is accordingly likely that funds were withdrawn from the loan market and used in the other ways suggested, when loan rates were already too high from the point of view of the borrower; and of course this withdrawal of funds would then make the position of the borrower more difficult still. We have here a cause of real scarcity of loan money, aggravating the effects of that tendency to over-investment in fixed plant which seems usually to make itself felt towards the end of a period of rising prices. On the other side, to counteract the stringency, were the ever extending credits of the Reichsbank. In the later stages the rapid shrinkage in the value of the currency, wiping out the value of all liquid balances faster than the Reichsbank could lend, undoubtedly overwhelmed this offsetting factor; and a state of acute shortage of short term capital was clearly revealed after stabilization. But neither in the movement of interest rates nor (apparently) by any other means, is it possible to trace the steps by which this shortage developed.

II

The influence of inflation upon bank deposits—including current account balances—was very striking, although the true nature of this influence was not at first apparent. As is shown by the following table relating to the great Berlin banks collectively, there was an enormous increase in the mark sums standing to the credit of customers.

DEPOSITS AND CURRENT ACCOUNT BALANCES OF BERLIN BANKS

Dec. 31, 1913	-	-	5,148·6 million marks
,,	1918	-	19,696·1 ,, ,,
,,	1919	-	39,149·7 ,, ,,
,,	1920	-	62,568·1 ,, ,,
,,	1921	-	115,568·9 ,, ,,
,,	1922	-	1,618,230·0 ,, ,,
,,	1923	-	1,088,795,806·0 billion marks

These figures do not indicate, however, a real increase in the resources entrusted to the banks. For one thing we have to allow for the transference of deposits from provincial banks to Berlin banks as a result of the amalgamations which took place during the period.[1] But much more important, of course, is the depreciation of the mark in which the deposits were reckoned. An attempt may be made to eliminate this second factor by converting the mark balances to their gold mark equivalents on the basis of the dollar exchange: and in a rough way this is done in the next table.

					Million Gold Marks.
Dec. 31, 1913	-	-	-	-	5,148·6
,,	1918	-	-	-	9,848
,,	1919	-	-	-	3,262
,,	1920	-	-	-	3,577
,,	1921	-	-	-	2,626
,,	1922	-	-	-	925
,,	1923	-	-	-	1,089

But unfortunately the dollar exchange is not a reliable index to the internal value of the mark: too

---

[1] On the other hand, in comparing post-war figures with those for 1913, the disappearance of the Schaaffhausen Bankverein from the Berlin banks has to be taken into account.

low (in marks to the dollar) in 1918, when the exchange was still effectively controlled, it was too high in most of the following years, and the relation between internal and external values varied a good deal within short periods. What can be taken as certain is that the great nominal increase in deposits covered a considerable fall in their real value. (The 1923 figure above may be taken as correct, for at that time internal prices were pretty closely adjusted to the exchange value of the mark.)

The increase in the mark figures for deposits above will be found to be more or less proportionate to the increase in note circulation. This would suggest that the fall in the real value of the deposits was entirely the outcome of the fall in the total value of the currency. In this connexion also, however, the deposit figures are misleading; the effect of amalgamations has again to be considered; and the deposits include, in addition to mark deposits proper, the so-called *Valutadepositen* at their current mark value. The latter were sums standing to the credit of customers in accounts kept in terms of foreign currency: they were not, as a rule, the result of payments to the banks in German money, nor were they as a rule available for employment by the banks in Germany. Unfortunately we do not know the amounts of the *Valutadepositen*, but from all accounts they were not negligible, and this means that the ordinary deposits did not increase as fast as the note circulation. The real value of these deposits must have been affected then, not only by the shrinkage in the value of the German currency, but also by the fact that people deposited a smaller proportion of their money with the banks.

Hand in hand with these changes in total deposits went a decline in the relative importance of the deposits subject to longer notice of withdrawal as compared with those withdrawable within seven days. This change, in which again it is easy to see the influence of inflation, is shown in the following table:

DEPOSITS AND CURRENT ACCOUNT BALANCES
OF BERLIN BANKS

		Short.	Percentages. Intermediate.	Long.
End of 1913	-	56·8	29·8	13·3
1918	-	60·6	26·1	13·1
1919	-	78·1	14·0	7·8
1920	-	76·7	15·1	8·2
1921	-	77·1	15·0	7·9
1922	-	93·0	4·9	2·1
1923	-	92·6	3·3	4·0

As some compensation for the declining resources at the disposal of the banks, there was an increase in the business which did not involve the employment of these resources—in the transactions which in German are conveniently called ' neutral,' because they do not affect either the asset or the liability side of the balance sheet. There are three branches of such business to be noticed here.

1. *Stock Exchange Commission Business.*

We have seen that there was a marked revival of stock exchange activity in the later years of the War; and had the War been followed by the restoration of normal conditions generally, a speedy completion of this recovery might have been expected. As it was, the increasing depreciation of the mark had the effect of converting this movement toward the normal into a quite abnormal expansion. In order to protect their savings from depreciation, people hastened to invest them in shares, which might be expected to rise in nominal value as the value of the money unit declined; at the same time the uncertainty of general conditions, the largely illusory appearance of business prosperity, and the desperation of the victims of depreciation, all combined to engender the spirit of speculation. Against these influences the increased taxation of bourse transactions had little effect; whilst the one remaining war restriction, the absence of official arrangements for time dealings, is as likely as not to have furthered speculative activity, since it precluded ' bearing ' operations, which might have steadied prices. The result was that, despite enlargements of their staffs and premises, the banks were hard pressed to cope with the stream of orders.

2. *Promotion and Issuing Business.*

The readiness of the market to buy industrial shares provided an exceptional opportunity for making new capital issues; and this was taken advantage of on a large scale by industrialists who saw a favourable chance of expanding their undertakings and effecting fusions. It is probable also that new issues took place with a view to watering capital. The part of the banks in such transactions is not normally a strictly ' neutral ' one; but at this time the placing of new industrial securities proceeded so smoothly and rapidly that the banks more than ever functioned as mere brokers in the capital market.

3. *Foreign Exchange Business.*

Partly as a result of the resumption of foreign trade, and partly because, despite all governmental prohibitions, foreign bills and foreign notes were the object of a great deal of speculation, there was also a great increase in dealings in foreign exchange (*Devisengeschäft*). It seems appropriate to mention this business here, because, so far as is known, the leading banks did not commit themselves to any large extent in connexion with it. It cannot be said of these, however, that they invariably kept an ' open position '; and it is known that certain other banks committed themselves very heavily, sometimes, as in the case of the *Pfälzische Bank*, with disastrous results.   It may be added that after 1919 the right to participate in this business was extended from the leading Berlin banks to all ' recognized ' banks and bankers.

Returning now to the development of the banking business proper, the accompanying tables show the changes in the relative importance of the main classes of assets and liabilities in the annual balance sheets.

CASH, ETC., AS PERCENTAGE OF TOTAL ASSETS

	1913.	1918.	1919.	1920.	1921.	1922.	1923.	Jan. 1st 1924.
Deutsche Bank - - -	5·7	6·0	4·7	5·2	3·7	5·4	10·4	6·6
Dresdner Bank - - -	4·5	8·5	6·3	5·5	4·0	4·9	10·3	7·2
Discontogesellschaft -	4·0	4·7	7·9	8·5	10·9	4·4	7·5	3·5
Darmstädter Bank - -	4·9	9·2	6·2	6·8	4·7	8·4	9·2	6·8
Berliner Handelsgesellschaft -	3·6	2·4	1·3	7·1	5·5	19·0	4·4	1·9
Commerz- u. Discontobank -	3·4	1·8	2·6	4·0	3·3	7·5	8·5	6·5
Nationalbank - - -	3·4	6·8	5·9	11·8	11·1	—	—	—
Mitteldeutsche Creditbank -	3·5	7·2	9·4	9·4	18·8	12·6	18·0	10·0
Average [1] - - -	4·6	6·3	5·8	6·4	6·0	6·1	9·5	6·1

BILLS AS PERCENTAGE OF TOTAL ASSETS

	1913.	1918.	1919.	1920.	1921.	1922.	1923.	Jan. 1st 1924.
Deutsche Bank - - -	28·5	58·9	61·6	69·9	60·4	25·2	3·3	2·1
Dresdner Bank - - -	24·4	51·6	49·5	55·9	41·1	14·0	3·3	2·2
Discontogesellschaft -	20·7	45·7	46·7	48·3	38·8	14·4	5·3	2·5
Darmstädter Bank - -	18·9	37·4	49·1	46·5	24·2	20·3	2·6	1·9
Berliner Handelsgesellschaft -	18·8	19·6	46·2	50·6	47·9	31·3	6·2	4·3
Commerz- u. Discontobank -	14·9	50·2	54·0	43·1	29·0	37·2	3·5	2·7
Nationalbank - - -	20·6	32·3	24·2	21·2	19·5	—	—	—
Mitteldeutsche Creditbank -	15·8	45·3	45·2	50·5	36·9	25·3	1·6	0·9
Average [1] - - -	22·8	49·6	52·4	55·4	42·8	21·3	3·5	2·3

[1] Percentages for eight banks together, 1913 to 1921 ; thereafter for seven banks.

BALANCES WITH CORRESPONDENTS AS PERCENTAGE OF TOTAL ASSETS

	1913.	1918.	1919.	1920.	1921.	1922.	1923.	Jan. 1st 1924.
Deutsche Bank - - -	2·8	3·6	7·5	5·2	9·6	29·0	36·8	28·5
Dresdner Bank - - -	4·0	2·3	8·8	7·3	13·3	43·4	37·6	28·0
Discontogesellschaft -	5·7	9·4	9·6	9·1	14·4	42·9	41·7	32·3
Darmstädter Bank - -	5·3	5·9	7·2	6·6	17·4	45·2	35·0	25·9
Berliner Handelsgesellschaft -	2·0	3·0	3·2	6·0	0·9	10·8	71·5	33·0
Commerz- u. Discontobank -	8·0	4·3	6·2	7·1	5·6	9·0	36·7	28·2
Nationalbank - - -	3·5	2·4	16·0	7·5	9·2	—	—	—
Mitteldeutsche Creditbank -	2·6	8·6	8·2	10·7	4·0	44·5	39·5	22·0
Average [1] - - -	4·1	4·8	8·5	7·2	11·7	42·1	38·6	27·3

BOURSE LOANS AS PERCENTAGE OF TOTAL ASSETS

	1913.	1918.	1919.	1920.	1921.	1922.	1923.	Jan. 1st 1924.
Deutsche Bank - - -	10·4	8·0	1·7	0·9	0·75	0·2	—	1·3
Dresdner Bank - - -	7·7	7·0	6·1	1·9	2·3	1·3	0·3	0·2
Discontogesellschaft - -	8·5	6·9	1·9	0·7	0·6	0·06	—	—
Darmstädter Bank - -	11·3	16·4	6·8	2·5	11·4	1·7	2·2	1·6
Berliner Handelsgesellschaft -	12·0	—	—	—	—	2·0	—	—
Commerz- u. Discontobank -	17·0	10·8	7·6	7·0	18·4	5·4	2·6	2·0
Nationalbank - -	11·6	20·7	16·3	13·2	18·4	—	—	—
Mitteldeutsche Creditbank -	9·6	7·2	2·5	1·2	6·2	1·8	1·3	0·7
Average [1] - - -	10·3	8·7	3·7	2·3	5·0	1·0	0·5	1·0

[1] Percentages for eight banks together, 1913 to 1921 ; thereafter for seven banks.

ADVANCES AGAINST COMMODITIES AS PERCENTAGE
OF TOTAL ASSETS

	1913.	1918.	1919.	1920.	1921.	1922.	1923.	Jan. 1st 1924.
Deutsche Bank - - -	9·6	0·7	2·2	1·2	2·3	4·0	6·0	4·2
Dresdner Bank - - -	7·6	0·3	7·7	3·8	8·7	14·0	9·7	8·0
Discontogesellschaft -	10·7	0·4	1·4	1·0	3·0	2·0	4·5	2·3
Darmstädter Bank - -	1·8	0·9	2·8	3·9	6·1	2·0	7·8	5·7
Berliner Handelsgesellschaft [1] -	—	—	—	—	—	—	—	—
Commerz- u. Discontobank -	4·2	0·2	1·4	3·6	3·6	1·6	2·4	1·9
Nationalbank - - - -	—	0·5	1·2	3·8	7·6	—	—	—
Mitteldeutsche Creditbank -	1·3	0·05	0·2	0·1		0·2	0·2	0·08
Average [2] - - - -	7·1	0·5	2·0	2·6	4·1	5·0	6·2	4·3

ADVANCES AS PERCENTAGE OF TOTAL ASSETS

	1913.	1918.	1919.	1920.	1921.	1922.	1923.	Jan. 1st 1924.
Deutsche Bank - - -	28·8	12·9	13·4	14·3	21·6	19·7	42·3	33·2
Dresdner Bank - - -	40·6	22·8	21·2	22·5	29·1	22·3	37·9	28·5
Discontogesellschaft - -	31·6	20·5	26·7	27·8	30·6	35·5	40·7	24·8
Darmstädter Bank - -	44·9	23·5	24·7	31·3	34·8	22·3	43·4	32·2
Berliner Handelsgesellschaft	42·2	54·9	38·6	29·6	31·3	35·7	17·2	25·8
Commerz- u. Discontobank -	38·8	24·8	24·9	30·3	32·7	33·1	44·0	33·9
Nationalbank - - - -	42·2	28·6	31·2	37·7	32·1	—	—	—
Mitteldeutsche Creditbank -	53·1	26·1	31·1	24·7	31·7	14·3	39·4	25·2
Average [3] - - -	36·8	20·5	21·1	23·2	28·3	24·4	41·2	30·5

[1] The Berliner Handelsgesellschaft did not return these advances separately.

[2] Percentages for seven banks together, 1913 to 1921 ; thereafter for six banks.

[3] Percentages for eight banks together, 1913 to 1921 ; thereafter for seven banks.

SECURITIES AS PERCENTAGE OF TOTAL ASSETS

(a) Own Securities. (b) Syndicate Participations.
(c) Bank Participations.

		1913.	1918.	1919.	1920.	1921.	1922.	1923.	Jan. 1st 1924.
Deutsche Bank	a.	7·2	3·1	1·1	0·7	0·3	0·07	0·7	2·7
	b.	2·4	0·3	0·2	0·2	0·15	0·09	0·2	1·8
	c.	3·7	0·5	0·3	0·3	0·4	0·07	0·3	4·5
Dresdner Bank	a.	2·8	3·2	1·4	1·4	0·6	0·3	—[2]	2·2
	b.	3·6	1·2	0·6	0·6	0·3	—[1]	—	5·1
	c.	2·4	1·5	0·6	0·6	0·6	0·5	—	7·9
Discontogesellschaft	a.	2·4	2·2	0·9	0·7	0·3	0·09	—[2]	1·6
	b.	4·9	1·1	0·4	0·6	0·8	0·24	—	6·8
	c.	9·3	5·1	2·3	0·2	0·1	0·12	—	19·9
Darmstädter Bank	a.	5·6	3·7	1·6	1·2	0·5	—[1]	—[2]	7·9
	b.	4·5	1·4	0·7	0·6	0·3	—	—	5·2
	c.	0·8	0·5	0·2	0·5	0·5	—	—	4·3
Berliner Handelsgesellschaft	a.	7·8	12·7	5·3	3·9	1·6	0·6	—[2]	6·8
	b.	9·5	4·2	3·6	1·6	1·1	0·4	—	15·6
	c.	1·8	1·1	0·7	0·6	0·5	0·2	—	—
Commerz- u. Discontobank	a.	5·5	5·0	1·3	1·4	1·9	0·7	—[2]	5·3
	b.	3·7	1·4	0·8	0·9	1·3	0·14	—	3·6
	c.	2·4	0·8	0·5	0·1	1·2	0·03	—	1·7
Nationalbank	a.	6·9	3·8	2·5	1·4	0·6	—	—	—
	b.	9·2	3·0	1·9	1·3	0·7	—	—	—
	c.	1·2	0·9	0·6	0·4	0·5	—	—	—
Mitteldeutsche Creditbank	a.	5·2	2·6	1·1	0·9	0·7	0·08	—[2]	2·6
	b.	4·4	1·4	1·0	1·1	0·4	0·12	—	10·8
	c.	1·0	0·2	0·2	0·1	0·3	0·05	—	0·7
Average [3]	a.	5·2	3·5	1·3	1·1	0·6	0·07	—	3·8
	b.	4·3	1·1	0·5	0·5	0·5	0·09	—	5·7
	c.	3·5	1·6	0·8	0·7	0·6	0·07	—	7·1

[1] No entry.   [2] Nominal entry only.

[3] Percentages for eight banks together, 1913 to 1921 ; thereafter for seven banks.

CAPITAL AND RESERVES AS PERCENTAGE
OF TOTAL LIABILITIES

	1913.	1918.	1919.	1920.	1921.	1922.	1923.	Jan. 1st 1924.
Deutsche Bank - - -	13·9	6·4	3·2	3·4	2·1	0·5	—[1]	36·2
Dresdner Bank - - -	17·0	7·4	3·9	2·8	4·5	0·3	—[1]	34·3
Discontogesellschaft -	22·7	10·3	5·0	3·9	3·3	1·3	0·2	44·7
Darmstädter Bank - -	19·7	8·5	4·4	4·2	3·7	0·4	—[1]	33·4
Berliner Handelsgesellschaft -	26·3	18·7	12·3	5·4	2·9	0·7	—[1]	45·1
Commerz- u. Discontobank -	19·5	6·9	4·4	4·5	6·5	2·8	—[1]	30·3
Nationalbank - - -	24·9	13·6	9·2	6·3	6·8	—	—	—
Mitteldeutsche Creditbank -	26·8	9·3	6·2	6·2	10·0	0·9	0·06	59·7
Average [2] - - -	19·0	8·3	4·1	3·8	3·7	0·7	—	37·0

DEPOSITS AND CURRENT ACCOUNT BALANCES AS
PERCENTAGE OF TOTAL LIABILITIES

	1913.	1918.	1919.	1920.	1921.	1922.	1923.	Jan. 1st 1924.
Deutsche Bank - - -	70·4	86·0	87·5	94·2	96·2	98·3	99·9	63·3
Dresdner Bank - - -	62·3	90·2	92·1	95·0	93·7	98·4	94·8	64·9
Discontogesellschaft -	54·4	84·5	90·2	93·2	95·2	97·5	99·8	54·5
Darmstädter Bank - -	62·1	88·3	91·3	92·9	93·2	97·4	93·6	65·2
Berliner Handelsgesellschaft -	53·9	73·7	81·0	88·3	78·6	96·7	95·2	53·0
Commerz- u. Discontobank -	62·2	89·0	89·3	91·1	89·2	89·1	95·8	69·4
Nationalbank - - -	56·5	82·6	83·9	88·7	89·9	—	—	—
Mitteldeutsche Creditbank -	50·6	88·6	91·0	90·5	86·3	94·9	90·1	40·1
Average [2] - - -	62·1	86·6	89·3	93·1	93·3	97·3	96·8	60·2

[1] Nominal entry only.

[2] Percentages for eight banks together, 1913 to 1921 ; thereafter for seven banks.

ACCEPTANCES AS PERCENTAGE OF TOTAL LIABILITIES

	1913.	1918.	1919.	1920.	1921.	1922.	1923.	Jan. 1st 1924.
Deutsche Bank - - ' -	13·4	0·9	0·9	0·7	0·5	0·2	0·16	0·1
Dresdner Bank - - -	18·7	1·4	3·4	0·9	0·8	0·4	0·06	0·04
Discontogesellschaft - -	20·2	1·6	1·4	0·7	0·9	0·3	0·18	0·1
Darmstädter Bank - - -	17·0	2·1	2·6	2·0	1·5	0·5	0·12	0·08
Berliner Handelsgesellschaft -	17·6	5·5	5·0	4·8	7·4	0·2	—	—
Commerz- u. Discontobank -	16·4	3·4	5·7	3·15	3·3	2·4	0·3	0·2
Nationalbank - - -	16·3	2·7	5·2	3·2	2·0	—	—	—
Mitteldeutsche Creditbank -	20·9	1·3	2·5	2·2	2·6	2·0	—	0·03
Average [1] - - - -	16·9	1·6	2·2	1·4	1·4	0·4	0·15	0·1

At once the warning must be given that there was a very considerable and progressive under-statement of Securities and Participations amongst the assets. In itself, as we have seen, the under-valuation of securities in the balance sheets was not new; but at this time it is understood to have been carried to un-precedented lengths, the purpose being presumably to build up special secret reserves to set against the losses arising from currency depreciation.[2]   The same effect would have been achieved, of course, if the securities had been booked at their full value and the difference carried to form reserves; but apparently it was con-sidered undesirable to allow the amounts set aside to appear in the profit and loss accounts.   As this indi-cates, the under-statement of these assets was balanced by an under-statement of the bank's own resources amongst the liabilities; and naturally in each case the under-statement affects the other percentages inversely.

[1] Percentages for eight banks together, 1913 to 1921; thereafter for seven banks.

[2] The securities were not necessarily 'written down'; hidden reserves would often be formed simply by refraining from writing them *up* in accordance with the rise in prices. This course may have been required by a strict adherence to the principles of the commercial code, which enjoins that assets shall be valued at their current price or cost price, whichever is *lower*.

We have no means of ascertaining the extent of the under-statement, except in the case of the 1923 figures: here the opening gold mark balance sheets for 1924, if not themselves entirely reliable, at least give us some idea of the correction required.   (See Appendix III.)

On the liability side only one feature calls for further notice: the dwindling into insignificance of the Acceptances.   In the main this is yet another effect of depreciation, which early made it impossible to use mark bills in foreign trade and eventually destroyed the bill market at home.   But the failure of the volume of acceptances to recover even temporarily after the Armistice may also reflect a policy on the part of the banks of withholding a cheaper form of credit than current account advances.   The smallness of the Acceptances explains in turn the relative decline in bill holdings on the other side of the accounts, when a comparison is made between the pre-war figures and those for 1922 and 1923; the falling-off from the high percentages of the first part of the inflation period, however, was due to the more restricted discounting of treasury bills.

Apart from the misleading investment percentages, the only other group of assets to decline continuously in relative importance was that headed *Reports und Lombards*—a result which is rather surprising in view of the activity of the stock exchanges.   It will be noticed that there was a temporary recovery here in 1921; one may surmise that at this stage of inflation the banks were transferring their money from bills to day to day loans, but that they soon realized that this form of investment gave them little more protection from the effects of depreciation.   Advances (*Debitoren*) and Advances on Goods (*Warenvorschüsse*) increased (relatively) during the period without reaching their pre-war importance, while the Cash percentage remained fairly constant and much the same as before the War (when the necessary correction is made for the under-statement in securities). There remain the *Nostroguthaben* or Balances with Correspondent Banks, which began the period with a percentage higher than that for 1913, and increased in importance as other assets declined. The rise in the percentage after 1921 is especially striking. In part these foreign balances (for this is what they mostly were) were accumulated to finance imports; but to a much greater extent, in all probability, they served as investments which were both liquid and safe from depreciation.

III

The policy of amalgamation adopted in the later years of the War was actively pursued in the following years, particularly between 1920 and 1922. Two mergers of especial importance were those of the Darmstädter Bank with the Nationalbank für Deutschland — both leading Berlin banks — and of the Commerz- und Discontobank with the *Mitteldeutsche Privatbank*, Magdeburg (not to be confused with the Mitteldeutsche Creditbank).

The fusion of the Commerz- und Discontobank and Mitteldeutsche Privatbank was carried out in June, 1920. The *Magdeburger Privatbank*, as it was often called, was one of the most important provincial banks, and had been notable for many years through its activity in building up a large network of branches. At one time it had been regarded as loosely attached to the Deutsche Bank group, but it repudiated the suggestion that it had surrendered its independence in any degree. Following the then English practice, the combination adopted a compound title—the *Commerz- und Privatbank*.

The other and yet more important merger mentioned above, that of the Darmstädter Bank and the

Nationalbank took place in July, 1922.   It was preceded by the amalgamation of the Nationalbank für
Deutschland and the *Deutsche Nationalbank*, Bremen,
in 1920, and by a 50-year 'community of interest'
compact between the Darmstädter and the enlarged
Nationalbank in 1921.   The Deutsche Nationalbank,
Bremen, had been organized as a *Kommanditgesellschaft
auf Aktien*, and this form was retained after both the
1920 and the 1922 fusions.   In each case there was a
formal absorption of the larger *Aktiengesellschaft* by the
smaller *Kommanditgesellschaft*, accompanied by a change
in the name of the latter.   The preference shown on
these occasions for the *Kommanditgesellschaft auf Aktien*
form of organization was probably due to the greater
independence of the *Geschäftsinhaber* (managing partners) of such a society as compared with the directors
of an *Aktiengesellschaft* in relation to the shareholders:
for this meant that there was less danger of the bank
being captured by outside interests.   The final amalgamation adopted the title *Darmstädter und Nationalbank*.

After these two changes the group of Berliner
Grossbanken consisted of seven banks as follows:

> Deutsche Bank
> Discontogesellschaft
> Dresdner Bank
> Darmstädter u. Nationalbank
> Commerz- u. Privatbank
> Berliner Handelsgesellschaft
> Mitteldeutsche Creditbank

Other important amalgamations were those of the
Discontogesellschaft with *Stahl, Federer & Co. Bank*,
Stuttgart, in 1919; of the Deutsche Bank with the
Braunschweiger Privatbank, the *Hannoversche Bank*
and the *Privatbank zu Gotha* in 1920; [1] and of the

---

[1] In 1922 the Deutsche Bank absorbed the *Deutsch-Petroleum A.G.* This
company had originally been a financing and holding subsidiary for the

Commerz- u. Privatbank with the *Vereinsbank Wismar* in 1920, with the *St. Pauli Creditbank* in 1921, with the *Chemnitzer Bankverein*, the *Bankverein Göttingen*, the *Loebauer Bank*, the *Hessische Bankverein*, the *Thüringer Landesbank*, and the *Vogtländische Kreditanstalt* in 1922, and with the *Freiberger Bankverein* in 1923. In most of these cases and certain others, the bank absorbed already belonged to the group of the Berlin bank; they exemplify once more, therefore, the tendency to substitute an organization of branches for the earlier group system. Perhaps the latter should be regarded as merely the first stage in the expansion of the Berlin banks, leading naturally to a more centralized form of organization, once the reputation of these had been established throughout the country and the fact of their penetration of the provinces had been accepted. Certainly the branch organization seems more appropriate to institutions which aim at small individual profits on a large turnover, rather than large profits from a few transactions[1]—and the development in the business of the creditbanks has been in this direction.[2] With regard to the years of inflation in particular, it is to be remarked that the uncertainty of the times weakened the resistance of the provincial banks; in some cases, as in that of the Pfälzische Bank, they found themselves in serious difficulties.[3]

Deutsche Bank's petroleum interests in Roumania. The issue of the War had largely deprived it of its importance in this respect ; but it had managed to emerge with large balances in foreign money, and it was to secure these that the bank took the company over. It was afterwards re-formed with a smaller capital, presumably to engage in the oil business in Germany and elsewhere as opportunities arose.

[1] *Cf.* French deposit banks with numerous branches and the Banques d'Affaires with no branches but a certain number of affiliations.

[2] See Fendler, *Zur Kapitalkonzentration der Berliner Grossbanken,* particularly pp. 64-74.

[3] The desire to escape double taxation may also have been a factor, but on the other hand the taxes levied in respect of the amalgamation transactions themselves acted as a deterrent.

In a number of other cases the Berlin banks incor-
porated small provincial banks or private banking firms
which had hitherto been independent.   All these amalgamations naturally increased the number of branches
of the Berlin banks, and the effect is shown in the
following table, taken from the *Deutsch-Oekonomist*,[1]
comparing the number of offices in 1913 with that at
the beginning of 1924.

OFFICES OF LEADING BERLIN BANKS

	1913.	1924.
Deutsche Bank - - -	15	143
Discontogesellschaft [2] - -	17	133
Dresdner Bank - - -	50	102
Darmstädter u. Nationalbank	60	182
Commerz- u. Privatbank -	8	246
Mitteldeutsche Creditbank -	19	29

These figures relate only to domestic branches.   The
number of foreign branches also increased slightly; for
against the loss of the three London branches and of
the Brussels and Antwerp offices of the Deutsche Bank
and Discontogesellschaft has to be set the opening of
new branches by the Deutsche Bank in Amsterdam and
Sofia and by the Dresdner Bank in Bukarest; while the
cession of the Saar region, Dantzig and part of Silesia,
had the effect of converting a number of German
offices into foreign ones.   The table also excludes
suburban sub-offices.   Here there was another substantial increase, the competition amongst banks for
street corner sites being the subject of general comment
at the time.   It is to be added that many of the offices,
particularly the central ones, were considerably en-

---

[1] *Die deutschen Banken in 1924*, p. 9.

[2] Disconto figure for 1924 includes 31 offices of Schaaffhausen Bankverein,
and 4 of Norddeutsche Bank.   Discrepancies will be noticed between some of
the 1913 figures and those given in Part I on Weber's authority.   It seems
to be peculiarly difficult to count branches ; statements relating to same
dates are frequently at variance.

larged to cope with the increased number of transactions. The effect of all these developments is to be seen in the increase in the numbers employed by the Berliner Grossbanken, from 30,000 at the end of 1913 to 140,000 at the end of 1923.

The extension of the banks' organization was accompanied by increases in their capital, as here shown:

SHARE CAPITAL OF BERLIN BANKS

	1913.	1923.
Deutsche Bank - - -	200	1,500
Discontogesellschaft - -	200	666·67
Dresdner Bank - - -	200	975
Darmstädter u. Nationalbank	250[1]	600
Commerz- u. Privatbank -	85	700
Berliner Handelsgesellschaft -	110	110
Mitteldeutsche Creditbank -	60	1,100

In many instances the increases in capital resulted from amalgamations; when this was not the case, the motive was probably to give a more reasonable appearance to large paper mark profits. As will have been seen from the table in the preceding section, no serious attempt was made to maintain the pre-war proportions between capital—or capital plus reserves—and external liabilities.

The developments related seem to point to a greater degree of concentration in German banking, and to an increased predominance on the part of the Berliner Grossbanken. This impression will be modified in a later section, when we come to deal with the establishment of specialized industrial banks and the growth of publicly-owned banking institutions. But it must be pointed out here that this impression requires correction, even with regard to the class of creditbanks alone.

In the first place we must notice two instances in which important provincial banks took steps likely to ensure

[1]Darmstädter and Nationalbank together.

them a more independent position *vis à vis* the Berlin banks.   One was the formation in 1921 of a 'community of interest,' based on the exchange of *Aufsichtrat* representatives, between the *Allgemeine Deutsche Creditanstalt* of Leipzig (Adca), the *Bayerische Hypotheken und Wechselbank* of Munich, and the *Barmer Bankverein*.   These were perhaps the three most important provincial banks and had been particularly active since 1917 in extending their organization, often by absorbing smaller banks and bankers in their region.   All three had been more or less closely associated with the Discontogesellschaft and this connexion was not now formally ended.   The intention may have been rather to increase the weight of the provincial banks in the partnership with the Discontogesellschaft. At the same time, however, the associated provincial banks asserted a new measure of independence by taking up shares in Hardy & Co. of Berlin; and when, almost by way of retaliation, the Discontogesellschaft opened its own branches in Leipzig and Munich,[1] it became clear that the old relationship had in fact been weakened.   The Barmer Bankverein withdrew from the 'community of interest' after a short time, but not to return to the orbit of the Discontogesellschaft. (See below, p. 233.)   In the other case, a second Bavarian bank, the *Bayerische Vereinsbank*, formed a 'community of interest' with the famous banking house, *Mendelssohn & Co.* of Berlin and (since the War) Amsterdam.   Mendelssohn's acquired shares in the Vereinsbank and also received representation on its *Aufsichtrat*: but the arrangement was definitely one between equals, and was justified on the Bavarian side on the ground that it assured as valuable support as could be desired in Berlin without any sacrifice of

---

[1] Strauss, *op. cit.* p. 86. According to Fendler, *Zur Kapitalkonzentration der Berliner Grossbanken*, p. 50, the Discontogesellschaft opened these branches first, thereby provoking the counter movement of the provincial banks.

independence. This compact was made in 1922: before this the Vereinsbank had already taken up a participation in *E. S. Friedman & Co.* of Berlin and had consolidated its position in Bavaria by a very close understanding with the *Bayerische Handelsbank.*

In the second place, the Berlin banks encountered rivals for the control of the provincial banks in the great industrialists. At the time, it will be remembered, large groups (*Konzerne*) of the most diverse undertakings were being built up by industrial leaders such as Stinnes, and it would have been surprising if the banks had been left altogether untouched by the movement. Actually in two cases the independence of leading Berlin banks was threatened: that of the Berliner Handelsgesellschaft by Stinnes, and that of the Mitteldeutsche Creditbank by Michael.[1] But these ambitious plans were defeated, and the industrialists then contented themselves with capturing a certain number of provincial banks and smaller Berlin institutions. Thus Stinnes[2] acquired control of the *Barmer Bankverein,* Michael control of the *Deutsche Vereinsbank,* Frankfurt am Main[3]—previously in the Deutsche group—and the Barmat Brothers control of the *Bremen Privatbank* and the *Allgemeine Handelsbank,* Magdeburg.[4]

Finally, the effect of the amalgamations in increasing the concentration of banking was partly offset by the formation of a number of new banks, chiefly in Berlin.[5]

---

[1] Neisser: *Das Deutsche Bankgewerbe,* pp. 43-4.   [2] *Ibid.*

[3] *Op. cit.* pp. 45-6.

[4] The last-named also secured the newly-formed Deutsche Merkurbank, Berlin—see below: an Austrian, Körner, captured the Kolonialbank, Berlin, later turned into the Deutsche Länderbank. Some of these conquests were made in 1924, strictly speaking after stabilization. But they belong essentially to the inflation era.

[5] Deutsche Unionbank ; Deutsche Merkurbank ; Hansabank ; Deutsche Handelsbank ; Spar u. Creditbank ; Privat u. Industriebank ; Allgemeine Bankverein (at first of Berlin and Düsseldorf, later withdrawn from the capital).

The incentive to promote these banks was provided by the apparently enormous profits earned by the leading banks, and the difficulty these experienced in handling the volume of business to be done. It is true that there was an obstacle to the formation of new banks in that the right to receive deposits, to take charge of securities, and to engage in exchange dealings was limited to recognized banks existing before a certain date. (This limitation was imposed to facilitate control of the banks, particularly with regard to the duties imposed on them on behalf of the tax administration.) But these rights were transferable, and it was possible to find established banks which would sell their rights, either because of the insignificance of their business or because they found themselves in difficulties. In several cases German industrialists were responsible for the establishment of new banks;[1] in others Austrian capital was concerned.[2]

There was also a considerable increase during this period in the number of private banking firms, aided by the fact that anyone who had been employed in a banking business for a certain time could claim recognition as a banker if he set up on his own.

IV

The declining value of the mark presents us with especial difficulties when we come to study the banks' real earnings and profits. At the time the directors of the banks seem to have been far from clear as to the true position of their institutions. Looking at the matter in retrospect, there is less danger of being

---

[1] *E.g.* Michael for that of the Industrie u. Privatbank ; Sichel for that of the Westbank, Frankfurt, which took over the rights of the Deutsche Palästina Bank.

[2] Körner in the Allgemeine Bankverein ; Österreichische Creditanstalt in the Bank für Auswärtige Handel ; Allgemeine Depositenbank (Vienna) in the Hamburger Handelsbank.

altogether misled by inflated figures: but the nature of the information available is such that only the broadest conclusions can be hoped for.

The circumstances of the inflation period were favourable enough for the banks, if the latter were solely concerned to make large immediate profits in terms of the depreciated mark; they were by no means so favourable if profits were to be measured by a stable standard, and an attempt was to be made to maintain the real value of the banks' own resources. Leaving aside the risks of depreciation to which those resources were exposed, the real earning capacity of the banks was affected adversely by two sets of influences, the one tending to reduce real gross profits and the other tending to increase real costs. With regard to the former, we have already noticed the decline in the real value of the deposits and current account balances. This reduced the basis—always in terms of real wealth—upon which interest could be earned. At the same time, since total turnovers seem also to have been below the pre-war level, when converted into gold marks,[1] there was probably some contraction in the main basis for charges (*Provisionen*). It is not possible, unfortunately, to say how far there was an offsetting expansion in the branches of business subject to special charges, particularly stock-broking: but it may be regarded as certain that the value of such business did not grow in anything like the same proportion as the number of transactions. This brings us to the increased costs of the banks, in which the chief factor was the increase in the number employed. So far as this was not the result of the amalgamations—which should have affected gross profits and expenses in

[1] There is some difficulty in converting 'turnover' to gold mark figures, since some kind of average rate of exchange has to be taken. The Deutsche Bank attempted the conversion in its report for 1921 : then the gold mark turnover was shown to be 85 milliard as against a turnover of 129 milliard in 1913.

about the same proportions—the enlargement of bank staffs seems to have been due to two causes: firstly the increase in the number of transactions to be performed; secondly the amount of assistance which the banks were called upon to render gratuitously to the Reich Finance Department.[1] Subject to the qualification that a large proportion of those employed were women, paid at lower rates than men, the real cost of salaries may be supposed to have increased more or less in the same proportion as the numbers employed.

It is not to be thought, however, that the banks made no effort to resist these influences. There could be no mistake about the increasing costs, and to meet these, probably also with a view to repairing the depreciation of their own assets, the banks frequently revised the terms of business in their own favour. In pursuance of this course the *Konditionen-Kartell* was extended, particularly by agreements in 1920 and 1922. It would be tedious to trace the changes in terms in detail, but one or two examples may be given to illustrate the scope of the modifications effected. In 1922 the interest charge on current account advances was 2% above Bank rate—or 8% on the average for the year—in comparison with a pre-war rate of 1% over Bank rate; on the top of this, *Provisionen*— now mainly interest under another name—had to be paid, amounting to at least 6% per annum, and sometimes to 12%, as against 1% before the War.[2] On the other side the interest allowed on current account balances remained at $1\frac{1}{2}$% to 2%.[3] Thus the interest

---

[1] According to the Report of the Discontogesellschaft for 1921: 'Calculations show that of every 100 persons on our staff, some 10 at least are engaged on work which serves the interests of the State, but not those of the bank.'

[2] See *Die Bank*, August 1922, p. 474. There was also an extra charge of 2% on unauthorized overdrafts.

[3] *Ibid.* This is for balances withdrawable at any time. Higher rates, say 3% to 4%, were paid on balances subject to notice of withdrawal, but demand balances predominated at this time.

margin in favour of the banks was widened from about
4% to 12% or 18%. At the same time a change had
been introduced in banking practice which increased
the occasions on which this margin was enjoyed: this
change was the adoption of the English (or rather
London) custom of crediting an advance to current
account as soon as it was made available to the customer and charging full interest (+charges) on it from
that date, in place of the pre-war German practice of
only charging for the advance as and when it was used.
To take another example relating to a different date
and a different branch of business, the commission
charged on an order to purchase a share was $58\ ^0/_{00}$ at
the end of the inflation period instead of one of $2\ ^0/_{00}$
before the War.[1] We see, then, that if the bases of
the earnings contracted—in terms of real wealth—the
rates levied on these bases very substantially increased.
The question is whether they increased sufficiently to
compensate for the increased costs and also to make
good any losses in the banks' capital resources.

In seeking an answer to this question practically no
help is to be obtained from the published profit and
loss accounts. In the first place the figures shown for
gross earnings were more than ever artificial, it being
generally reported (without contradiction) that the
actual income under all heads was drastically curtailed
in order to build up secret reserves. We meet here
in an enhanced degree a difficulty which we have
already encountered in dealing with the pre-war and
war accounts. But with the later years of inflation we
come upon another difficulty. Owing to the rapid
depreciation of the mark, x marks of income or expenditure at one date was in reality far from equal to
x marks of income or expenditure at another date:
accounts, therefore, which add or compare mark sums
on the assumption that the mark was equal at all dates

[1] Schacht, *Stabilisierung*, p. 148.

within a year can only yield meaningless results.   In
the light of these considerations we shall pass over the
profit and loss accounts and test the financial success
of the banks over this period, firstly by reference to the
dividends paid, and secondly—since dividends may be
sacrificed to strengthening capital, or the maintenance
of capital neglected in the interest of dividends—by
reference to the state of the banks' own resources as
revealed by the 1924 revaluations.

(1) The dividends declared during the period by
the leading Berlin banks were as follows:

BANK DIVIDENDS, 1918-1923

	1918.	1919.	1920.	1921.	1922.	1923.
Deutsche Bank -	12	12	18	24	300	o
Discontogesell-						
schaft - -	9	10	16	20	250	o
Dresdner Bank -	7	9	12½	16	200	o
Darmstädter Bank	6	8	10	14⎱	200	o
Nationalbank -	5	7	10	14⎰		o
Commerz- u. Dis-						
contobank -	7	9	12	16	150	o
Berliner Handels-						
gesellschaft -	8	10	12½	16	200	1 [1]
Mitteldeutsche						
Creditbank -	7	8	10	12½	150	o
Depreciation factor	2	12	17·5	44	1,750	1 billion

We first notice that, except in the case of the Berliner
Handelsgesellschaft, no dividends at all were paid in
1923.   For the preceding years the dividends, at first
sight so large, need to be corrected by taking into
account the depreciation of the money in which they
were paid.   So far as the real return on pre-war
capital is concerned, this correction is easily effected

[1] 1 gold mark per cent. of capital.

by dividing the nominal dividends for each year by the
ratio of depreciation at the end of that year—given
(roughly) in the bottom line of the table. In result
we get real dividends of 1% and under in the first two
years, 1919 and 1920, falling to ones of a fraction of
1% in the later years. Probably we should not be far
wrong in applying the same divisors to the dividends
on those war and post-war additions to capital which
originated in amalgamation transactions; since this
new capital was for the most part a substitute for the
pre-war capital of provincial banks. In respect of the
dividends on the remainder of the post-1914 capital,
which was subscribed in money already more or less
depreciated, less drastic revision is called for. It
would involve too much unprofitable labour to calculate the real rate of return on each block of new capital
by reference to the depreciation subsequent to the date
of subscription: as a sample we may take the return
on the 200 million mark shares offered by the Discontogesellschaft in March 1922 at a price of 300%.
In the course of 1922 the mark declined in the proportion 40:1, and although some of this decline had
taken place before the shares were sold, we may
conveniently take 40 as the divisor for depreciation,
since the 1922 dividends were not paid out until about
May 1923, when yet further depreciation had taken
place.[1] On this basis the real rate of return for the
eight or nine months would be 250 divided by 120
(40 × 3) or a little more than 2%. Had we taken as
our sample the case of a capital increase in an earlier
year, the price would have been lower, and also, at
first, the depreciation factor, but the dividend to be
corrected would also have been much lower in the first
years: later depreciation would have proceeded faster

---

[1] Really the divisor should be greater than 40 ; for most of the depreciation in 1922 occurred in the second half of the year, while there was very
rapid depreciation in the first part of 1923.

than the nominal dividend rate increased. Our conclusions as to real dividend are, then, firstly that prewar capital received a scanty return at first which subsequently dwindled into insignificance; and secondly, that even in its first years newly subscribed capital received but a modest return.

(2) The accompanying table shows the capital and reserves of the Berlin banks at the end of 1913, and in the opening ' gold mark ' balance sheets of 1924, also the capital at the end of 1923.

| | 1913. | | | 1923. | 1924. | | | Ratio at which Capital was Converted. |
	Capital.	Reserves.	Together.	Capital only.	Capital.	Reserves.	Together.	
Deutsche Bank	200	112·5	312·5	1,500	150	50	200	10 : 1
Discontogesell-schaft	200	81·3	281·3	111·67	100	34	134	8⅔ : 1
Dresdner Bank	200	61	261	975	78	22	100	12¼ : 1
Darmstädter with Nationalbank	250	48	298	600	60	40	100	10 : 1
Commerz- u. Discontobank later Commerz -u. Privatbank	85	14	89	700	42	21	63	16⅔ : 1
Mitteldeutsche Creditbank	60	9·15	69·15	1,100	22·02	2·22	24·24	50 : 1
Berliner Handels-gesellschaft	110	34·5	144·5	110 (Gold M. nomin-ally)	22	5	27	5 : 1

It will be seen that by drawing upon reserves—open and secret—it was possible to convert the share capitals into gold mark capitals at ratios varying from 5 : 1 (Berliner Handelsgesellschaft) to 50: 1 (Mitteldeutsche Creditbank). These ratios are low compared

with the general conversion ratio of 1 billion : 1, and
show the extent of the reserves at the end of 1923.
But the fact remains that the reserves accumulated were
far from adequate to offset the losses caused by depreciation.   Stated broadly, the table shows that the
banks lost more than half of their pre-war capital
resources, together with the whole of the capital subscribed after 1914.   Strictly there should be included
with the latter a large part of the pre-war capital
of the banks absorbed: but this item may perhaps
be represented by secret reserves in the January
1924 balance sheets in excess of those at the end
of 1913.

These losses were proportionately smaller than those
of the mass of depositors: further they were not
peculiar to banking undertakings.   Since banks deal
almost entirely in money claims, it may be suggested
that they necessarily lose with the depreciation of the
currency, and that efforts to withstand this necessity
are hopeless from the first.   Against this view, however, it may be argued that, so far as they are not
embodied in buildings and equipment—which ought
to retain their value whatever happens to the currency
—the capital resources of a bank serve chiefly to provide a guarantee for its creditors, and that it would be
consonant with this purpose to separate them from the
deposit moneys employed in banking proper and to
invest them in any way which seemed safe.   The
question then arises as to what opportunities of safe
investment were in fact open to the banks during this
period of rapid depreciation.   Two possibilities which
suggest themselves are investment in industrial shares
and investment in foreign countries with (relatively)
stable currencies.   To both of these courses the banks
appear to have resorted, but both had their serious
limitations.   In the one case, as Helfferich has shown,
industrial shares did not retain anything like their

original gold value,[1] and therefore by no means fulfilled the requirements of the situation: in the other, the *Kapitalfluchtgesetz*—law against the export of capital—could not be simply ignored, although it might to some extent be evaded. It is further to be observed that much of the new investment of this period in bank premises—in part necessitated by the pressure of the abnormal volume of transactions upon the existing accommodation, in part inspired by the desire to embody wealth in ' real ' forms—proved in the end to be unremunerative. On the whole it would appear, therefore, that the circumstances hardly allowed the banks to do more to protect their resources, short of converting their whole business into transactions on a valorised basis (as was urged by Hauser, Dalberg, and others). The latter course they refused until the very end to take.[2]

The losses due to depreciation were masked losses, which only came to light when assets had to be revalued in a stable unit of account. Losses of the more ordinary kind, in terms of the unit of account in continuous use, were of much less importance during this period, and would hardly need mention if they had not been responsible for a certain number of failures. Speculation in foreign exchanges occasioned most of these losses, and the banks to fail were mostly of small account. But unsuccessful gambling on the fall of the franc in 1921 brought about the downfall of two banks of importance in West Germany. One of these, the *Pfälzische Bank*, was an old and well-reputed institution belonging to the Deutsche group. On its liquidation its offices were divided between the Deutsche Bank

---

[1] See *Money*, vol. ii. pp. 587 *et. seq.* Measured by their dollar value, at rate of exchange, by the spring of 1923 shares had fallen to 7% or 8% of their pre-war value, all allowances being made for watering.

[2] In this matter the savings banks showed themselves more adaptable than the creditbanks.

and the *Rheinische Creditbank*—another member of the
Deutsche group which had for some time been closely
associated with the Pfälzische Bank in a ' community
of interest ' arrangement.   The other important failure
was that of a post-war creation under Austrian influence, the *Allgemeine Bankverein* of Düsseldorf.

Apart from these cases, it is clear that the period
was a disastrous one from the point of view of the bank
shareholders.   The curtailment of ' real ' dividends did
not prevent drastic reductions in their capital.   The
evidence only allows us to reach this definite conclusion
with regard to the period as a whole, without distinguishing the results obtained in particular years.   It
seems probable that the heaviest losses were incurred
during the later years of rapid depreciation, but that,
measured in terms of real wealth, the results were also
unsatisfactory in the earlier years.

V

To complete this survey of the inflation years it is
necessary to refer to certain developments, as a result
of which the business field of the creditbanks was
invaded by institutions of other types.

The institutions in question fall into three classes:

1. Banks   for   particular   industrial   groups
   (*Konzerne*).
2. Banks for particular branches of trade or
   industry.
3. Public banks on a communal or state basis.

1. In addition to acquiring control of existing creditbanks and establishing new creditbanks, as described
in a previous section, the great industrialists in a
number of cases set up special organs, often called
banks, to do the banking business of their groups.

In so far as these organs did not act as banks for the

general public (it is not always clear whether they did
or not), but only for certain financially interconnected
undertakings, they resemble the financial companies
established by the electrical groups before the War.
But they were less concerned than the latter with the
raising of long term capital: and their chief function
seems to have been to find direct employment for
temporary balances, and generally to organize lending
and borrowing within the group. Their creation may
be regarded in part as an expression of the general
desire of the industrialists to make their groups self-
sufficient. But in part also it was provoked by the
abnormal margin between the rates which the creditbanks charged their debtors and those they allowed
their creditors. On the whole, as we have seen, these
terms failed to yield the banks even adequate profits;
none the less they may have been exorbitant considered
in their application to the larger transactions alone,
since it was almost certainly the small transactions
which were unprofitable.

2. In several trades special banks were promoted,
having as their object the financing of the one trade.
(*Banken für Branchen*). These represented a form of
co-operation between independent firms engaged in
the same trade and were presumably organized by the
trade associations. As examples may be cited the
Getreidekredit A.G. (Corn Credit Company) in Berlin
associated with local ' corn banks ' in several parts of
Germany; the *Holzwirtschaftsbank* (Timber Trade
Bank); and the *Zuckercreditbank* (Sugar Credit Bank).
These new institutions are not to be confused with
much older ones with a similar form of title, such as
the *Bank für Brauindustrie* (Bank for Brewing Industry)
or the *Metallbank*, which were in reality holding companies for particular capitalist groups.

In most, though not all, cases the formation of these
new banks was justified on the ground that the existing

banks failed to give sufficient consideration to the
requirements of the particular trade.[1] As the firms in
the trades in question are mostly of moderate size, they
may have felt that their needs were not receiving the
same attention from the banks as those of larger
concerns. Perhaps the main purpose of these trade
banks, however, was to give easier access to the
comparatively cheap credit provided by the Reichsbank.[2]

3 (a). The expansion of the functions of the communal savings banks which took place during the War
was continued during the following years, until it
resulted in an almost complete transformation of these
institutions.

A number of different factors appear to have contributed to this development.

(1) The extension of the communal *Giro* (payment
by transfer) system, called for a different investment
policy from that appropriate to a pure savings bank:
particularly it required the cultivation of short term
lending.

(2) This apart, new modes of investment had to be
sought in place of mortgage and other long term fixed
interest loans, the value of which was likely to be
annihilated by depreciation. Only in the case of short
term loans could interest rates be revised with sufficient frequency to give the lender any hope of compensation for the fall in the value of his principal. The
influence of depreciation was similarly responsible for
a great contraction in the long term investments made
with the savings banks.

(3) Their own urgent financial needs suggested to
the municipal authorities the desirability of developing

---

[1] The big creditbanks were associated with the formation of the corn and
sugar banks. Strauss, *Die Konzentrationsbewegung*, p. 26.

[2] Somewhat similar were the banks formed at this time by trade unions
and associations of officials.

their banking institutions both as a source of loans and a source of income.

(4) The development was favoured by socio-political ideas at the time prevalent: belief in socialization and hostility to the more developed forms of capitalism.

The movement encountered a certain check in the necessity of securing the consent of the higher administrative authorities for each new step, the granting of this consent being in turn controlled by state ordinances. This check by no means impeded all progress, but it was sufficiently effective to lead a number of municipalities to set up separate *municipal banks*, distinct from the savings banks and often alongside of them, with a most general banking programme.[1] With a view to putting a stop to this latest development and to keeping the whole movement within certain channels, the Prussian Government in April, 1921, replaced the earlier restrictive ordinances by a new one, under which the savings banks might be allowed to assume very general banking powers: at the same time, sanction was only to be given to the creation of municipal banks in cases in which a special need for the new type of institution could be shown to exist. By a later Prussian ordinance of April, 1923, savings banks were allowed to form separate banking departments.[2]

Above the savings banks and municipal banks, the primary organs of the communal banking system, had

---

[1] Apparently the consent of the supervising provincial authorities could often be obtained for the establishment of a new bank, when it would have been denied for the expansion of a savings bank (there being no general rules to govern their decision in the former unforeseen case). It is said, however, that a number of the new municipal banks were formed without any sanction from above. Neisser, *op. cit.* p. 86.

[2] It should be borne in mind that the regulation of savings banks is a state and not a federal affair. In the other states the general course of development was similar to that in Prussia, but naturally the details differed.

been erected the district *Giro Zentralen* and (in 1918) the *Deutsche Giro Zentrale*, Berlin. The main purpose of this higher organization was to operate payments by book transfer (*Giro* payments) between one local bank and another,[1] to which the task of distributing liquid balances between the banks was easily added. But during the inflation period the *Zentralen* also came to engage directly in banking transactions with private business.

(*b*) Finally, new state-owned banks were formed in Bavaria—where the *Königliche Bank* of Nuremberg was moved to Munich and transformed into the *Bayerische Staatsbank* in 1920—in Saxony (*Sächsische Staatsbank*, 1922), and Thuringia (*Thüringische Staatsbank*). All these banks act as repositories and financial agents for their state governments, but all of them also deal to a greater or less extent with private customers. In Saxony and Thuringia particularly, the relations between the state banks and industry have been very close: and in both cases the state bank has also participated in other banks and in insurance companies.[2]

In Prussia no new state bank was established, although the *Königliche Seehandlung* changed its title to that of *Preussische Staatsbank (Seehandlung)* after the Revolution, and later departed from its conservative policy of dealing only with the leading banks. A new publicly-owned bank appeared in Berlin, however, in 1922, when the *Reichskredit und Kontrollestelle G.m.b.H.* was turned into the *Reichskreditgesellschaft m.b.H.* The earlier organization, formed in 1919, had been an agency for exercising financial supervision over various Government works, which were converted after the War from military to civil production and put on an

---

[1] See Appendix II.

[2] The Braunschweigische Staatsbank—an older institution—also took a larger part in private finance during the inflation years. The Brunswick and Thuringian State Banks are also mortgage institutions.

independent footing (whilst remaining in the ownership of the Reich). In 1922 this supervisory work was handed over to a new organ (*Deutsche Revisions u. Treuhand G.m.b.H.*) and the *Kontrollestelle* became under the title of *Reichskreditgesellschaft* a banking agency (*Konzernbank*) for the Reich group of trading undertakings. The whole group, including the Reichkreditgesellschaft, is controlled by a holding company, *V.I.A.G.* (*Vereinigte Industrieunternehmungen A.G.*), which is in turn owned by the Reich. In the years from 1922 to 1924, the Reichkreditgesellschaft engaged in certain other transactions on behalf of the Reich government, in addition to its business in connexion with V.I.A.G., but it did not cultivate extensive relations with private firms or persons.

It will be seen, then, that the inflation period witnessed a great expansion of banking organization, and that the creditbanks emerged from it not only with heavy financial losses, but faced with many new competitors.

CHAPTER VIII

THE CREDITBANKS SINCE STABILIZATION

I

THE exchange value of the mark was stabilized at
4·2 billion (million million) to the dollar, i.e. one
billionth of its pre-war value, from the end of November
1923, rigid control being maintained at first by the
Reichsbank to prevent further fluctuations. At the
same time a new paper currency was introduced, notes
denominated in *Rentenmarks* and covered by interest
charges or mortgages imposed on all business undertakings in Germany, agricultural, industrial, commercial, and financial. These mortgages were on a
gold mark basis and were represented by gold mark
mortgage bonds bearing interest at 5%: the *Rentenmark* was declared to have the value of one gold mark,
and the *Rentenmark* notes were convertible into the
gold mark bonds at par.[1] The new notes were universally accepted at their official value, and the *Rentenmark*,
synonymous with the gold mark, became the general
unit of account The Reichsbank held itself ready to
convert its own notes into *Rentenmark* notes at the rate

---

[1] The convertibility of the *Rentenmark* notes into gold bonds did not
really secure that the notes should have the value of one gold mark for each
Rentenmark of their denomination ; for while the interest on the bonds was
on a gold mark basis, the rate of interest was only 5% at a time when the
prevailing rate even for valorized loans was more than twice as high. Thus
the value of the *Rentenmark* might have fallen to 50 gold *pfennige* or
less, before it would have been worth while to exercise the right of
conversion.

of one billion marks to the *Rentenmark*, and at this rate the Reichsbank notes continued to circulate.[1]

The *Rentenmark* notes came into circulation through loans given by the new *Rentenbank*. Of the authorized maximum issue of 2·4 milliard *Rentenmark*, 1·2 milliard was to be lent to the Reich government to enable it to redeem its floating debt with the Reichsbank— this required about 200 million *Rentenmark*—and to dispense with further assistance from this institution whilst bringing its budget into equilibrium. The remainder was to be lent as required to the Reichsbank and the four minor note-issuing banks (in certain proportions), to be re-lent by them to private business.

These loans were absolutely necessary in the circumstances, because the government required time to re-establish the machinery of taxation, and business was practically brought to a standstill for lack of liquid capital. At the same time the shrinkage in the value of the old mark notes had left a void in the currency, which tended to grow as returning confidence brought about a decline in the velocity of circulation and the retirement of money substitutes.[2] The existence of this currency shortage provided, then, the possibility of giving loans in new money without causing further inflation. But unfortunately the need for capital and the need for currency did not precisely balance, and in endeavouring to satisfy the former the Reichsbank did actually put money into circulation more rapidly than it could be absorbed.[3] The effects of this course

---

[1] The demand for Reichsbank notes was to some extent maintained by the fact that they alone could be tendered at the Reichsbank in purchase of foreign exchange.

[2] The latter was also enforced by law.

[3] The increase in circulation between the end of November, 1923, and the end of March, 1924, has been put at not less than 2½ milliard *Rentenmarks* by Prof. Harms, who does not, however, give details. Only 2 milliard *Rentenmarks* were issued in the new notes—business only getting 800 million of its 1·2 milliard—and 225 million of these remained with the Reichsbank ;

showed themselves in the spring of 1924. Prices rose and the balance of trade became heavily adverse. Exchange rates could not rise because they were artificially pegged; but the Reichsbank had to ration the supply of foreign exchange, and, in fact, could only allot a small proportion of the amount applied for.[1]

To remedy the situation Dr. Schacht, the new Reichsbank President, decided to put a drastic check on further currency expansion. The rate of discount was left unchanged at 10%, but the total credit to be given by the Reichsbank (including *Rentenmark* loans) was limited to the amount outstanding on April 7th, while the distribution of this total was effected by rationing the individual clients, mainly on the basis of the credit they were then receiving. As the trouble had arisen rather through a too rapid expansion of currency, than from the volume being in excess of normal requirements, an actual contraction of currency was not called for, and the measure adopted soon brought about a reaction in prices. From the end of May the Reichsbank was able to meet the applications for foreign exchange in full, and with this the process of stabilization was completed.

In October, 1924, the note issue and currency was re-organized in accordance with the recommendations of the Dawes Committee, and the unit of account became henceforth the *Reichsmark*. Like the

but the latter's own circulation increased by 597 million gold or Rentenmarks. This points to a net increase of 2·3 milliard Rentenmarks. Further elements in the situation were, on the one hand, the withdrawal of emergency money, and on the other hand, the issue of new token money (*Rentenpfennige*). But the *amount* of the increase in circulation was less important than the *rate* of increase. (See controversy in *Hamburger Wirtschaftsdienst*, Nos. 16 and 27-31, 1924.)

[1] At one time only 1%. Little importance attaches, however, to the precise proportion allotted, because applicants over-stated their requirements in anticipation of only receiving a certain fraction. The rationing of *Devisen* was introduced almost as soon as the rate of exchange was fixed, but at first it was only necessitated by the continuance of speculation against the mark.

Rentenmark, the *Reichsmark* has the same gold value as the pre-war mark.

At the end of 1924 the system of foreign exchange control was relaxed to allow of sales of German currency abroad and to give freedom to all to acquire foreign money claims without special authorization. With the permission of time dealings in foreign exchange and free quotation of rates granted in May, 1926, the system of control was brought to an end, except that only authorized banks and bankers can deal professionally.[1]   With the similar exception that only authorized banking institutions can receive deposits and administer securities, little remains of the other special laws of the inflation period, such as the law against the exportation of capital (*Kapitalfluchtgesetz*).

II

The shortage of capital, the most serious of Germany's economic difficulties on the stabilization of currency, was a consequence of the preceding period of depreciation.   So far as short term or circulating capital is concerned, this is not difficult to understand. As already explained, liquid resources had been converted as far as possible into *Sachwerte*, and, on the top of this, the value of such balances as remained was almost completely wiped out by the final collapse of the mark (excepting, of course, balances in terms of foreign currencies, or in foreign currencies themselves). But it is perhaps surprising to find that, notwithstanding the stimulus given by inflation to investment in capital goods, there was also an acute scarcity of long term capital.   A considerable part of the explanation is probably to be found in the existence of certain

---

[1] Not by official means of control, but by its willingness to deal without limit at the price, the Reichsbank pegged the dollar exchange at parity until August, 1926.

classes, such as local authorities and landowners, who cannot obtain the capital they require by offering participating rights in profits. . Their demands had necessarily to accumulate during the inflation period, and were ready to make themselves felt as soon as conditions allowed of borrowing against a fixed rate of interest. On the other side of the market, the supply was restricted, firstly by the destruction of temporary balances awaiting investment and secondly by the attraction of the high rates of interest prevailing on the short loan market. A further factor affecting the investment market was the large proportion of the capital expenditure of the inflation period which proved ultimately to be uneconomic; but this showed its influence more when the 'rationalization' movement began in 1925, than immediately after stabilization. Whilst in the short term market scarcity expressed itself in almost fantastic rates of interest—e.g. 100% for day to day money at the beginning of 1924—the long term market, with its more elastic demand, showed the effect rather in the suspension of its business.

Relief of this dearth of capital has been provided chiefly by loans from abroad, although German savings have doubtless helped to ease the situation in later years. Down to the end of September, 1926, the net foreign borrowing of Germany has been estimated by Dr. Schacht to have amounted to 4¾ milliard marks, of which 3½ milliard was in the form of long term loans.[1] Foreign assistance may correctly be said to have begun with the English and American credits given to the *Golddiskontbank*, which was established to assist the German export trade just at the time when

---

[1] *Die Stabilisierung der Mark*, p. 170. The latter figure seems to include the 800 million Dawes Loan, which was not really a loan to Germany at all. It does not include shares and other participations in German concerns purchased by foreigners ; but on the other hand the re-purchases by Germans of securities sold abroad have not been subtracted.

the Reichsbank introduced its credit restriction (April 7th, 1924). But this first transaction was largely the result of urgent representations made by the President of the Reichsbank, and it was not until after the adoption of the Dawes Plan that the free movement of capital towards Germany commenced.

In the first phase the foreign loans came chiefly to the money market, where the disparity between German and foreign rates was the most striking and the investor's risks most limited. This phase did not last long—perhaps not six months from September, 1924 —and later the proportion of long term loans steadily increased; but the proceeds of the latter often came into the money market in the first instance, whilst awaiting their ultimate employment. From the middle of 1925 two further influences helped to produce a state of ease in the money market which did not correspond with the condition of the capital market as a whole.

(1) *Public balances.* The government of the Reich had accumulated a large surplus by raising money in excess of expenditure. This may have been due in part to a natural desire to avoid at all costs a repetition of the deficits of the pre-stabilization period. But it may also be regarded as a provision for unforeseen contingencies, necessitated by the restrictions imposed in the new Bank Act upon the Reich's borrowing powers.[1] The raising of this money in excess of current requirements probably aggravated the shortage of ready money in industry and commerce, but the need to employ the surplus in liquid forms brought an access of funds to the money market. Large balances held by the Post Office, the Railway Company, semi-public insurance institutions, and the like were similarly offered in Berlin on short terms.

[1] See author's note on Amendment of German Bank Act, *Economica,* No. 18, Nov. 1926.

(2) *Trade depression.* In the summer of 1925 trade received a check, which was followed by a period of acute depression in the autumn of that year and the first part of 1926.

The turn in the course of trade at this time has been described by some as a 'stabilization' crisis and by others as a 'deflation' crisis. Neither term, however, seems to fit the facts satisfactorily. The stabilization process was completed, as we have seen, at least a year earlier, and at that time there was a crisis which might be called a 'stabilization' crisis.[1] But after this period of difficulty the influence of foreign credits brought about a recovery in the autumn of 1924 which lasted some time into the following year. Again the decisive restriction of credit (deflation) was introduced in the spring of 1924, and the subsequent changes in the policy of the Reichsbank were in the direction of relaxing this restriction. With a view to restoring the Private Discount Market, the Bank agreed to re-discount first-class bank acceptances outside the otherwise fixed credit total in the summer of 1924; the following September the total of credits allowed was increased by 10%; apart from individual concessions there was no other change until the whole system of credit rationing was abandoned at the end of 1925. Neither stabilization nor deflation explains, therefore, a change which came about in the course of 1925. Some importance may perhaps be attached to the collapse of the Stinnes group and one or two other survivals from the inflation period in the early summer. For although these failures do not appear to have had considerable direct repercussions on German industry,

---

[1] It may well be argued, however, that many of the difficulties which are commonly attendant upon stabilization were experienced by Germany *before* stabilization took place, at the time when German prices came to be automatically adjusted to the exchange value of the mark. It would be at this point that the premium on exports due to exchange undervaluation would disappear. *Cf.* Aftalion, *Monnaie et Industrie*, pp. 44-45.

they may have been responsible for a temporary check in the flow of foreign loans.   But there is evidence that the general course of trade was already changing before the difficulties of these concerns came to light—the most sensitive indices in fact record a change of trend in February.   The causes of this change must, therefore, be sought further.   Probably the most decisive cause was the fact that the expanding tendency of German trade had not been paralleled by a similar movement in the other countries with which Germany now had stable exchange relations; for it is hardly possible for one (virtual) gold standard country to have a boom which is not shared by the rest.   Another may be found in the technical deficiencies of German industry; a boom normally requires to be preceded by a more thorough process of weeding out the inefficient than was induced by the brief period when German prices were falling in 1924.   The Reichsbank might indeed have enabled the boom to continue by expanding the currency; but the refusal to adopt a policy of inflation, which must have been fatal to the stabilization of the exchanges, ought not to be spoken of as *deflation*.   If the bank is to be blamed, it should not be for depressing prices in the summer of 1925, but rather for allowing them to rise during the preceding months.[1]

Whatever its causes, the depression contributed considerably to the easing of the short loan market.   The long term capital market is normally affected to a less degree by changes in trade: and in this case the difference between the two sections of the capital market was accentuated by the fact that industry at

---

[1] The rise in prices was due to foreign loans, the *Devisen* proceeds of which were exchanged at the Reichsbank for notes.   Where the Bank may be criticized is for buying the foreign bills without limit at par price down to August, 1926.   Had the exchange value of the dollar been allowed to fall to gold import point, commodity imports would have been encouraged and the tendency to rising prices and expanding trade might have been checked before it had proceeded to serious lengths.   (See Hahn, *Aufgaben u. Grenzen der Währungspolitik*, pp. 13-20.)

once endeavoured to meet its difficulties by adopting a wholesale policy of reorganization and reconstruction (rationalization), which called for new investments on a large scale.

The movements of the various interest rates may be followed in the accompanying table.

BERLIN MONEY MARKET RATES, 1925–1928
(Monthly averages from *Frankfürter Zeitung Wirtschaftskurven*)

	Day to Day Loans.	Monthly Loans.	Private Discount Rate.[1]	Trade Bills.	Mortgage Interest.
1925.					
January -	9·64	11·28	8·37	9·0	
February -	10·59	12·15	8·00	9·44	
March -	8·98	11·25	8·00	8·83	
April - -	8·50	10·25	8·00	8·85	
May - -	8·88	10·46	8·00-7·87	8·93	
June - -	8·73	10·59	7·83-7·69	8·68	
July - -	9·40	10·81	7·87-7·86	9·08	
August -	8·87	10·64	7·78-7·61	9·05	
September -	8·51	10·55	7·27-7·09	8·85	
October -	8·99	10·55	7·16-7·02	8·91	16·00
November -	8·36	10·57	6·78-6·77	8·68	
December -	8·07	10·29	6·75	8·66	15·00
1926.					
January -	7·04	8·07	6·28-6·26	7·66	15·00
February -	6·03	6·66	5·46	6·79	13·77
March -	5·63	6·73	5·00	6·32	11·72
April - -	4·77	6·02	4·88	5·79	10·71
May - -	4·80	5·53	4·69	5·38	10·31
June - -	4·68	5·82	4·52-4·51	5·23	10·65
July - -	4·88	5·75	4·56-4·50	5·05	10·40
August -	4·85	5·61	4·66-4·55	5·09	10·15
September -	4·75	6·21	4·97-4·79	5·43	10·31
October -	4·81	6·12	4·93-4·75	5·35	9·50
November -	4·45	6·12	4·69-4·57	5·10	9·50
December -	6·03	7·24	4·83-4·61	5·38	9·25

[1] Where there are two quotations, the first is for short bills, and the second for long.

BERLIN MONEY MARKET RATES, 1925-28—*cont.*

	Day to Day Loans.	Monthly Loans.	Private Discount Rate.[1]	Trade Bills.	Mortgage Interest.
1927.					
January -	4·03	6·16	4·26	4·62	8·05
February -	5·33	5·82	4·27-4·19	4·43	7·50
March -	4·87	6·91	4·68-4·48	4·92	7·75
April - -	5·65	6·57	4·67-4·57	4·89	8·00
May - -	5·99	6·91	4·90	5·00	8·60
June - -	5·80	7·73	5·39	5·67	8·75
July - -	7·06	8·48	5·90	6·15	9·00
August -	5·82	8·38	5·83-5·81	6·15	9·50
September -	6·02	8·29	5·90	6·21	9·50
October -	7·19	8·72	6·69	7·04	10·0
November -	6·03	8·72	6·76	7·29	10·0
December -	7·95	9·09	6·85	7·36	9·75
1928.					
January -	5·29	7·77	6·25-6·27	6·82	9·75
February -	6·76	7·34	6·20	6·69	9·75
March -	6·46	7·56	6·72	7·00	9·75
April - -	6·53	7·66	6·70	6·89	9·75
May - -	6·98	7·59	6·66	6·91	9·75
June - -	6·34	8·09	6·58	6·89	9·75
July - -	7·43	8·07	6·75-6·73	7·01	9·75
August -	6·14	8·19	6·68	6·98	
September -	6·67	8·62	6·64	6·99	
October -	6·70	8·41	6·58	6·92	
November -	6·70	8·16	6·28	6·76	Series discontinued.
December -	7·29	8·74	6·29	6·98	
1929.					
January -	5·17	7·48	5·67	6·37	
February -	6·23	7·11	5·80	6·22	
March -	7·15	7·40	6·31	6·56	
April - -	7·01	8·05	6·63	6·87	
May - -	9·58	9·85	7·50	8·57	
June - -	8·10	9·90	7·50	8·30	

[1] Where there are two quotations, the first is for short bills, and the second for long.

In the money market, day to day money, which had still cost about 33% in the first part of 1924, was quoted at 11% at the end of that year, at 8% at the end of 1925, and averaged a little over $4\frac{1}{2}$% in April, 1926. Later in the summer it went at times below 4%. Monthly loans continued to pay rates rather above 10% down to the end of 1925, but cheapened rapidly in 1926 to about $5\frac{1}{2}$% in July. Finally, the private discount rate, which stood at 9% when the market was re-opened at the beginning of 1925, had declined to $4\frac{1}{2}$% by July, 1926.

Changes were made in the discount rate of the Reichsbank to follow the movements of the market.

REICHSBANK DISCOUNT RATE

From end of 1923	-	10%	(at first for valorized
„ Feb. 26, 1925	-	9	loans)
„ Jan. 12, 1926	-	8	
„ Mar. 17, 1926		7	
„ June 7, 1926	-	$6\frac{1}{2}$	
„ July 6, 1926	-	6	

The rapidity with which the reductions succeeded one another in 1926 will at once be noticed.

The interest charge on current account advances followed the Bank rate, being 2% above Bank rate until March, 1926, when it became 1% above Bank rate. In addition to what is expressly called interest, however, a *Kreditprovision* or charge has been levied since the War, which is really interest under another name. In October, 1924, the Berlin banks fixed this credit charge at 6%: subsequently it was reduced to 3% in January, 1925; to 2·4% in October, 1925, and to 2% in September, 1926.[1] Thus there was a steady decline in the price of this kind of loan

---

[1] Schacht, *Stabilisierung*, p. 155.

also, but in the summer of 1926 it was still between 9% and 10%.[1]

The rates of interest prevailing in the long term capital market are more difficult to measure. Probably the *Frankfürter Zeitung* calculation of the interest cost of mortgage loans reflects the trend of rates as correctly as any other figures. This showed an interest rate of about 15% at the end of 1925, declining to $10\frac{1}{2}\%$-$10\frac{3}{4}\%$ in the summer of 1926. Rates of interest on first-class bonds were lower, and in some cases were not more than 8% at the period of greatest ease. Most of the 8% fixed interest bearing securities issued in 1926, however, were placed at a discount. (On loans placed abroad, of course, the rate of interest was lower.)

To sum up: whilst the decline in interest rates was general from stabilization to the summer or autumn of 1926, this was most marked in the case of money market rates and left an abnormal margin between these and both the long term rate of interest and the charge for current account advances.

Since the end of 1926 the situation has changed more than once, but the general result has been to bring the various rates nearer together. Encouraged by the greater borrowing facilities accorded the Reich by the 1926 amendment of the Bank Act,[2] taxes were

---

[1] The *Frankfürter Zeitung Wirtschaftkurven*, 1926, i. p. 40, gives the following table of current account charges plus interest, which agrees with the above account :

From	1.10.25	-	-	-	-	-	-	13·4%
„	13. 1.26	-	-	-	-	-	-	12·4
„	1. 3.26	-	-	-	-	-	-	11·4
„	27. 3.26	-	-	-	-	-	-	10·4
„	7. 6.26	-	-	-	-	-	-	9·9
„	6. 7.26	-	-	-	-	-	-	9·4
„	1. 9.26	-	-	-	-	-	-	9·0

These appear to be the standard Berlin charges. Provincial customers probably paid more in many cases.

[2] See note in *Economica*, No. 18, Nov. 1926.

reduced: and owing to this and the heavy expenditure on unemployment relief, the government surplus disappeared in 1927. At the same time, in response to the representations of Dr. Schacht, the balances of the Reichspost and other semi-public institutions were invested to a greater extent in mortgages, whilst other steps were taken to divert funds to meet the long term credit needs of agriculture. On the other side the demand for short term loans increased with the recovery of trade which set in during the latter part of 1926—aided by the British coal strike—and with an accompanying boom on the Stock Exchange. The Bank rate, it is true, was further reduced to 5% during the slack period after the new year in 1927: but this reduction led almost immediately to greatly increased credit demands on the Reichsbank. Not wishing to increase the charge for credit to legitimate trade and industry, Dr. Schacht endeavoured to meet the situation by inducing the other banks to make a drastic reduction of 25% in their stock exchange loans (May, 1927). Carried out in a somewhat merciless fashion, this plan had the effect of converting the boom on the security market into a temporary slump. But owing to the continued expansion of trade, the demand for credit continued to grow, and the Reichsbank was called upon to increase its short term credits by almost a milliard reichsmark in the course of the year. At the same time the Bank lost part of its foreign exchange reserve (200 million in 1927), so that its reserve ratio was reduced from 63% at the end of 1926 to 47% at the end of 1927. These developments made it necessary to raise the Bank rate, first to 6% in June and then to 7% in October. During the latter part of 1927 the Berlin money market rates were also 1% or 2% higher than at corresponding dates in the previous year.

The higher rates prevailing in Berlin had the effect of attracting considerable further supplies of short term money from other centres.   During 1927 Germany's short term debt to foreign countries is estimated to have increased by something like 2 milliard reichs-mark,[1] and, despite repayments to New York, there was a further net increase of about $1\frac{1}{2}$ milliards[2] in 1928.   These borrowings strengthened the reserves of the Reichsbank, and, aided by a certain slackening of trade activity, eased money market conditions to-wards the close of 1928; at the opening of 1929 the Bank rate was reduced by $\frac{1}{2}\%$ (to $6\frac{1}{2}\%$).   Market rates did not decline, however, to the level of 1926, and the easier conditions were only short lived.   Bor-rowing by the Reich government, the recall of short loans to take advantage of the high rates in New York, and finally the Reparations crisis, brought about a sharp reversal of tendency in the spring of 1929.

With respect to long term investment, there has been a considerable improvement in the domestic market since the end of 1925; indeed for the four years 1925-1928 inclusive the German securities placed at home have totalled two and a half times the amount placed in foreign markets.[3]   None the less, conditions in the capital market have continued to be influenced to a great extent by the supplies of foreign loans.

In this connexion, official policy with regard to foreign borrowing has been of considerable impor-tance.   On various grounds, but particularly because of the effect of future interest charges on Germany's balance of payments, repeated warnings against ex-cessive borrowing from abroad have been uttered by Dr. Schacht and the Agent General for Reparations

---

[1] 1·9 milliard according to German Statistical Office calculations quoted by the Commissioner of the Reichsbank. Report for July, 1929, p. 39. Other estimates agree fairly well.

[2] 1·6 according to above authority.

[3] Report of Agent General, Dec. 1928, p. 115.

Payments; and the Reich government, without adopting the views of these officials on all points, has been led to take certain steps restricting resort to foreign capital.   The most important of these concern borrowing by subordinate public authorities, particularly municipalities.   By agreement with the States an Advisory Committee (*Beratungsstelle*) was set up at the beginning of 1925, to which municipal loans to be placed abroad (optionally, also state loans) were to be submitted for approval.[1]   It has been the task of this body to sift the applications and pass only those required for genuinely ' productive ' purposes.   Despite a steady tendency to raise the ' pass ' standard of urgency and productivity, it was found impossible to limit municipal foreign borrowing to the required degree by this piecemeal method:[2]   accordingly the individual consideration of applications was suspended in November, 1927, to allow of a general census of municipal loan requirements being taken, preparatory to the adoption of some form of rationing of the supply deemed to be available.   As the first result of this inquiry a large collective municipal loan and a loan each for the cities of Berlin and Frankfürt a M. were approved in May, 1928.   These measures concerned, of course, only the foreign borrowing of public authorities.   Private borrowing received a certain check at the end of 1926, when the Reich Finance Minister ceased to grant further exemptions from Reich direct taxation (*Kapitalertragssteuer*) in respect of loans placed

[1] The precise constitutional position of this Committee is rather complicated.   (See Kuczynski, *American Loans to Germany*, pp. 5-7.)

[2] It has naturally been found very difficult to arrive at a satisfactory definition of a productive purpose for borrowing.   It may, for instance, mean (1) productive of revenue to borrower, (2) productive of material wealth for the community, (3) productive of an improved balance of trade ; and it may be these things either directly or indirectly.   Further, the whole system of restricting foreign borrowing alone must be largely abortive, since excessive borrowing by municipalities at home may force industry to borrow abroad on a larger scale than would otherwise be necessary.

abroad; but this privilege was restored in the following summer.   In more recent times, however, these
various measures have had less effect in restricting
borrowing than the reduced capacity of America to
lend.

It is becoming increasingly difficult to measure the
volume of foreign investment in Germany, because it
is more and more the practice for foreign investors to
purchase securities in the German markets.   According to returns from the banks, securities valued at
2,300 million reichsmarks were bought by foreigners
in this way in the course of 1928.[1]   The statistics for
loans placed abroad since the beginning of 1925 show
an increase to a total of approximately 6 milliard by
the end of 1928;[2] but a deduction should be made
from this figure for loans redeemed and securities
purchased abroad on German account (1,900 millions
in 1928, according to the same source of information).

In relation to the demand, long term capital has
continued to be painfully scarce in Germany.   The
tendency for the rate of interest to decline slowly continued during the first month or so of 1927.   But a
500 million loan of the Reich government in February
exhausted the absorptive capacity of the home market,
and thereafter conditions became more stringent.
Throughout 1928 the rate of interest has been rather
higher than in 1926, and in 1929 it has risen still
further.

III

One of the first tasks of the banks after stabilization
was to convert their accounts from depreciated marks
into gold marks, in order to make a new beginning.
In the uncertain conditions still prevailing in 1924 it

[1] Report of Agent General for Reparations Payments, July 1929, p. 104.
[2] *Ibid.*

was not easy to arrive at a satisfactory valuation of assets, and for this reason the opening gold mark balance sheets for January 1st, 1924, did not appear until late in the year and were then of doubtful accuracy.   The conversion of the (external) liabilities, on the other hand, was a more or less mechanical operation.

The following figures compare the deposits and current account balances at December 31st, 1913, with those at January 1st, 1924, firstly for the group of Berlin banks—9 in 1913 and 7 in 1924—and secondly for all creditbanks—160 with at least 1 million marks capital in 1913 and 101 with at least ¼ million marks capital in 1924.

DEPOSITS AND CURRENT ACCOUNT BALANCES

		Berlin Banks.	All Creditbanks.
31.12.13	- -	5,148·63	9,641·59
1. 1.24	- -	1,089·36	1,923·83
		million marks (gold) [1]	

Immediately after stabilization the resources entrusted to the banks were only about one-fifth of what they had been before the War.   The next table shows the recovery made in the years 1924 to 1928 by the leading Berlin banks.

DEPOSITS AND CURRENT ACCOUNT BALANCES
WITH THE BERLIN BANKS

					Million Marks.
End of 1913	-	-	-	-	5,148·6
Beginning of 1924	-	-	-	1,089·4
End of 1924	-	-		-	3,323·7
„ 1925	-	-	-	-	4,730·2
„ 1926	-	-	-	-	6,318·7
„ 1927	-	-	-	-	7,950·5
„ 1928	-	-	-	-	9,843·2 [2]

[1] *Deutsch-Oekonomist* Annual, 1924, pp. 13-14.

[2] Without figures for Mitteldeutsche Creditbank.

The post-war figures are higher than they would otherwise be as a result of the amalgamations effected by the Berlin banks since 1914: but on the other hand the Schaaffhausen'scher Bankverein has dropped out of the class of Berlin banks, and in 1928 the deposits of the Mitteldeutsche Creditbank are not included, because no balance sheet was published for this year. It seems safe to assume that if the effect of these changes were eliminated, the present volume of deposits with the Berlin banks would still surpass that of the pre-w years.[1]

Of the several factors which may be supposed to have contributed to this recovery, first place must be given to the expansion which has taken place in the volume of the currency. The total supply of means of payment has increased year by year, as shown in the following table (based on Reports of the Commissioner of the Reichsbank).

TOTAL VOLUME OF MEANS OF PAYMENT IN
GERMANY

End of 1913	-	-	6,453·2 million marks
„ 1923	-	-	probably under 2 milliard marks
„ 1924	-	-	4,000·4 million marks
„ 1925	-	-	5,208·5 „ „
„ 1926	-	-	5,829·7 „ „
„ 1927	-	-	6,304·2 „ „
„ 1928	-	-	6,614·7 „ „

This exceptionally rapid increase in the amount of money in circulation, accompanied by a return to

---

[1] It would be interesting to have the figures for all the banks to set beside those given above. Unfortunately such statistics are only available for 1913 and 1924-1925:

End of 1913	-	-	-	-	-	10·3 milliard
Beginning of 1924	-	-	-	-	2·1 „
End of 1924	-	-	-	-	-	5·8 „
End of 1925	-	-	-	-	-	8·3 „

From publication of the Statistisches Reichsamt : *Die deutschen Banken,* 1924-26, p. 16. *Guthaben von Banken* are here included with *Kreditoren* as in previous tables.

normal methods of using banking facilities, might be expected to produce an exceptional increase in deposits. Probably the increase of currency and the resumption of ordinary practice in entrusting money to the banks, are together sufficient to account for the growth of deposits during 1924. The increase of currency later must also have contributed to their subsequent expansion.

Other possible factors to be considered are:

(1) *Increased use of banking accounts*, as compared with a pre-inflation standard (i.e. over and above a return to what was normal previously). Probably there has been progress in this direction, but means have not been found to measure it. The reports of the leading banks often give figures showing an increase in the number of customers having accounts, but no allowance is made as a rule for the effect of amalgamations.

(2) *Saving*. The post-inflation growth of deposits is not uncommonly cited as an expression of the amount of saving which has been done in Germany since 1923. This seems incorrect in theory—since saving is not necessarily done by saving up cash and paying it into a bank, to be left there—and does not square well with the fact that the savings accounts with the Sparkassen still (in April, 1929) total only 40% of their pre-war amount,[1] nor with the fact that the long term deposits with the creditbanks are just those which have increased least. The process of saving may certainly be expected to lead to some increase in bank deposits: money may be accumulated with a bank prior to its investment in securities; recently the Berlin banks have opened special savings accounts. But the amount saved annually in Germany must now be appreciably less than was saved in a pre-war year; hence saving

[1] See Report of Agent General for Reparations Payments, July 1929, p. 111.

can hardly explain the recovery of deposits to their pre-war level.

(3) *Foreign Loans.* According to Lansburgh [1] 25% of the deposits of the Berliner Grossbanken in 1925 and again in 1926 were of foreign origin. In the following two years the proportion increased: according to the same authority two-thirds of the increase in deposits during 1927 was due to money from abroad, whilst the proportion of foreign deposits was 40% at the end of 1928 and had been higher during that year.[2] Assuming these statements as to the proportion of deposits in foreign ownership to be correct, however, there remains for us a question as to the nature of these foreign deposits. If they are what is called *Valutadepositen*, i.e. deposits made by surrendering claims on foreign money (usually with a right to repayment in that money) valued in marks at the current rate of exchange, they clearly represent a net addition to the recorded deposits of the German banks. If, on the other hand, the foreigners first obtain claims to marks and then lodge them with German banks, there may only result a transfer of deposits from native to foreign ownership. It is certain that a considerable part of the foreign deposits have been of the former type, almost certainly more than half, but the precise proportion is not known, except to the Reichsbank.

Foreign loans, granted to others than the banks, have also exercised an indirect influence on the amount of deposits at certain times through their effect on the volume of currency The borrowers have exchanged their *Devisen* at the Reichsbank for the notes of the latter, and some of these notes would find their way

---

[1] Annual reviews in *Die Bank*.

[2] According to *Frankfürter Zeitung Wirtschaftskurven*, 1929, i. p. 44, 1·75 out of 2·3 milliards increase in bank deposits in 1928 was to be attributed to foreign deposits.

to the banks to form deposits. But this effect has been of a temporary character, for the most part: usually the process has been reversed after a while by an outflow of *Devisen* from the Reichsbank. In any case, full account has been taken of this effect in considering the influence of currency changes.

(4) *The expansion of bank credit*. According to a theory widely accepted amongst economists, when payments are largely effected by means of book transfers between bank accounts, deposits may originate in loans granted by banks, just as bank notes come into circulation through such loans. This is not the place in which to examine this theory and define its limitations; but it may be said that the validity of the conclusion that banks can create deposits varies from one country to another, and that no satisfactory test has yet been devised to determine the extent (if any) to which deposits have originated in this way in any particular case.

In Germany little was heard of this theory before the War, but it is now very generally adopted, and is often used to explain the increase in deposits in recent years. While allowance may be made for a mere change in ideas, it must be recognized that the attention given since the War to developing the practice of making payments by book transfers (*Bargeldlosezahlungsverkehr*) should, so far as successful, have extended the scope for this kind of credit creation. It may be mentioned that whilst some writers (Dalberg, Hahn) consider this factor to have operated throughout the period, others (e.g. Lansburgh) more or less confine its application to the time (1926-27) when bourse speculation was particularly active. It is argued by the latter that bourse credits more easily lead to expansion of deposits than others, because the money borrowed is transferred in large sums, not disbursed in small cash payments. Whatever may be thought

of the theory of this view, it is noteworthy that there
was a temporary check to the expansion of deposits
after the bourse credits were restricted in 1927.[1]   But
the resumed growth of deposits later weakens the force
of this argument.

Whilst the increase in deposits has been a common
feature of the five years completed since stabilization,
in other respects the business of the banks has varied
considerably between one year and another. In 1924,
banking consisted chiefly in granting current account
credits, including here the discounting of bills for
customers—a branch of business which then showed
a considerable revival, aided perhaps by the restriction
of Reichsbank discounts.   The resources of the banks
were still small, but rates of interest, the interest
margin in favour of the banks and bank charges were
all very high.   1925 was in several respects a less
favourable year, notwithstanding the increase in the
funds handled by the banks, for the crisis in trade
must have brought many losses, whilst interest rates
and charges were lower. The year 1926 was
characterized by a revival of the typical transactions
of German banking in connexion with the Stock
Exchange—the emission of securities, loans to speculators and stock-broking (commission) business. As
circumstances helping to induce this revival we may
notice especially the process of reorganization
(rationalization) through which industry was passing,
the resumption of official time dealings on the bourse
at the end of the previous year, and the partial recovery
of the home investment market. General trade conditions also improved during the year, which was
altogether a prosperous one for the banks, despite

---

[1]   Kreditoren.

	Berlin Banks.	All Creditbanks.
30.4.27 –	– 6,551·8	8,398·5
30.6.27 –	– 6,408·8	8,270·3

further concessions in terms to their customers.[1]   The
year ended in a remarkable stock exchange boom
which continued into 1927, until curtailed by the May
restriction of credits.   Compensation was found, however, for the subsequent decline of business in this
direction in the continued expansion of trade, reflected
in large increases in advances against goods (*Warenvorschüsse*) and ordinary current account advances
(*Debitoren*).   As from the beginning of 1927, the
banks relaxed yet further the stringency of their terms
to customers,[2] but their revenue benefited both from
the increase in their funds and from the higher interest
rates.   Finally, in 1928, conditions became less favourable to the banks owing to the reduction in the volume
of internal trade and the accompanying bourse depression.   In making up their balance sheets for this
year it is probable that they had to write off many
losses.   The deposits held by the banks grew very
remarkably—more rapidly even than before—and the
interest margin was favourable so far as German funds
were concerned, but the proportion of foreign deposits
on which higher interest rates had to be paid was
higher than before.

In the last year or two (1927-1929) there have
been some interesting developments in the part played
by the banks in the mediation of foreign investment

---

[1] It is particularly to be noticed that in many cases the year's turnover
figures equalled those for 1913—though here again allowance must be made
for the intervening amalgamations.

[2] As a result of conferences between the *Centralverband des deutschen
Bank- u. Bankiergewerbes* and the *Reichsverband der deutschen Industrie* it was
agreed that the interest should not be charged on credits granted but not
yet used.   This is a reversion to the previous German practice, departure
from which after the War was felt to be burdensome to industry.   *Kreditprovision*—or a credit charge—of 2% is still charged, however, for the whole
term of the credit.   At the same time it was agreed that the *Ueberziehungs
Provision* or charge for unauthorized overdrafts should not be levied for
more than one week.   After this, the relation must be regularized either by
repayment or by an ordinary credit.   *Magazin der Wirtschaft*, 3rd year,
No. 1, Jan. 6, 1927, p. 5.

in Germany. It has always been difficult for the smaller industrial firms, and even those of moderate size, to raise loans abroad; since 1928, moreover, the large firms have found the New York market slow to take up their debentures. Under pressure of the demand for capital there has been some tendency for the banks to take up short loans abroad and re-lend the sums for development at home, but there were obvious dangers attaching to such a course of borrowing short and lending long. In several instances the banks have, therefore, resorted to the plan of intervening to raise long term loans abroad. In the first cases they did this directly in their own names. In the autumn of 1927 the Deutsche Bank with the assistance of Dillon, Read & Co. raised a loan of 25 million dollars for five years in New York, and proceeded to re-lend the proceeds for a similar term in Germany.[1] Shortly afterwards the Commerz u. Privatbank negotiated a loan of 20 million dollars for ten years through the Chase National Bank for the same purpose.[2] Although emergency measures, and in themselves preferable to the practice of receiving short term foreign credits, these transactions were regarded with some misgiving; the confusion of the functions of a bank and an investment company seemed undesirable. Latterly, therefore, the banks have sought a solution of the problem more in accordance with their traditions by establishing, again in conjunction with foreign financiers, special investment companies to raise money abroad. Thus in 1928 the Commerz u. Privatbank, working with the Chase National Bank as before, promoted the *General Mortgage and Credit Corporation*,[3] whilst a large group of

[1] *Magazin der Wirtschaft*, iii. 37, Sept. 15, 1927, pp. 1409-11.

[2] *Magazin der Wirtschaft*, iii. 41, Oct. 13, 1927, p. 1573.

[3] *Magazin der Wirtschaft*, iv. 39, Sept. 27, 1928, p. 1504.

banks, exclusive of the Berliner Grossbanken, formed the *Centralbank deutschen Industrie A.G.*[1]

In the second half of 1929 the Deutsche Bank and Harris, Forbes & Co., New York, have formed a larger investment trust, the *United States and Overseas Corporation.* A number of American, Swiss, and Scandinavian banks have participated, namely the Banca-America-Blair Corporation and the Central Hanover Bank Trust Co. of New York, the First National Corporation (Boston), the Guardian Detroit Co., the Basler Handelsbank, the Schweizerische Kreditanstalt (Zürich), and the Skandinaviska Kredit A.B. (Stockholm). This is to be a general international investment trust with very wide functions; although it will in no way confine its interests to Germany, it is supposed that it will invest there largely.[2]

CASH, ETC. AS PERCENTAGE OF TOTAL ASSETS

	1913.	Jan. 1st 1924.	Dec. 31st 1924.	1925.	1926.	1927.	1928
Deutsche Bank - - -	5·7	6·6	6·2	5·4	3·2	3·8	3·3
Dresdner Bank - - - -	4·5	7·2	4·1	3·7	2·5	2·4	2·7
Discontogesellschaft - - -	4·0	3·5	2·3	3·4	4·4	4·5	4·5
Darmstädter und Nationalbank -	4·5 {4·9 / 3·4	6·8	6·3	5·3	5·1	3·7	4·0
Berliner Handelsgesellschaft -	3·6	1·9	4·0	3·1	2·1	2·0	2·5
Commerz- u. Privatbank - -	3·4	6·5	4·2	2·9	2·5	3·8	2·6
Mitteldeutsche Creditbank - -	3·5	10·0	12·0	13·8	9·7	7·1	—
Seven Berlin Banks - - -	4·6[3]	6·1	5·0	4·5	3·6	3·6	3·8

---

[1] The last named institution has never functioned, owing to the unfavourable condition of the American market, and now the promoters have decided to go no further with the project. The *Centralbank* remains nominally in existence, but the capital has been repurchased by the principal promoters, who apparently hope to sell the title later, and thus recover their promotion expenses. See *Magazin der Wirtschaft,* vi. 3, Jan. 17, 1930, p. 152.

[2] See *Magazin der Wirtschaft,* v. 38, Sept. 19, 1929, pp. 1456-7.

[3] Eight banks.   [4] Six banks.

BILLS AS PERCENTAGE OF TOTAL ASSETS

	1913.	Jan. 1st 1924.	Dec. 31st 1924.	1925.	1926.	1927.	1928
Deutsche Bank - - -	28·5	2·1	21·0	22·3	21·9	18·6	23·0
Dresdner Bank - - - -	24·4	2·2	19·3	21·8	24·1	21·8	21·2
Discontogesellschaft - - -	20·7	2·5	18·1	20·4	19·9	22·8	25·6
Darmstädter und Nationalbank -	19·5 {18·9 / 20·6}	1·9	25·0	24·4	21·9	24·1	24·1
Berliner Handelsgesellschaft -	18·8	4·3	21·9	30·4	18·5	17·0	13·9
Commerz- u. Privatbank - -	14·9	2·7	29·8	27·1	21·6	18·6	19·1
Mitteldeutsche Creditbank - ·	15·8	0·9	21·3	23·3	14·4	13·9	—
Seven Berlin Banks - - -	22·8[1]	2·3	22·0	23·2	21·7	20·8	22·4

BALANCES WITH CORRESPONDENTS AS PERCENTAGE
OF TOTAL ASSETS

	1913.	Jan. 1st 1924.	Dec. 31st 1924.	1925.	1926.	1927.	1928.
Deutsche Bank - - -	2·8	28·5	20·8	13·2	9·4	10·2	8·2
Dresdner Bank - - - -	4·0	28·0	17·2	13·2	12·7	12·0	13·2
Discontogesellschaft - - -	5·7	24·8	14·6	11·6	9·5	11·0	8·2
Darmstädter und Nationalbank -	4·8 {5·3 / 3·5}	25·9	15·1	11·3	13·3	12·3	11·7
Berliner Handelsgesellschaft -	2·0	33·0	25·7	14·4	13·2	11·5	13·0
Commerz- u. Privatbank - -	8·0	28·2	8·1	7·9	9·2	12·0	10·1
Mitteldeutsche Creditbank - -	2·6	22·0	11·6	8·6	15·3	20·7	—
Seven Berlin Banks - - -	4·1 [1]	27·3	16·5	11·9	11·2	11·6	10·4 [2]

BOURSE LOANS AS PERCENTAGE OF TOTAL ASSETS

	1913.	Jan. 1st 1924.	Dec. 31st 1924.	1925.	1926.	1927.	1928.
Deutsche Bank - - -	10·4	1·3	0·9	1·0	9·5	5·7	5·4
Dresdner Bank - - - -	7·7	0·2	0·5	3·0	9·3	4·6	4·8
Discontogesellschaft - - -	8·5	—	0·1	0·7	7·9	4·9	6·0
Darmstädter und Nationalbank -	11·4 {11·3 / 11·6}	1·6	1·3	1·9	10·5	6·2	6·0
Berliner Handelsgesellschaft -	12·0	—	—	1·5	16·9	11·2	8·8
Commerz- u. Privatbank - -	17·0	2·0	3·2	6·1	14·3	9·2	8·0
Mitteldeutsche Creditbank - -	9·6	0·7	3·1	2·6	13·0	7·5	—
Seven Berlin Banks - - -	10·3[1]	1·0	1·0	2·2	10·4	6·2	6·0 [2]

[1] Eight banks.   [2] Six banks.

ADVANCES AGAINST COMMODITIES AS PERCENTAGE OF TOTAL ASSETS

	1913.	Jan. 1st 1924.	Dec. 31st 1924.	1925.	1926.	1927.	1928.
Deutsche Bank - - -	9·6	4·2	6·6	7·1	6·7	7·7	10·8
Dresdner Bank - - - -	7·6	8·0	9·7	-2·0	8·2	11·2	16·2
Discontogesellschaft - - -	10·7	2·3	6·1	8·5	5·3	9·3	13·4
Darmstädter und Nationalbank -	1·2 { 1·8	5·7	5·3	6·6	5·6	7·4	11·5
Berliner Handelsgesellschaft -	—[1]	—	—	11·5	8·4	16·1	20·7
Commerz- u. Privatbank -	4·2	1·9	6·0	6·8	6·4	9·5	12·7
Mitteldeutsche Creditbank - -	1·3	0·08	0·3	2·5	1·3	1·6	—
Seven Berlin Banks - - -	7·1	4·3[2]	6·4[2]	8·3	6·5	9·0	13·1

SECURITIES AS PERCENTAGE OF TOTAL ASSETS
(a) Own Securities. (b) Syndicate Participations. (c) Bank participations.

		1913.	Jan. 1st 1924.	Dec. 31st 1924.	1925.	1926.	1927.	1928.
Deutsche Bank - - -	a.	7·2	2·7	1·4	1·0	1·6	1·4	1·2
	b.	2·4	1·8	0·9	1·0	0·8	1·5	1·3
	c.	3·7	4·5	2·1	1·5	1·2	1·1	0·8
Dresdner Bank - - -	a.	2·8	2·2	1·4	1·2	1·6	1·4	1·2
	b.	3·6	5·1	1·6	1·0	0·7	0·7	0·5
	c.	2·4	7·9	2·8	2·0	1·7	1·5	1·3
Discontogesellschaft - -	a.	2·4	1·6	0·8	0·4	0·6	0·7	0·7
	b.	4·9	6·8	3·3	2·1	1·6	1·7	1·9
	c.	9·3	19·9	9·0	7·2	6·2	5·0	4·0
Darmstädter u. Nationalbank -	a.	6·0 { 5·6 / 4·5 / 0·8	7·9	2·3	1·9	1·2	1·3	1·1
	b.	6·0 {	5·2	1·8	1·6	1·0	1·35	1·1
	c.	0·9 { 6·9 / 9·2 / 1·2	4·3	2·6	2·1	1·4	1·2	1·0
Berliner Handelsgesellschaft -	a.	7·8	6·8	1·7	1·3	2·9	5·2	3·9
	b.	9·5	15·6	5·8	4·0	1·6	—	1·2
	c.	1·8	—	—	—	—	—	—
Commerz- u. Privatbank -	a.	5·5	5·3	2·4	1·5	1·5	1·4	1·4
	b.	3·7	3·6	1·7	0·9	0·7	1·0	1·0
	c.	2·4	1·7	0·9	0·6	0·4	0·5	0·6
Mitteldeutsche Creditbank -	a.	5·2	2·6	1·4	0·6	1·6	0·8	—
	b.	4·4	10·8	—	—	—	—	—
	c.	1·0	0·7	—	—	—	—	—
Seven Berlin Banks -	a.	5·2[1]	3·8	1·6	1·2	1·4	1·4	1·3[2]
	b.	4·3[1]	5·7	1·9	1·4	1·0	1·2	1·1[2]
	c.	3·5[1]	7·1	3·2	2·4	1·9	1·6	1·5[2]

[1] Eight banks.   [2] Six banks.

ADVANCES AS PERCENTAGE OF TOTAL ASSETS

	1913.	Jan. 1st 1924.	Dec. 31st 1924.	1925.	1926.	1927.	1928.
Deutsche Bank - - -	28·8	33·2	35·7	44·3	43·1	48·0	40·6
Dresdner Bank - - - -	40·6	28·5	39·3	39·7	37·1	42·7	37·0
Discontogesellschaft - - -	31·6	24·8	40·8	41·7	41·3	37·4	33·1
Darmstädter und Nationalbank -	44·2 $\begin{cases}44·9 \\ 42·2\end{cases}$	32·2	37·2	42·5	38·4	41·1	38·5
Berliner Handelsgesellschaft -	42·2	25·8	35·7	30·7	32·4	35·1	34·5
Commerz- u. Privatbank - -	38·8	33·9	37·9	42·3	40·5	41·9	41·7
Mitteldeutsche Creditbank - -	53·1	25·2	38·3	40·2	38·1	42·1	
Seven Berlin Banks - - -	36·8[1]	30·5	37·8	41·7	39·6	42·5	39·2[2]

CAPITAL AND RESERVES AS PERCENTAGE OF TOTAL LIABILITIES

	1913.	Jan. 1st 1924.	Dec. 31st 1924.	1925.	1926.	1927.	1928.
Deutsche Bank - - -	13·9	36·2	18·3	13·3	11·9	9·7	7·8
Dresdner Bank - - - -	17·0	34·3	12·6	8·7	8·2	6·9	5·6
Discontogesellschaft - - -	22·7	44·7	19·5	14·7	16·3	13·2	11·0
Darmstädter und Nationalbank -	21·3 $\begin{cases}19·7 \\ 24·9\end{cases}$	33·4	12·7	9·9	6·6	6·2	5·0
Berliner Handelsgesellschaft -	26·3	45·1	16·8	11·0	7·0	7·0	9·3
Commerz- u. Privatbank - -	19·5	30·3	14·0	9·2	7·1	7·4	5·9
Mitteldeutsche Creditbank - -	26·8	59·7	27·3	19·4	15·4	11·4	—
Seven Berlin Banks - - -	19·0[1]	37·0	16·0	11·5	10·0	8·6	7·0[2]

DEPOSITS AND CURRENT ACCOUNT BALANCES AS PERCENTAGE OF TOTAL LIABILITIES

	1913.	Jan. 1st 1924.	Dec. 31st 1924.	1925.	1926.	1927.	1928.
Deutsche Bank - - -	70·4	63·3	79·3	80·5	81·5	80·7	84·0
Dresdner Bank - - - -	62·3	64·9	86·2	86·5	86·3	87·0	90·0
Discontogesellschaft - - -	54·4	54·5	77·8	79·0	77·1	80·8	84·3
Darmstädter und Nationalbank -	60·6 $\begin{cases}62·1 \\ 56·5\end{cases}$	65·2	85·3	85·1	87·8	88·4	90·1
Berliner Handelsgesellschaft -	53·9	53·0	81·6	86·1	90·5	88·4	86·8
Commerz- u. Privatbank - -	62·2	69·4	84·2	86·4	87·5	87·4	83·8
Mitteldeutsche Creditbank - -	50·6	40·1	69·7	71·9	80·9	83·8	
Seven Berlin Banks - - -	62·1[1]	60·2	81·9	83·0	84·3	85·9	86·7[2]

[1] Eight banks.   [2] Six banks.

ACCEPTANCES AS PERCENTAGE OF TOTAL LIABILITIES

	1913.	Jan. 1st 1924.	Dec. 31st 1924.	1925.	1926.	1927.	1928.
Deutsche Bank - - -	13·4	0·1	0·5	4·8	5·0	3·9	3·6
Dresdner Bank - - - -	18·7	0·04	0·05	4·1	4·6	5·2	3·7
Discontogesellschaft - - -	20·2	0·1	0·8	4·8	4·9	4·8	3·6
Darmstädter und Nationalbank -	16·9 {17·0, 16·3}	0·08	0·7	3·6	3·8	4·1	3·5
Berliner Handelsgesellschaft -	17·6	—	—	1·7	1·3	3·4	3·3
Commerz- u. Privatbank - -	16·4	0·2	0·7	3·6	4·6	4·4	4·3
Mitteldeutsche Creditbank - -	20·9	0·03	1·3	7·5	2·7	4·1	—
Seven Berlin Banks - - -	16·9[1]	0·1	0·5	4·2	4·4	4·4	3·7 [2]

Comparing the composition of assets and liabilities in the balance sheets for the last four years with the percentages for 1913, the following points are to be noticed.

(1) There is a striking decline in the relative size of Own Securities and Syndicate Participations. At first sight this would appear to indicate a revolution in the business of the banks, bringing them more into the category of pure deposit banks. As has been said, however, the banks have not abstained from participation in the issue business when the state of the market allowed, as in 1926 and the first part of 1927. The explanation of the low percentage for security holdings must be found therefore in the fact that securities taken over by the banks have been rapidly passed on to the public. But this of itself means in all probability that the banks have been more cautious in taking over securities.

(2) The outstanding Acceptances are also of much smaller relative importance than in 1913. It is possible that a more restrictive policy in granting acceptance credit in domestic trade (instead of the dearer current account credit) explains part of this decline, but a larger part is to be ascribed to a falling off in

[1] Eight banks.   [2] Six banks.

foreign trade acceptances. The loss of the London branches is a factor of importance in the latter respect, others being an increase in the proportion of foreign trade conducted on a cash basis and an increase in the proportion of German trade financed by foreigners. (In the balance sheets acceptance liabilities have been to a great extent replaced by 'credits opened with other banks on behalf of customers,' a sub-heading of *Kreditoren.*)

(3) The *Nostroguthaben* or Balances with Correspondents, now mainly balances with foreign banks, are very much larger than before the War. (According to the report of Deutsche Bank for 1928, 81·5% of *Nostroguthaben* were in foreign money.) This again is partly due to the loss of the London offices and changes in methods of financing foreign trade; but to a greater extent the foreign balances represent reserves held against foreign deposit liabilities.

(4) The greater relative importance of Deposits and Current Account Balances amongst the liabilities reflects the comparative smallness of the other two constituents, Acceptances and Own Resources (capital and reserves). Between stabilization and the end of 1928, four banks increased their capital: the Discontogesellschaft from 100 million to 135 (Sept. 1926), the Dresdner Bank from 78 million to 100 million (in the same month), the Commerz- u. Privatbank from 42 million to 60 million (Feb. 1927), and the Berliner Handelsgesellschaft from 22 million to 28 million (November, 1928). There have also been certain increases in the open reserves. The absolute amount of change in Own Resources during the five years is shown in the table on page 279.

The lower percentage of Own Resources on the liabilities side must be considered, of course, in relation to the lower percentage of Securities and Participations on the assets side.

(5) Lastly it is to be noted that Cash Reserves (including Reichsbank balances) are proportionately lower even than they were before the War. This comparative deterioration first appeared in 1926 and gave some justification for demands by Dr. Schacht for a more conservative credit policy. On the other hand, it is to be remembered that a considerable proportion of the deposits is now owed to foreigners, and foreign bank balances (*Nostroguthaben*) are a better reserve against liabilities of this kind than cash in hand in Germany.

	1. 1. 24.		31. 12. 28.		Change : Capital and Reserves Together.
	Share Capital.	Reserves.	Share Capital.	Reserves.	
Deutsche Bank - - -	150	50	150	77·5	+27·5
Discontogesellschaft - -	100	34	135	52·0	+53·0
Dresdner Bank - - -	78	22	100	32·0	+32·0
Darmstädter Bank - -	60	40	60	55·0	+15
Commerz- u. Privatbank [1] -	42	21	60	35·6	+32·6
Berliner Handelsgesellschaft	22	5	28	15·0	+16

Million Reichsmark

Owing to the 'trimming' of receipts in the profit and loss accounts, net profits and dividends show a stability which masks the vicissitudes above described. From the table on page 280 it will be seen that the dividends, after increasing in most cases in 1926, have remained constant for the last three years. On the whole the disclosed profits—and with this the allocations to dividends—have probably been considerably lower in recent years than the actual profits earned,

[1] The capital of the Commerz- und Privatbank was increased by 15 millions to 75 millions in February, 1929, in connexion with the absorption of the Mitteldeutsche Creditbank. At the same time its reserves were raised to 58·1 million.

the difference having been used to form secret reserves. This would appear to be true for all the leading Berlin banks in 1927, and in 1926 for all except the Deutsche Bank, which in this year incurred losses of about 20 million marks in connexion with the *U.F.A.* Film Company. In 1928 undisclosed losses probably offset undisclosed profits. The dividend rates themselves can be considered very satisfactory from the point of

DIVIDENDS

	1913.	1924.	1925.	1926.	1927.	1928.
Deutsche Bank - -	12½	10	10	10	10	10
Discontogesellschaft -	10	10	10	10	10	10
Dresdner Bank - -	8½	8	8	10	10	10
Darmstädter Bank - -	6½ ⎫	10	10	12	12	12
Nationalbank - -	6 ⎭					
Berliner Handelsgesellschaft	8½	10	10	12	12	12
Commerz- u. {Discontobank / Privatbank -	6	8	8	11	11	11
Mitteldeutsche Creditbank	6½	8	8	9	9	—

view of the shareholders, if the losses involved in converting the capitals after stabilization are accepted as final. On the other hand, judged by pre-war standards, the net profits have recently been very small in relation to the total funds administered and total turnover figures.

The net profits have been relatively small, not because of deficiencies in gross profits—on the contrary these compare favourably with those for 1913, despite under-statements in the accounts—but because so large a proportion of the gross profits has been absorbed in expenses of administration and taxes. The table on page 281 shows this proportion for each of the Berliner Grossbanken for 1913 and the last five years.

The striking increase in the expense ratios in comparison with previous years reveals one of the most serious difficulties with which the banks are at present faced. During the last three years there has been some improvement, owing to the curtailment of expenses, but hardly enough to modify the gravity of the problem.

In the main the difficulty appears to result from two causes: firstly, excessive expansion in staff and offices during the inflation period, and secondly, the comparatively small average value of the transactions. In the first case the remedy is clearly to reverse the steps taken; in the second case the staff can hardly be reduced faster than the efficiency of each member is

EXPENSES AND TAXES AS % OF GROSS PROFITS

	1913.	1924.	1925.	1926.	1927.	1928.
Deutsche Bank - - -	35·4	81·6	81·9	78	73·8	73·7
Discontogesellschaft - -	36·4	83·5	81·7	77	78·1	78·7
Dresdner Bank - - -	38·2	84·7	84·6	83·2	83	83·0
Darmstädter Bank - -	49·7	88	86·8	73·6	79·8	79·8
Commerz- u. Privatbank -	46·9	91·5	89·9	85	83·5	82·4
Mitteldeutsche Creditbank	36·6	86·2	81·8	78·4	78·2	—
Berliner Handelsgesellschaft	23·3	75	71·1	61·3	58·3	35·5[1]

raised by improved organization and mechanical appliances, unless, of course, business is to be abandoned. As will be shown in the next section, numbers both of offices and staffs have been considerably reduced since 1924; but staff expenses have not fallen in proportion, because the employees dispensed with have usually been the juniors, and in other cases special retiring allowances have been granted. (In 1927 there were also salary increases.) The burden of taxation imposed upon the banks is also a source of regular complaint, the proportion of gross profit absorbed in meeting taxes having increased from about 5½% before the War to nearly 11% in 1927.[2]

[1] Gross profits swollen in 1928 by 8 million Rm., compensation for property confiscated in U.S.A.

[2] See article by Kroszewski, in *Bank-Archiv*, 1928, No. 22, pp. 426-7 (27th year).

Early in 1928 an important advance was made in the publicity of German banking operations. After a conference between the Reich Ministry for Economics, the Reichsbank and the other banks, it was agreed that interim balance sheets should be published at the end of every month, excepting December and January, instead of at the end of alternate months. (Publication of two-monthly interim balance sheets had been resumed in February, 1925.) At the same time a number of changes were introduced in the form of the balance sheets, almost all in the direction of making them more detailed and informative.

The following is the scheme of the new balance sheets:

ASSETS

1. *Unpaid Capital* -   -   -   -   -
2. *Cash, Foreign Currency and Coupons due for payment* -   -   -   -   -
   Balances at Issuing and Clearing banks -
3. in total   -   -   -   -   -   -
4. of this total, with German banks of issue -
   Cheques, Bills and Treasury Bills (unverzinsliche Schatzanweisungen) -   -   -
5. (*a*) Cheques and Bills (excluding following categories)   -   -   -   -   -
6. (*b*) Treasury Bills of Reich and States in total   -   -   -   -   -   -
7. of these, rediscountable with Reichsbank
8. (*c*) Own acceptances   -   -   -   -
9. (*d*) Own drawings   -   -   -   -
10. (*e*) Promissory notes drawn by customers to bank's order   -   -   -   -   -
11. in total (*a*), (*b*), (*c*), (*d*), (*e*)   -   -   -
    Balances with Other Banks and Bankers, due within three months -   -   -
12. in total   -   -   -   -   -   -
13. due within seven days -   -   -   -
    Reports and Lombards against quoted stock exchange securities -   -   -   -
14. in total   -   -   -   -   -   -
15. of this total, Reports proper   -   -   -

Advances on Goods in transit or in warehouse
   (*a*) Acceptance credits -   -   -   -
16. (1) secured by shipping or warehouse warrants
17. (2) covered by other securities -   -   -
18. (3) without real security -   -   -   -
19. 16-18 together   -   -   -   -   -
20. (*b*) other short term credits on pledge of
     particular, defined marketable goods   -
21. Total advances on goods (19 and 20 together)
Own Securities   -   -   -   -   -
22. (*a*) Loans and interest-bearing bonds of
     Reich and States -   -   -   -   -
23. (*b*) other securities pledgeable at Reichs-
     bank and other central banks -   -   -
24. (*c*) other quoted securities -   -   -   -
25. (*d*) other securities -   -   -   -   -
26. own securities in total (22-25) -   -   -
27. *Syndicate Participations*   -   -   -   -
28. *Permanent Participations in Banks and*
     Bankers -   -   -   -   -   -
     Advances   -   -   -   -   -   -
29. in total   -   -   -   -   -
30. of this, advances to banks, bankers, savings
     banks and other credit institutions -   -
31. of total (*a*) covered by quoted securities   -
32. (*b*) covered by other securities -   -   -
33. *Long term loans on mortgages or to munici-*
     palities   -   -   -   -   -
34. *Bank premises*   -   -   -   -
35. *Other real property* -   -   -   -   -
36. *Other assets*   -   -   -   -   -
37. Sum of all assets   -   -   -   -
38. *Claims as guarantor (Aval- Bürgschafts-*
     debitoren) -   -   -   -   -   -

LIABILITIES

39. *Share Capital*   -   -   -   -   -
40. *Reserves*   -   -   -   -   -   -
     Due to Creditors (Deposits, Current Account
     balances) -   -   -   -   -   -
41 (*a*) in respect of credits obtained for custo-
     mers with other banks -   -   -   -

42. (b) due to German banks, bankers, savings
      banks, other credit institutions   -   -
43. (c) due to other creditors   -   -   -
44. (b) and (c) together   -   -   -   -
45. total sum due (a), (b), (c)   -   -   -
      of (b) and (c) or (44)   -   -   -   -
46. (1) due within seven days   -   -   -
47. (2) due after seven days within three months
48. (3) due after three months   -   -   -
49. *Acceptances* -   -   -   -   -   -
      Long-term Borrowings -   -   -   -
50. (a) mortgage bonds outstanding   -   -
51. (b) other long term borrowings   -   -
52. Total long term borrowings   -   -   -
53. *Other Liabilities* -   -   -   -   -
54. Sum of liabilities -   -   -   -   -
55. *Guarantees given* (not included in total of
      balance sheet) -   -   -   -   -
      Contingent Liabilities on Endorsements   -
56. (a) on discounted bank acceptances -   -
57. (b) on promissory notes of customers to
      bank's order   -   -   -   -   -
58. (c) on other rediscounted bills   -   -
59. in total   -   -   -   -   -   -
60. on this total, due within fifteen days   -
      Liabilities on own drawings   -   -   -
61. in total   -   -   -   -   -   -
62. of this total, on account of others   -   -

The new features in this scheme may be summarized as follows:

ASSETS.

Cash is separated from balances at clearing banks, and of
the latter those with German note-issuing banks are shown
separately.

Other Bank Balances (*Nostroguthaben*) are restricted to
those due within three months, and those due within seven
days are shown separately.

Treasury bills are again separated from other bills.

Reports or Contangoes are separated from other loans against
the pledge of securities (the distinction between the latter and
' advances covered by securities ' remains obscure).

Advances against goods are divided into *Rembours* or acceptance credits and others : the former are subdivided in more detail as to cover.

Under Advances (*Debitoren*) those to credit institutions are shown separately; covered advances are subdivided according as the cover consists in quoted securities or not. A heading is included for long term mortgage loans. This enables the same ' scheme ' to be used by mixed institutions, such as the *Bayerische Hypotheken und Wechselbank*, which combine mortgage with short term credit business. The Commerz- u. Privatbank, moreover, appears to include here some of the loans granted out of the special American funds referred to above.

LIABILITIES

Under *Kreditoren* (deposits and current account balances) the division into *provisionspflichtige* and *provisionsfreie*—subject to or free from charges—has been abandoned as no longer significant. More regrettably, perhaps, the subdivision *Nostro-verpflichtungen* (debts to other banks) has also been abandoned. On the other hand the division according to terms of withdrawal (due within seven days, etc.) has been extended to cover the balances of other banks. The latter now include the balances of savings banks. A new heading appears for long term obligations.

Contingent liabilities on endorsements are now to be shown in much greater detail. This perhaps is the chief improvement which has been made.

The new balance sheets still leave many interesting matters in darkness: none the less they represent an appreciable advance on the old. In addition to the new information to be published through them, the banks are to make periodical returns to the Reichsbank showing the extent to which their debtors and creditors are foreign. This information will be confidential so far as the position of each individual bank is concerned, but apparently the Reichsbank is to publish the figures for the banks collectively.

The new balance sheets appeared for the first time at the end of March, 1928. As before, their publication is voluntary in principle, but is a condition for the admission of new shares to quotation on the bourses. The Berliner Handelsgesellschaft has now agreed to come into line with the other large banks, and its first interim balance sheet has appeared, relating to August 31st, 1929.

IV

As in the preceding years, there have been a number of instances since stabilization of the absorption by a Berlin bank of a provincial member of its group. It is again the Deutsche Bank which has been responsible for most of these amalgamations, this bank absorbing the *Württembergische Vereinsbank* in 1924, the *Essener Creditanstalt* and the *Siegener Bank* in 1925, the *Lübecker Privatbank* in 1927, and the *Hildesheimer Bank* in 1928. The report for 1928 also announced the absorption of the *Osnabrücker Bank* in the near future. In 1926 the Discontogesellschaft effected a fusion with the *Bank für Thüringen, vormals B. M. Strupp*.

In this direction there has been an extension, in some respects only nominal, of the organization of the Berlin banks. The characteristic tendency of recent years, however, has been to scale down organization with a view to reducing expenditure. Many small offices have been altogether closed, and at the offices retained the staff has generally been curtailed. The total number of offices of all kinds maintained by six Berliner Grossbanken (excluding the Berliner Handelsgesell-schaft) declined from 1,033 at the beginning of 1924 to 777 at the beginning of 1927:[1] the staff of the seven Berlin banks would seem to have fallen from a maximum of 140,000 to a figure under 50,000 at the beginning of 1928. These striking reductions have

[1] Obst, *Das Buch des Kaufmanns*, p. 223.

been made, it must be remembered, in spite of the counteracting effect of the amalgamations mentioned above. The policy of retrenchment was applied most drastically in 1924 and 1925; since then there has been an appreciable slackening in the rate at which reductions have been made.[1]

According to the number of branches and sub-offices maintained, the several Berlin banks assumed the following order at the beginning of 1927:[2]

1st.	Commerz- und Privatbank -	with	315
2nd.	Deutsche Bank - - -	„	288
3rd.	Darmstädter u. Nationalbank	„	207
4th.	Dresdner Bank - - -	„	191
5th.	Discontogesellschaft - -	„	163
6th.	Mitteldeutsche Creditbank -	„	48

Taking into account only branches (*Filialen, Zweigniederlassungen*),[3] and of these only the ones within Germany, the position at the beginning and the end of 1928 was as follows:[4]

1928.	Beginning.	End.
Commerz- u. Privatbank -	198	241
Deutsche Bank - - -	170	170
Darmstädter u. Nationalbank	116	108
Discontogesellschaft - -	95	91
(including offices of Schaaff-hausen Bankverein and Norddeutsche Bank)		
Dresdner Bank - - -	84	79
Mitteldeutsche Creditbank -	22	22

[1] The 1926 Reports generally spoke of the completion of the programme of retrenchment. In most cases further reductions have been made, in consequence probably of the slump in bourse transactions : on the other hand the Commerz- und Privatbank has expanded its organization.

[2] Kaul in *Die Bank*, April 1927, p. 215.

[3] Including, however, co-ordinate head offices, e.g. office of Dresdner Bank at Dresden.

[4] Figures for the beginning based on data in Strauss, *Die Konzentrationsbewegung im deutschen Bankgewerbe*, pp. 149 *et seq* ; for the end on information from the banks.

Abroad the Deutsche Bank maintains 7 branches (Dantzig 3, Kattowitz, Amsterdam, Sofia and Constantinople), the Dresdner Bank 4 (Dantzig, Kattowitz, Konigshütte, and Tarnowitz; the Bukarest branch has been given up), the Discontogesellschaft 2 (Dantzig and Kattowitz), the Darmstädter Bank 1 (Kattowitz), and the Commerz- und Privatbank 1 (Dantzig). The Berliner Handelsgesellschaft has continued to be a completely centralized institution.[1]

The relative importance of the several banks from the point of view of resources administered is shown by the following table, based on the annual balance sheets. For purposes of comparison, the leading independent provincial banks have been included, and also the *Reichskreditgesellschaft* (see next section).

| | | 1927. | |
	Capital.	Reserves.	Deposits.
Deutsche Bank - - -	150	75	1,977·3
Dresdner Bank - - -	100	30·4	1,640·1
Darmstädter Bank - -	60	50	1,563·9
Discontogesellschaft - -	135	65·5	1,421·4
(including Schaaffhausen'scher Bankverein and Norddeutsche Bank)			
Commerz- u. Privatbank -	60	34·1	1,101·7
Berliner Handelsgesellschaft -	22	5	343·1
Mitteldeutsche Creditbank -	22	2·3	179·3
Reichskreditgesellschaft -	40	17	487·5
Allgemeine Deutsche Kreditanstalt - - - -	40	11	294·4
Barmer Bankverein - -	36	18	221·5
Bayerische Hypotheken und Wechselbank [2] - - -	45	19·8	197·7
Bayerische Vereinsbank [2] -	21	9·3	178·8

Million marks.

[1] It has an interest now, however, in the *J. F. Schroeder Bank* of Bremen. Its interests in certain foreign banks are mentioned below.

[2] Mixed bank with mortgage business.

	Capital.	1928. Reserves.	Deposits.
Deutsche Bank - - -	150	77·5	2,453·9
Dresdner Bank - - -	100	32	2,112·5
Darmstädter Bank - -	60	55	2,082·6
Discontogesellschaft - -	135	66·5	1,767·6
(including Schaaffhausen'scher Bankverein and Norddeutsche Bank)			
Commerz- u. Privatbank -	60	35·6	1,357·8
Berliner Handelsgesellschaft -	28	15	399·4
Mitteldeutsche Creditbank -	—	—	—
Reichskreditgesellschaft -	40	19	584·3
Allgemeine Deutsche Kreditanstalt - - - -	40	11	363·8
Barmer Bankverein - -	36	18	327·5
Bayerische Hypotheken und Wechselbank [1] - - -	45	19·9	239·4
Bayerische Vereinsbank [1] -	30	12·3	197·2

Million marks.

In these tables five banks stand out above the others: the four D-banks and the Commerz- und Privatbank, each with a large network of branches and over a thousand million marks in deposits. Since the close of 1928 the tendency to concentration has been carried a great deal further, firstly by the absorption of the Mitteldeutsche Creditbank by the Commerz- und Privatbank in February, 1929, and secondly by the absorption of the Discontogesellschaft by the Deutsche Bank at the beginning of October. These amalgamations between Berlin banks have obviously a different significance from fusions of Berlin banks and provincial banks.

The Mitteldeutsche Creditbank had for some time been surpassed in importance by the larger provincial banks, and had only retained its rank as a Berliner Grossbank on historical grounds. Since 1924 there

---

[1] Mixed bank with mortgage business.

had been the further peculiarity in its position, that a large proportion of its capital (although not a controlling interest) had been in the hands of one financier, Jarislowsky.[1] The latter does not seem to have attempted to exercise any serious influence over the bank; but the concentration of its shares was considered to endanger its independence, and on Jarislowsky's death it was deemed wise to accept an offer from the Commerz- u. Privatbank.[2]

The amalgamation of the Deutsche and the Discontogesellschaft—two of the very largest banks—was more surprising, and is much more important. In addition to the main organizations of the two banks, the fusion embraces the subsidiaries of the Discontogesellschaft—the A. Schaaffhausen'scher Bankverein, the Norddeutsche Bank, and the Suddeutsche Discontogesellschaft—and also the Deutsche Bank's affiliation, the Rheinische Creditbank. The chief justification put forward for the amalgamation, apparently, is that it will lead to considerable administrative economies through the closing of overlapping offices. The hope may be entertained, moreover, that the amalgamated banks will enjoy greater credit abroad. But since neither the Deutsche Bank nor the Discontogesellschaft has been developing so rapidly as the Darmstädter in recent years, the motives may be in part competitive. The last consideration suggests that this move may call forth a reply from the other large banks, and yet further concentration.[3]

[1] Jarislowsky had more than half the ordinary shares, but this did not give control because of the existence of a small class of special shares, carrying 300 votes apiece, in the hands of the directors and their friends. (*Magazin der Wirtschaft*, iv. 13, March 29, 1928, p. 508.)

[2] A rather strange consequence of this amalgamation has been that the Mitteldeutsche Creditbank published no balance sheet for 1928.

[3] More than once in recent times rumour has suggested that the Berliner Handelsgesellschaft is to lose its independence. The retirement of its leading partner, Carl Fürstenberg, may make this more likely. On the other hand, it has a strong position in its special field and is in some ways stronger than the larger banks.

According to Strauss,[1] at the end of October, 1926, the big Berlin banks showed collectively 72·5% of the capital and reserves, and 82·5% of the deposits of all the banks (85) then publishing interim balance sheets. The Berlin banks here do not include the Berliner Handelsgesellschaft (nor the Reichskreditgesellschaft), whilst the two leading Bavarian banks are not included in the remainder. In February, 1913, the corresponding proportions were 47% and 60% (out of 91 banks). For this purpose the Berlin banks are taken without the members of their groups, except that the Norddeutsche Bank and (in 1926 only) the A. Schaaffhausen'scher Bankverein are included with the Discontogesellschaft.

Turning now to the groups of banks more or less controlled by the Berlin banks, their composition at the end of 1926 is given in the following lists, taken from a publication of the *Statistisches Reichsamt*.[2] An asterisk indicates that a bank has since been absorbed.

DEUTSCHE BANK

Deutsche Ueberseeische Bank.
Georg Fromberg & Co., Berlin.
Deutsche Treuhandgesellschaft.
Niederlausitzer Bank, Kottbus.
Mecklenburgische Deposten- u. Wechselbank, Schwerin.
    (*a*) Mecklenburgische Treuhand, g.m.b.H.
    (*b*) Mecklenburgische Hypotheken u. Wechselbank.
    (*c*) Rostocker Bank.

  * Lübecker Privatbank.

Oldenburgische Spar- u. Leihbank.
    (*a*) Treuhand A.G. Oldenburg.
    (*b*) Bremen-Banter Landges. m.b.H.
    (*c*) Franz Neelmeyer & Co., Bremen.

---

[1] *Op. cit.* p. 19.

[2] *Konzerne usw im deutschen Reiche*, 1926, pp. 198 *et seq.*

Osnabrücker Bank.
 (*a*) Meller Volksbank.
 (*b*) Ibbenbürener Volksbank.

* Hildesheimer Bank.
 (*a*) H. Brandt, Lamspringe.
Elberfelder Bankverein.
G. C. Trinkhaus, Düsseldorf.
Deutsche Vereinsbank, Frankfurt a. M. [1]

* Rheinische Creditbank, Mannheim.
 (*a*) Bankhaus J. A. Krebs, Freiburg i. B.
 (*b*) Mannheimer Bank.
 (*c*) Rheinische Treuhand A. G.

Abroad—
Tiroler Hauptbank, Innsbruck.[2]

* DISCONTOGESELLSCHAFT

* A. Schaaffhausen'scher Bankverein, Cologne ⎱entirely
* Norddeutsche Bank, Hamburg   ⎰owned.
* Süddeutsche Discontogesellschaft, Mannheim
 (*a*) E. Ladenburg, Frankfurt a. M.
 (*b*) C. Schmitt & Co., Pforzheim.
 (*c*) Handels- u. Gewerbebank, Heilbronn.
 (*d*) Badische Bank, Mannheim.
 (*e*) Frankenthaler Volksbank.
 (*f*) Bodencreditbank, Basle.
Revision Treuhand A. G., Berlin.
L. Pfeiffer, Kassel.

---

[1] It is doubtful whether this bank belonged to the Deutsche group in 1926. In April, 1929, it was absorbed by the rising *Effekten- und Wechselbank*, of Berlin and Frankfurt.

[2] Strauss (*op. cit.* pp. 149-50) gives also :
 Bankverein fur Schleswig-Holstein.
 Kieler Bank (in liquidation—October, 1929).
 Oberschlesischer Bankverein (Poland).
 Commerzbank in Lübeck.
 Danziger Bank.
 Plauener Bank (Commerz- u. Privatbank also interested since 1927).
 British & German Trust, Ltd. (with others).

Geestemünder Bank.
P. Elimeyer, Kom. Ges., Dresden.[1]

Abroad—

Ephrussi & Co., Vienna.
Handels Maatschappy, H. A. de Bary & Co., Amsterdam.
Kreditbank, Sofia.
Banco Brasileiro Alemao, Rio de Janeiro.
Banco de Chile y Alemania, Valparaiso.

DRESDNER BANK

Deutsche Orientbank.
Deutsch-Südamerikanische Bank.
Hardy & Co.[2]
Mecklenburgische Bank.
   (*a*) Neuvorpommersche Spar- u. Kreditbank.
Oldenburgische Landesbank.
   (*a*) Friedrich Brüning, Bremen.
   (*b*) Schiff & Co., Elsfleth.
   (*c*) Bank für das Nahethal.
   (*d*) Deutsche Schiffsbeleihungsbank, Hamburg.
Dürener Bank.
Landgräfliche Hessische Landesbank, Homburg.
Sächsische Bodencreditanstalt, Dresden.

Abroad—

Proehl & Gutmann, Amsterdam.
Internationale Bank, Luxemburg.
Internationale Rigaische Bank, Riga.

DARMSTÄDTER UND NATIONALBANK

Hagen & Co., Berlin.
Deutsche Hypothekenbank, Berlin.
Schwarz, Goldschmidt & Co., Berlin.
Deutsch- Südamerikanische Bank.
Deutsche Orientbank.

---

[1] Strauss also gives the Vereinsbank, Hamburg, and the Preussische Centralbodencredit A.G.   The connexion of the former at present with the Discontogesellschaft is doubtful.

[2] ADCA and the Bayerische Hypotheken u. Wechselbank also very largely interested.

Mecklenburg-Strelitzsche Hypothekbank, Neustrelitz.
Gebr. Hammerstein, Essen.
Otto Hirsch & Co., Frankfurt a. M.

Abroad—

Danziger Bank für Handel u. Gewerbe.
Danziger Hypothekenbank.
Merkurbank, Vienna.
Internationale Bank, Amsterdam.

COMMERZ- UND PRIVATBANK

E. Kaufmann & Co., Berlin.
Treuhand A. G., Leipzig.
Vereinsbank, Colditz.

Abroad—

N. V. Hugo Kaufmann & Co.'s Bank, Amsterdam.
Internationale Rigaische Bank.

In comparing these lists with those given in Part I, the chief differences—apart from the inclusion of private banking firms and some very small banks in the survey made by the Statistical Office—are due to the absorption of provincial banks between 1914 and 1926. The disappearance of the Barmer Bankverein and the Bayerische Disconto- und Wechselbank from the group of the Discontogesellschaft, however, marks a reaction against the predominance of Berlin. The case of the Barmer Bankverein has already been mentioned above; the Bayerische Disconto- und Wechselbank has belonged entirely to the Bayerische Hypotheken und Wechselbank since 1923. The Barmer Bankverein, the Bayerische Hypothek- und Wechselbank, the Allgemeine Deutsche Creditanstalt, and the Bayerische Vereinsbank, each appears with a group of its own in the survey of the Statistical Office.

It will be noticed that the groups still include the overseas banks (with the exception of the Deutsch-Asiatische Bank and the colonial banks), and also certain foreign banks; and it may be in place to give some account of these in recent times before concluding this section.

Of the overseas banks, those operating in South America were least affected by the War. Only in Brazil did they find themselves—from the end of 1917—in a country at war with Germany; and there they received comparatively lenient treatment, and were given full freedom to resume business before the end of 1919.[1] Their business in the other states was naturally very much restricted by the severance of intercourse with the home country, and also by loss of access to the London money market; but their local connexions brought sufficient business to maintain them. In the Near East the Deutsche Orientbank at once lost its Egyptian branches at the outbreak of the War, but gained a great access of business in Turkey, owing to the closing of the French and British institutions. Its position was further strengthened in 1917 by the entry of the Deutsche Bank into its *Konsortium*, whereby a consolidation of the German interests in this region was effected. At the end of the War, however, all its offices outside Germany were closed, and even since the Treaty of Lausanne it has only been able to recover part of its business at Constantinople.[2] In the Far East the Deutsch-Asiatische Bank had its business entirely suspended during the War by the sequestration of its offices.[3] Two Japanese branches have been re-opened since the Armistice, and some kind of agreement had been come to with the Chinese Government for the restoration of property in that country before the present confusion arose. When more normal conditions are established in the Far East, it will be necessary to re-organize this institution in view of the

[1] Benfey, *Die neuere Entwicklung des deutschen Auslandsbankwesens,* pp. 199 *et seq.*

[2] *Ibid,* p. 95.   [3] *Ibid,* pp. 80 *et seq.*

abandonment of Germany's extra-territorial rights; until then it can have little more than a nominal existence. Finally, the colonial banks have definitely lost their *raison d'être*, although not all of them have yet been liquidated.[1]

In the years following the War, some of the German offices of the overseas banks developed an independent, domestic business, quite unconnected with their original purposes. This was particularly the case with the Berlin office of the Deutsche Orientbank.[2] Only the South American banks were able to carry on any part of their normal work abroad, and they had considerable difficulties to contend with, first in the economic crisis which affected South America with especial severity in 1920, and, in the following years, in the depreciation of both the South American and the German currencies. The part taken by them in financing Germany's overseas trade was smaller than it had been before the War,[3] and the absence of an export of capital from Germany meant that they had few opportunities for engaging in large financial transactions.[4] On the other hand, there was a period after the War when many securities were sold by Germany to South America, mainly through these institutions;[5] and throughout the inflation years there was much South American speculation in marks. But the mainstay of the German offices abroad has probably been their local business. While the number of offices has on the whole somewhat declined, some new ones have been opened.[6]

---

[1] Benfey, *Die neuere Entwicklung des deutschen Auslandsbankwesens*, p. 213.

[2] *Ibid*, p. 208.   [3] *Ibid*. p. 209.

[4] They were, however, responsible for floating a wireless company to erect two large stations, *ibid*. p. 50.

[5] *Ibid*. p. 208.

[6] *Ibid*. pp. 212-3. In 1920 the Südamerikanische Bank formed a subsidiary in Madrid—the *Banco Germanico de la Amerika del Sur, ibid*. p. 58.

Neither the Deutsch-Asiatische Bank nor the Deutsche Orientbank paid any dividends during the years 1914-1924. The dividends of the South American banks were as follows:[1]

	1914.	1915.	1916.	1917.	1918.	1919.	1920.	1921.	1922.	1923.	1924.
Deutsche Ueberseeische Bank - - -	6	6	6	6	30	30	40	40	600	4	6
Deutsch - Südamerikanische Bank - -	—	—	—	—	—	9	10	16	300	—	—
Brasilianische Bank für Deutschland - -	6	8	8	8	—	—	15	25	40	1000	—
Bank für Chile u. Deutschland - - - -	—	—	6	—	—	—	8	10	50	—	—

Since stabilization, the two overseas banks for South America in general—the Deutsche Ueberseeische Bank and the Deutsch-Südamerikanische Bank—have issued gold mark balance sheets which show their pre-war capital intact—in view of all the circumstances a considerable achievement. The two localized South American banks, on the other hand, the Brasilianische Bank für Deutschland and the Bank für Chile und Deutschland, were converted after stabilization into Brazilian and Chilean companies respectively, with capitals in terms of the currencies of those countries. The new capital, which remained in German hands, in each case represented a considerably lower gold value than the pre-war mark capital. These specialized banks have therefore been less successful than those with a wider field of activity. The re-organization under South American registration suggests a desire to assume a larger part in local finance, even at the expense of weakening the connexion with the home country. But, in the case of Chile, this plan has failed to free the overseas bank from the restrictions imposed in the interests of the native banks, and

[1] From Benfey, *op. cit.* p. 211.

accordingly its liquidation has now been decided on.[1]
The Deutsche Orientbank retains its original constitution, but (despite post-war increases) its capital has
been written down to one-tenth of the pre-war figure
in the gold mark balance sheet.

The Deutsche Ueberseeische Bank paid a dividend
of 7% for 1925; since this year the Deutsche Bank
has reported that its returns have been satisfactory
without giving the actual rate.   The Deutsch-
Südamerikanische Bank paid no dividends in 1925 and
1926, but 5% in 1927 and 6% in 1928.   Dividends
of other overseas banks have been: Banco Brasileiro,
1924-25 and 1925-26 8%, 1926-27 4%, 1927-28
5%; Chile Bank, 1926 and 1927 6%, 1928 4%;
Deutsche Orientbank, 1925 to 1928, 5%.

In the altered political conditions and with no
surplus of capital in Germany, there seems to be no
likelihood that either the Deutsch-Asiatische Bank or
the Deutsche Orientbank will regain anything like its
former importance.   The prospects are more hopeful
for the South American institutions, which were always
more dependent on pure commerce; but these have
new competition to face from overseas banks set up by
other countries.

The existing German participations in foreign banks
(apart from the new one in Brazil) are given more fully
in the following list extracted from Benfey's book.[2]

GERMAN PARTICIPATIONS IN FOREIGN BANKS [3]

AUSTRIA

Foreign Bank.	German Bank.
Niederösterreichische Escomptegesellschaft.	Berliner Handelsgesellschaft.
Mercurbank. A.G.	Darmstädter Bank.
Rosenfeld & Co.	Deutsche Bank.

---

[1] As a result of the amalgamation of the Deutsche Bank and Discontogesellschaft the Banco Brasileiro has now (Jan., 1930) been merged in the
Deutsche Ueberseeische Bank.

[2] Pp. 174-177.   [3] This list relates to 1925.

Foreign Bank.	German Bank.
Ephrussi & Co.	Discontogesellschaft.
Kux, Bloch & Co.	Mendelssohn & Co. and Bayerische Vereinsbank.
Ullman & Co.	Hardy & Co., Barmer Bankverein and Bayerische Hypotheken u. Wechselbank.
J. Liebig & Co.	Allgemeine Deutsche Creditanstalt.
M. L. Biedermann. A.G.	Gebr. Arnhold.

All of Vienna

Tiroler Hauptbank, Innsbruck.	Deutsche Bank.
Bank für Oberösterreich u. Salzburg, Lenz.	Bayerische Vereinsbank.
Steiermärkische Escomptebank, Graz.	Bayerische Vereinsbank.
Kärntner Kredit u. Wechselbank, Klagenfurth.	Bayerische Hypotheken u. Wechselbank.
Salzburger Kredit- u. Wechselbank.	Bayerische Hypothek- u. Wechselbank.

HOLLAND (Amsterdam)

Handels Maatschappy H.A. de Bary.	Discontogesellschaft.
Proehl & Gutmann.	Dresdner Bank.
Internationale Bank te Amsterdam.	Darmstädter Bank.
Internationale Crediet Cie.	Deutsche, Disconto and Dresdner.
N. V. H. Kaufmann & Co.'s Bank.	Commerz u. Privatbank.
Amsterdamsche Crediet M'tsch'y (v.d. Heydt Kerstens Bank).	Bleichröder, Barmer Bankverein, A.D.C.A., Bayer Hypotheken u. Wechselbank.
Disconto-en Effectenbank.	Barmer Bankverein.
Mendelssohn & Co.	Mendelssohn & Co.
M'tsch'py voor Bank en Handelsonderneemingen.	Bayerische Vereinsbank and Mendelssohn & Co.
Nederlandsche Accept M'tsch'py.	Mendelssohn & Co.

NEW YORK

Foreign Bank.	German Bank.
Speyer & Co.	Lazard Speyer-Ellissen.
Strupp & Co.	J. Dreyfus & Co.
G. H. Burr & Co.	Hardy & Co.
J. A. Sisto & Co.	Dresdner Bank.

DANTZIG

Danziger Bank.	Deutsche Bank.
Danziger Bank für Handel u. Gewerbe.	Darmstädter Bank and Ostbank für Handel u. Gewerbe.
Danziger Privataktienbank.	Berliner Handelsgesellschaft.

POLAND

Oberschlesischer Bankverein, Pless.	Deutsche Bank.
Oberschlesische Bank, Kattowitz.	Dresdner Bank.
Oberschlesische Diskonto-bank, Königshütte.	Darmstädter Bank.

LITHUANIA

Memeler Bank für Handel u. Gewerbe.	Ostbank für Handel u. Gewerbe.

CZECHO-SLOVAKIA

L. Wolfrum & Co., Aussig.	ADCA.

LUXEMBURG

Luxemburger Unionbank.	Delbrück, Schickler & Co. and J. H. Stein.

BULGARIA

Kreditna Banka, Sofia.	Discontogesellschaft.

The important Italian and Roumanian connexions which existed before the War have been forcibly terminated, and the only remaining participation of this type is that of the Discontogesellschaft in the Bulgarian *Kreditna Banka*. The others in the list fall into two classes: (*a*) participations in banking institutions in important financial centres—Amsterdam, Vienna, and New York; (*b*) participations in banks in ceded territories or other adjacent regions which are closely connected with Germany economically. Attention may be called especially to the foreign connexions of the South German provincial banks.

Against these German participations abroad must be set the American holdings of shares in German banks, and some less important Austrian and Swiss participations. In the former case the holdings appear to be in the hands of business friends who do not aim at exercising control.

V

It remains to describe the recent changes in the position of the banks in relation to the other elements in the economic system.

The shortage of capital immediately after stabilization caused most industrial and commercial firms to be in a high degree dependent upon the institutions which had money to lend. At first they could look to the Reichsbank for help; but with the restriction of Reichsbank credit in the spring of 1924, they were forced to lean upon the creditbanks. Thus, whatever the difficulties of the period, the banks had the satisfaction of becoming more influential *vis à vis* their customers. The controllers of the great industrial groups resisted this change for a certain time, aided in varying degrees by their prestige, by reserves in foreign currencies, and also by loans obtained from public banks (see below). But just the more ambitious and aggressive of these industrialists were in a fundamentally unsound position. They had not been able to give sufficient attention to maintaining the technical efficiency of the various undertakings which they had agglomerated; the share holdings upon which they had borrowed heavily were shrinking in value; and such uncovered advances as they obtained only postponed their downfall until the summer of 1925. In several cases, particularly that of the Stinnes group, it then fell to the banks to liquidate their interests; and the protests of certain members of the Stinnes family against the despotism of the banks were significant of a revolution in the distribution of economic power.

As exceptions to this general account, there were some concerns, better financed than the others, which were never in such a helpless predicament; and because their credit was good, these were naturally amongst the first to receive assistance in the form of foreign loans. As the latter became the chief factor in the capital market, the situation was somewhat modified. On the whole the dependence on the banks was mitigated, but this effect was not spread uniformly, since only certain firms could borrow abroad, and of these again not all could do so without the mediation of a bank. These differences with regard to financial dependence or independence—by no means a new feature—have continued to exist; but the tendency towards a relaxation of the banks' domination appears to have been strengthened by the partial recovery of the home capital market and the revival of confidence in the prospects of industry. It is hard to define, however, a situation which changes rapidly: the recent acceleration in tendency towards concentration amongst the banks, and the greater part played recently by the latter in mediating foreign investment, may again have shifted the balance in their favour.

The process of industrial 'rationalization,' the basis of the more hopeful outlook, has involved considerable transformations in the relations between particular undertakings. On the one hand, those industrial groups (*Konzerne*) which possessed sufficient organic unity to survive the difficulties of 1924-25, have been obliged to rid themselves of many unassimilated accretions. On the other hand, the need to increase efficiency through the sub-division and concentration of production has given a new stimulus to the union of establishments engaged in like or closely related processes. The latter phase of re-organization has been the more conspicuous since 1925. In very many cases (numerically no doubt the majority) combination has not yet been carried beyond the stage at which the shares of a number of distinct companies are largely in common ownership; that is to say, the method is still that of forming groups. But in some of the most important cases the union has been of a more intimate kind. Thus in the great chemical combine the chief concerns have been completely amalgamated into the *I. G. Farbenindustrie A.G.*, which further rents and operates a number of other works ; and in the great steel combine a new company, the *Vereinigte Stahlwerke* has taken over most of the plants, leaving the original companies as its shareholders.

This latest movement towards industrial concentration has been regarded with favour by the banks, and indeed some of the bank directors, notably Herr Goldschmidt of the Darmstädter u. National Bank, have been its strongest advocates. It being known that this is their attitude, it is not unreasonable to suppose that in certain cases they have used their influence directly to further the movement, although evidence is not available to show how common or important such cases have been.[1]   But it is questionable whether it is true

---

[1] A recent example of an important fusion dictated by a bank is that of the Austro-Cosmos Line with the Hamburg-Amerika Line. The general directors of both lines were opposed to amalgamation, but it is said to have been forced on them by Herr Goldschmidt of the Darmstädter Bank

to assert, as some writers in the Press have done, that
the whole development has been initiated and enforced
by the banks. The leaders of the larger industrial
concerns are not now so helpless;[1] and further it
would appear that they are themselves decidedly in
favour of concentration, not only on the ground that
it increases efficiency, but also because it makes it
easier to raise capital abroad and is a necessary prelude
to agreements with foreign rivals. It may be said,
moreover, that the general tenor of the banks' policy
since stabilization has been such as to make far-
reaching control unlikely. The industrial influence
of the banks is always largely dependent on the extent
to which they are prepared to assume responsibility
and risks: and on the whole the policy of the banks
in recent years has been one of caution. At least in
comparison with the pre-war period, it can be said that
the banks have become more conservative, whether as
a result of the greater uncertainty of trade conditions,
the relative smallness of the banks' own resources, or
the temperament of many of their present directors.
It must be admitted that this caution on the part of the
banks may often tell on the side of industrial amalgamations, given favourable circumstances; but it is
hardly compatible with the initiation of important
schemes.

(Strauss, *op. cit.* p. 49). Without there being any suggestion of dictation,
Herr Goldschmidt is also known to have played a large part in bringing
about a close liaison between the American General Electric Company and
the A.E.G. and between the G.E.C. and the Osram Lamp Coy. (*Magazin
der Wirtschaft*, v. No. 28, July 4, 1929, pp. 1096-7.)
As has been said, however, Herr Goldschmidt has been conspicuous
amongst bank directors for his activity in this direction. It may also be
said with respect to the former case cited that the big shipping lines are
exceptionally under the influence of the banks.

[1] Of the great *I. G. Farbenindustrie* it can certainly be said that it is
independent of the control of the banks, no bank director being even on
its *Aufsichtrat*. The position of the *Vereinigte Stahlwerke* in this respect is
less clear. The fact that a number of banks, themselves rivals, are interested
in it would seem to make dictation from their side difficult.

It is no doubt a further consequence of this attitude of the big banks that there has been an increase in the importance of certain private banking firms in industrial finance. Mention may be made of *Sal. Oppenheim Jr. & Cie.* and *A. Levy*, of Cologne (both guided by Herr Louis Hagen); of *Lazard Speyer-Ellissen* (originally of Frankfurt am Main, now also of Berlin as a result of a fusion with *Schlesinger Trier & Co.*)—the pioneers in financing the artificial silk industry; and the firm *Gebr. Arnhold*, Dresden, influential in the brewing and porcelain industries—also controlling many hotels. The recent rise to a prominent position of the *J. F. Schroeder Bank* of Bremen may also be attributed to the adoption of a more active industrial policy than that pursued by most of the well-established Grossbanken.

The dissolution or dismemberment of the inflation *Konzerne* has set free most of the important banks which had come under industrial control. Even the Michael group, which has held together to an exceptional degree, has parted with the *Deutsche Vereinsbank*, Frankfurt a. M. However, as is shown by the accompanying list of examples extracted from the official survey already mentioned (*Konzerne, Interresengemeinschaften und ähnliche Zusammenschlüsse in Deutschen Reich, Ende* 1926) many of the industrial groups now existing include institutions more or less of the nature of banks.

GERMAN INDUSTRIAL GROUPS AND THEIR BANKS

J. MICHAEL & Co. (chiefly metal industry).
    Industrie und Privatbank, Berlin,
        and through this,
  * Hannoversche Bodencreditbank.
    Textilkredit A.G., Berlin.
    Internationale Handelsbank K.a.A., Berlin.
    Bankverein für Kredit u. Handel, Hamburg.
    Rheinland Bank, Biebrich.
  * Mitteldeutsche Bodenkreditanstalt, Greiz.

KLOECKNER WERKE (coal and iron).
 * Bodenkreditbank, Duisburg.
ROECHLING (coal and iron).
 Gebr. Roechling Bank, Saarbrücken.
ILSEDER HUTTE (coal and iron).
 Ilseder Bank Sandow & Co., Grossilsede.
GEBR. MANNESMANN (machinery).
 Bank für Innen und Aussenhandel, Berlin.[1]
I. G. FARBENINDUSTRIE (chemicals).
 Deutsche Länderbank, Berlin.
EVAG (chemicals).
 Münchener Bankverein.
HUTSCHENREUTHER (china, etc.).
 Bank für Keramische Industrie, Dresden.
BLUMENSTEIN (textiles).
 Bank für Textilindustrie, Berlin.
SCHULTHEISS-PATZENHOFER (brewing).
 Ostdeutsche Bank, Berlin.[2]
HUGENBERG (publishing).
 Ostdeutsche Privatbank, Berlin.
 Deutsche Kreditverein, Berlin.
 * Landwirtschaftliche Pfandbriefbank,
   and through this,
 * Getreiderentenbank (in liquidation).
 Agrar- u. Commerzbank.
 * Preussische Pfandbriefbank.[3]
WINTERSHALL (potash).
 Kali Bank, Cassel.
 Bank für Landwirtschaft, Berlin.
LOTHRINGEN KONZERN (coal).
 Westfalenbank, Bochum.
 * Rheinisch-Westfälische Bank für Grundbesitz, Essen.[4]

---

[1] Strauss gives also Depositen u. Handelsbank, *op. cit.* p. 170.

[2] Strauss gives also Getreidekreditbank, Berlin, and Deutsche Landwirtschaftliche Handelsbank, *ibid.* p. 170.

[3] Strauss includes the Ostbank für Handel u. Gewerbe in this group, *ibid.* p. 171.

[4] Strauss gives another example—Haniel-Gutehoffnungshütte and the Bank fur Bergswerks- u. Hüttenwerke, Düsseldorf. He also mentions that several private banking firms are controlled by industrialists, e.g. Delbrück by Merton and v.d. Heydt by Thyssen.

A number of these institutions, the names of which are marked with an asterisk, specialize in real estate (mortgage) credit: so far as membership of the groups is concerned, they are probably merely survivals, having been acquired at an earlier time when such institutions were to be bought up very cheaply. The remainder are mainly important as the financial organs of their particular groups.[1] In this capacity, however, they carry on short-term banking as well as capital transactions, thus depriving the ordinary banks of a good deal of business. It may also be mentioned here that even where no separate banking or financial organ is formed, the central offices of the big combines, such as the *Vereinigte Stahlwerke*, serve as intermediaries for the distribution of balances between the affiliated undertakings, and also for the investment of balances in the money market. The progress of industrial concentration is thus detrimental, in this direction, to the interests of the banks.

The other type of institution through which firms not primarily engaged in finance have attempted to do their own banking, the banks for the whole of a particular trade, have had a mixed history. As might be expected, in view of the impossibility of diversifying credit risks, there have been cases in which the banks have found themselves in difficulties—e.g. the *Holzwirtschaftbank* has recently been obliged to write down its capital.[2] But other banks of this class, amongst them the *Zuckercreditbank*, are reported to be quite successful.[3] Furthermore, there has been a new development in this field since 1924 in the form of companies

---

[1] Two only publish interim balance sheets—the Bank für Textilindustrie and the Westfalenbank. Their deposits etc. at end of March, 1929, were respectively 45·4 and 65·1 million marks. But 11·8 and 30·7 million respectively represented debts incurred on behalf of customers.

[2] *Magazin der Wirtschaft*, iii. 31, August 4, 1927, p. 1213.

[3] *Ibid.*

to finance purchases (*Absatzfinanzierung*) from particular branches of industry, particularly those supplying relatively expensive machinery.   Examples are the *Kreditanstalt für Verkehrsmittel*, the *Automobilbank*, and the *Finanzierungsgesellschaft für Landkraftmaschinen*— the last assisted by government guarantees on behalf of agricultural purchasers.   Generally the ordinary creditbanks have stood aloof from these developments, but an exception has been made by the participation of the Deutsche Bank, Discontogesellschaft, Dresdner Bank, and Commerz- u. Privatbank in the promotion of the *Finanzierungsgesellschaft für Industrielieferungen* in 1928.   This company is intended to assist the purchase of machinery by 18-month bill credits and is to be financed partly by the participating banks themselves and partly by recourse to re-discount facilities abroad.[1]

Turning now to the public banking institutions, reference may first be made to the appearance of the following new banks in Berlin.

1. *The Golddiskontbank*.   This bank was originally formed in the spring of 1924 to assist the export trades by providing them with credits for the importation of raw materials.   In addition to this immediate object— which was likely to be of only temporary importance— there was an idea that it might be developed into a note-issuing bank on a gold basis, eventually to replace both the Reichsbank and the Rentenbank.   The reorganization of the Reichsbank under the Dawes scheme has, of course, removed all possibility of this development, and the Golddiskontbank has long since become superfluous for its original purpose in connexion with foreign trade.   It is retained in existence, however, as a useful adjunct to the Reichsbank,

---

[1] *Magazin der Wirtschaft*, iv. 43, October 25, 1928, p. 1665.   In the latter part of 1929 the big Berlin banks have proceeded considerably farther in this direction.   See *Magazin der Wirtschaft*, v. 44, October 31, 1929, p. 1511.

through which the latter can indirectly engage in transactions which lie outside its own scope as defined by the Bank Act. Since its own re-organization in 1924, the Reichsbank has owned the entire capital of the Golddiskontbank.

2. *The Rentenbankkreditanstalt.* Amongst the statutes passed in 1924 to give effect to the Dawes plan was one dealing with the liquidation of the Rentenbank; out of its somewhat complicated provisions has arisen the Rentenbankkreditanstalt, designed to serve as a feeder for the various institutions concerned with providing credit for agriculture.

Since the activity of the Rentenbank itself was henceforth to be limited to the liquidation on behalf of the Reichsbank of the private Rentenmark credits, it no longer had any need of working funds, and the amount in hand could therefore be taken to form the capital of the new institution. This capital is to be increased by an annual contribution not exceeding 25 million marks out of the mortgage interest which agricultural undertakings have still to pay to the Rentenbank until the withdrawal of its notes has been completed.[1]

On its own credit the new bank raises money which is then dispensed in agricultural loans through other agencies. It does not lend to individual landowners or farmers directly, and, except for the employment of its liquid balances, it can only deal with certain specified institutions. It gives both short term (' personal ') credit and long term (' real ') credit, but, unless prolonged, its authority to grant the former expires at the end of 1930.

3. *The Deutsche Verkehrskreditbank.* This is not strictly a public bank, but is conveniently regarded as

---

[1] The mortgages imposed in favour of the Rentenbank upon commerce and industry were cancelled in view of the new burden these had to assume in the form of the ' Industrial obligations ' under the Reparations Plan. The agricultural mortgages have been retained primarily to provide the means of redeeming the Rentenmark loan to the Reich.

such, since roughly three-fourths of its capital is in the hands of the Deutsche Reichsbahn A.G. (German Railway Co.), and the latter largely retains its public character despite its formal separation from the Government.

The original function of the Verkehrskreditbank, and one which it still retains, was to manage a peculiar system of giving credit for freight payments. (*Frachtstundenverkehr.*[1]) Customers admitted by the Verkehrskreditbank to the scheme make their payments to the Railway by written orders (on special forms) addressed to the Verkehrskreditbank, and settle with the latter once a fortnight. In turn the Verkehrskreditbank also settles fortnightly with the Railway Co., so that it does not actually make advances but simply administers a system of book credit on behalf of the Railway. However, this function has been subordinate in importance to that of managing all the funds of the Railway Co., including the sums accumulated for interest payments on the (Reparations) Railway Debentures. These funds are invested in first class bills or lent to other banks. The *Deutsche Verkehrskreditbank* has a large number of offices spread over the Reich.[2]

These three new banks are additional to the public banks already existing in Berlin, namely (apart from the Reichsbank) the Seehandlung (Staatsbank), the Preussenkasse (Preuss. Zentral Genossenschaftskasse), the Deutsche Girozentrale, the Berliner Stadtbank (the *Girozentrale* for Berlin) and the Reichskreditgesellschaft. The last-named was re-organized as an Aktiengesellschaft (instead of a G.m.b.H.: the differ-

---

[1] It was formed for this purpose, apparently on a private basis but by arrangement with the Reichsbahn, in 1923. The participation of the Deutsche Reichsbahn A.G. dates from the autumn of 1924.

[2] Another new public bank established in Berlin, but of less importance, is the *Deutsche Landesbanken-Zentrale*—a central institution for the provincial banks and the *Landschaften*.

ence is roughly that between a public and a private company in England [1]) in 1924, with a view to the greater development of its general banking business. The *Reichspost* (P.O.), which of course has its headquarters in Berlin, is also a bank to a certain extent, having large funds to handle in the form of balances of those who have postal cheque accounts.

Apart from these public banks in Berlin there are, of course, the state and provincial banks in other parts of Germany, as mentioned in the previous chapter. They seem to have rather expanded their general activity and have been particularly concerned with raising capital abroad for smaller German interests.

This group of public banks has been the subject of a considerable amount of criticism. In a brief treatment the main points at issue can be most conveniently considered under three headings, according as they relate to the general business management of these banks, to their relations with the Reichsbank, or to their relations with other banks, particularly the creditbanks.

1. Misgivings have been aroused with regard to the management of public banks in general by certain losses which came to light in 1924-1925. The most serious case is that of the Seehandlung, which had made extensive advances to the financiers Barmat and Kutisker. On the failure of both of these it was found that the loans were only partly covered by collateral, and the bank was left with heavy losses.[2] In this case, in addition to the obvious charge of recklessness, there

---

[1] See Appendix I.

[2] Sums amounting to 45 million R.M. had been lent to Barmat, Kutisker and Michael. The Michael loans, which also occasioned considerable anxiety, were repaid in full. According to the Report for 1924, the amount in danger was 17 million R.M. : and the following Annual Report stated that all losses except 4¼ million had been met out of revenue. Presumably the Barmat Kutisker loans were between 17 and 4¼ million, but the exact figure is not known. (See *Die Bank*, sub. *Seehandlung*, February and July, 1925, August 1926.)

was at least a suspicion that the directors of the bank, or one of them, had yielded to improper influences; and public opinion was the more shocked because the Seehandlung had always been reported to conduct its business on particularly conservative lines. Another of these banks to be involved in losses was the Deutsche Girozentrale, the cause in this case being peculation on the part of its own officials. One of the delinquents, who robbed the institution of several million marks, was its chief cashier.

As a result of these cases and the public discussion they received, internal reforms have been effected in both the Seehandlung and the Deutsche Girozentrale, which should make their repetition unlikely. Moreover the rehabilitation of the money market has made it possible for the Seehandlung to re-direct its business into the pre-war channels.[1] The abnormal conditions prevailing in 1923 and 1924 must certainly be borne in mind in judging the conduct of public and private banks alike at this time. Further, it must be emphasized that it is only certain of the public banks which have incurred losses of importance. According to general report, the Reichskreditgesellschaft has been as well managed throughout as any bank in Germany.[2]

2. With regard to the relations between the public banks and the Reichsbank, the line of criticism has been that the former are used as repositories for public moneys which ought to be lodged with the Reichsbank, and that their employment of these moneys often

---

[1] Some departure from tradition may appear to be indicated in its recent participation in the *Frankfürter Bank*. But the latter has been in the past a very conservative institution, acting to a large extent as a banker's bank in the Frankfurt money market.

[2] As this book is passing through the press, a further case of rash lending by a public bank in Berlin has come to light. The Berliner-Stadtbank has admitted losses of 9 million Rm. arising from loans to the Brothers Sklarek. For the future a limit (50,000 Rm.) is to be imposed on the amount this bank may lend to one person or firm. See *Die Bank*, March 22, 1930, pp. 470–1 ; also *Magazin der Wirtschaft*, vi. 13, March 28, 1930, p. 615.

thwarts the Reichsbank's credit policy.   Such a view is to be found repeatedly in the Reports of the Agent General for Reparations Payments.

In considering this matter it is important to grasp the elementary point that the public banks have in no way been responsible for the existence of government surpluses.   This is important, because certain critics have been disposed to blame these banks for disturbances which are properly attributable to the mere presence of large liquid balances.   Given that the government departments had large balances which they had to keep liquid and which they expected to earn interest, a depressing effect on money market rates appears to have been inevitable.   The requirement of interest precluded deposit with the Reichsbank, and if no other channel of investment had been available the authorities would have lent to the money market direct.   Actually they did do this to quite a large extent.[1]   The Reichsbank might, and did, adopt the plan of investing money at interest on behalf of the authorities.   But by so doing it did not in any way alter the effect on the money market until it succeeded in diverting some of the money to the long term market.   Then, of course, the balances ceased to be liquid.   Perhaps the authorities should have agreed to this earlier; perhaps they should not have insisted so much on receiving interest; but the decision of these questions of policy did not rest with the public banks.

With the decline in their amount, the whole question of public balances has lost much of its importance.[2]

[1] To strengthen their case critics sometimes speak as though the government departments themselves were banks in such cases.   But this is to confuse the issues.

[2] To be revived somewhat by the raising of a Reich loan in the spring of 1927, the proceeds of which were not immediately required.   This transaction has been criticized with much point by the Agent General for Reparations in his Report for June, 1927.

The Reichspost (P.O.) and, at times, the Railway Company, have still large sums in hand, however, and the demand continues to be made in certain quarters that these should be held by the Reichsbank.   Against this it is to be pointed out that the funds of the P.O., arising chiefly out of its cheque-and-transfer system, must earn interest in order that the expenses of operating that system shall be met.   With regard to the railway balances the position is different, but it may be asked on what ground the Reichsbank has a greater right to hold these than the balances of electricity undertakings or soap companies.   The Reichsbank did not manage surplus railway funds (which in Prussia were often considerable) in Germany before the War; nor are the corresponding funds managed at present by the central banks of England or the U.S.A.[1]

Apart from funds which are in any sense public, some of these banks also hold considerable private balances.   Thus the Reichskreditgesellschaft, apart from holding the balances of the V.I.A.G. companies, receives deposits from provincial banks and bankers (who do not care to do their Berlin business through banks which compete with them at home), and also obtains credits abroad.   The deposits of the Deutsche Girozentrale and Preussenkasse are also largely of private origin.[2] In employing these resources there is no evidence to show that the public banks are less amenable to the guidance of the Reichsbank than the privately-owned

---

[1] In January, 1928, an agreement was made between the Reichsbank and the Railway Company, according to which most of the funds in the Verkehrskreditbank are to be invested through the Reichsbank (Agent General for Reparations Payments, Report June 1928, pp. 80-1). According to the argument above, the change is of little importance ; the funds will come to the money market as before.

[2] Again the Seehandlung has recently been offering special terms for deposits placed for a period which extends over the end of the month or quarter.   Incidentally this illustrates the efforts of the public banks to contribute to the stability of the money market.

joint stock banks. On the contrary, it is known that the Seehandlung and the Reichskreditgesellschaft gave the Reichsbank considerable support in re-establishing the private discount market and also in its campaign for the reduction of bank charges.

The one case in which the relations between the Reichsbank and another public bank have been clearly unsatisfactory, concerns the Golddiskontbank; and here the ground of criticism is not that policies have conflicted, but on the contrary, that a common policy and management have enabled the Reichsbank in effect to overstep the limits imposed on it by the Bank Act. As an example we may cite the assistance given to agriculture, nominally by the Golddiskontbank, at the beginning of 1926. The Golddiskontbank made loans from three to five years to the Rentenbank-kreditanstalt, receiving mortgage bonds in exchange. In order that it should have the means to lend, the Reichsbank paid up the capital of the Golddiskontbank in full,[1] payment being actually made in *Devisen* or foreign bills. The *Devisen* were handed over by the Golddiskontbank to the Rentenbankkreditanstalt, but as the latter required German money it exchanged them at the Reichsbank for bank notes. Thus the transaction left the Reichsbank's stock of *Devisen* the same as before; its note circulation was increased, and against this it held shares in the Golddiskontbank which were represented by the mortgage debt held by the latter. The note circulation was therefore increased to give long term credit to agriculture. More recently the Golddiskontbank has made further advances to the Rentenbankkreditanstalt, obtaining the money by selling bills re-discountable at the Reichsbank. Altogether the amount advanced by the

---

[1] £3,000,000 to £4,000,000 was paid up to complete capital of £10,000,000. It does not seem, however, that this amount was lent to the Rentenbankkreditanstalt.

Golddiskontbank to the Rentenbankkreditanstalt totalled 220·7 million R.M. for the year 1926: but it is not clear to the author how much of this sum was provided by the Reichsbank and how much by the market.

3. With regard, finally, to the relations between public and private banks, the question is whether the creation of new public banks has led to undue competition and overlapping. This question has to be considered separately in relation to each of the public institutions likely to be concerned.[1]

(a) It can hardly be doubted that the Reichskreditgesellschaft does compete with the big private banks [2] in Berlin, particularly, of course, through its private connexions. However, it must be remembered that the number of Berliner Grossbanken has been reduced from nine before the War to five now (1929), so that there may be room in the money market for one or two new institutions. Certainly the competition of the Reichskreditgesellschaft cannot be regarded as in any way unfair, since it pays precisely the same taxes as the ordinary banks and is in no way subsidized.

(b) From the Verkehrskreditbank, on the other hand, the ordinary banks can receive no serious competition. Its speciality, the *Frachtstundenverkehr*, is, as we have seen, not really a branch of banking at all, and in its other function, the investment of railway balances, it very largely uses the other banks. Its alternative method of employing the balances is investment in *Privatdiskonten*, and this too is of advantage to the private banks, since it widens the market for their acceptances. The big private banks own

[1] The question hardly applies to old banks such as the Seehandlung and Preussenkasse, which had a definite place in the credit system before the War, to which they have now returned. It does not seem to apply either to the Golddiskontbank.

[2] ' Private bank ' here means private as opposed to public (or Government-owned), not, as opposed to joint stock : so throughout this section.

about 20% of the capital of the Verkehrskreditbank, and are strongly represented on its Aufsichtrat.

(c) The Rentenbankkreditanstalt has a special sphere which only touches that of the creditbanks indirectly in the matter of ' personal ' credit to agriculture, and there only slightly. Further, in this direction its activities are to be curtailed in the near future. Whether it will in time become superfluous in the organization for providing long term agricultural credit is a question which need not be discussed here.

(d) The Deutsche Girozentrale, considered simply as a member of the Berlin money market and apart from the whole system of which it is the head, chiefly competes with the private institutions in the business of floating municipal loans. Here it works in closest agreement with the Seehandlung and has won for itself a strong, and perhaps dominant, position. It is obliged, of course, to leave the private banks some part in the distribution of municipal stock, and there does not seem to be any objection of principle if it deprives them of the leading rôle in these transactions.

It is difficult, however, to consider the Deutsche Girozentrale apárt from the communal system of banking as a whole, and this brings us to the development of public banking which is most serious from the point of view of the creditbanks.

Like certain of the public banking institutions in Berlin, many of the savings banks throughout the country made rather rash advances to industrialists in the years 1923-24;[1] and again, like the former, a number of them incurred losses.[2] This experience

---

[1] It is said that one industrialist sent emissaries round the country after stabilization offering attractive terms to communal bank officials for loans.

[2] Information is very scanty with regard to these. It does not appear that the communal authorities, as guarantors of the savings banks, have been called upon to any serious extent, except in the case of the Berliner Stadtbank mentioned above (p. 312, footnote).

has doubtless had a certain sobering effect; and a return to more traditional forms of business has been further encouraged, on the one hand by the partial recovery of pure savings deposits, and, on the other hand by the re-establishment of normal conditions for mortgage loan transactions.[1]　But at the same time, these communal institutions show no disposition to surrender the new ground which they have occupied since 1914 in the field of general banking.　In Prussia at least this attitude has received official support, for the regulating decree of May, 1924, allows them even more scope than before in performing their task of ' providing banking facilities for those of moderate means.' (' *die notwendige bankmässigen Geschäfte des Mittelstandes zu besorgen.*')

From the point of view of securing the most economical organization of banking it seems clearly desirable that there should be a more definite delimitation of the sphere of the communal banks in relation to that of other types of institution—co-operative credit societies and Landesbanken as well as creditbanks.[2]　Commercial bankers appear still to cherish the hope that this will be achieved by undoing the developments of a dozen years and restricting the savings banks to their pre-war activities.　The latter seem to be too well entrenched in their new position, however, and to have too many supporters, for such a course to be practicable.　And its desirability is not beyond question.

---

[1] Particularly by the settlement of the *Aufwertung* question, i.e. the question of reviving debts paid off in depreciated money.

[2] With regard to the general necessity for a more or less scientific delimitation of spheres of rival organizations, a distinction may be made between a competitive situation resulting from gradual evolution and one resulting from a comparatively sudden change.　In the former case a tolerably satisfactory equilibrium between the two competing forces may be expected to establish itself without conscious planning ; in the latter case a general redundancy of organizations may occur which calls for rational curtailment, if appalling waste is to be avoided.　Cf. the position after the War in certain British industries.

It may be agreed that there are dangers of undue political control, of abuse of influence, and of mistakes arising from the management of officials inexperienced in banking. But it may be possible to devise rules and methods of organization which remove these dangers, or at least mitigate them; and, if this can be done, there are grounds for allowing the communal banks a field of activity which extends beyond the mere encouragement of thrift. In the first place there is the idea adopted in the last Prussian decree of making better provision for small customers than is made by the big banks with their inherent tendency to prefer large transactions. Co-operative credit societies, of course, have a part to play here and competition with them is undesirable; but there are probably business firms of the smaller size which are not very satisfactorily catered for by either co-operative or commercial banking. Closely allied with this idea is that of resisting an excessive centralization of loanable funds. In its extreme form, as a claim that ' local money ought to be employed locally ' there is little indeed to be said for this second idea; the promotion of the mobility of short term capital is one of the main functions of the banking system. But it may be admitted that the centralized banking organizations which have grown up in most European countries in the last fifty years are more efficient in absorbing money even in the smallest sums from all parts of their territory, than they are in re-distributing it evenly according to need; and on this ground there is something to be said for withdrawing a certain part of the available funds from the general process of centralization. Lastly, it is thought that as public institutions the communal banks may serve as a useful check on the banks which are primarily concerned with making profits for their shareholders. Here again the argument requires careful qualification. In the sphere of banking, unlimited competition is not merely wasteful but dangerous; and an important advantage of the definition of the respective spheres of savings banks and creditbanks would be that it would prepare the way for general understandings between them.   But the public would in that case still have the assurance that the publicly owned banks would not be parties to a policy which was in any way extortionate; and now that the creditbanks are so well organized amongst themselves this assurance might be of value.

If there is to be any reversal of public banking developments perhaps the strongest case could be made out for depriving the Reichpost of its cheque and transfer system, and dividing this work between the creditbanks and the savings banks according to the size of the account.   In addition to relieving the present congestion of banking organizations, this would probably lead ultimately to greater efficiency both in the system of making payments and in banking generally.   At the moment, however, such a change seems hardly to lie within the field of practical politics.[1]

The delimitation of the scope of the various types of credit institution is one of the great mass of questions which are being considered at present by the Commission of Economic Enquiry.   (A special sub-committee is dealing with the credit system.)   Nothing is known yet, however, of the conclusions, if any, which have been reached.   Meantime, whilst no agreement has been attained with regard to the proper division of functions between public and private banks—on the contrary, the creditbanks have recently advanced the war into the enemy's country by opening special savings accounts   for   their   customers—the   representative

[1] None the less it has been more or less advocated quite recently by Diplom Kaufmann M. Schönwandt in the *Magazin der Wirtschaft*, iii. 31, Aug. 4, 1927, p. 1202.   The fact that the postal system has not recently been paying its way is a small but practical point in favour of the change suggested.   (See, however, Appendix II.)

organizations of the creditbanks and the communal savings banks have come to an understanding early in 1928 with regard to the *methods* of competition. The main points of this treaty are as follows:[1]

(1) Propaganda or advertisement in favour of one type of institution is not to involve depreciation of another type.

(2) The making or receiving of payments on behalf of customers is not to be used as a means of capturing customers from other institutions.

(3) Neither public authorities in granting contracts, nor savings banks in granting mortgage loans, are to press for the maintenance of accounts with public banks.

(4) Banks of one class are not to attract customers by suggesting that they are less scrupulous than those of a rival class in making returns to the tax authorities.

Instances, both local and central, are established for the settlement of disputes; and in addition to dealing with questions of interpretation under the above agreement, these may also prepare the way for agreements as to the actual terms charged to customers. The co-operative credit societies are also parties to this understanding. The present position is, then, that neither party to the dispute will abandon its claims without a fight, but that some agreement has been reached as to the weapons to be used in the struggle. Unfortunately the issue can hardly be decided by purely economic means; for the fact that the Sparkassen are subject to legal regulation and have always had certain privileges in respect of taxation, inevitably leads each side to bring its political influence into play. (It is significant that the number of *Bank-Archiv*—the official organ of the *Zentralverband des deutschen Bank- und Bankiergewerbes*—which announces the above

---

[1] See *Magazin der Wirtschaft,* iv. 21, May 24, 1928, p. 816. *Bank-Archiv* xxvii. 16, May 15, 1928.

agreement, also contains an attack on the tax privileges of the savings banks.)

From the point of view of the creditbanks, it is important that at least the main lines on which the division of functions is eventually to be effected should be determined as soon as possible; for on these depend their future requirements in organization, in respect of which no final adjustment can be made in the present state of uncertainty. One thing that seems clear is that the creditbanks are not destined to evolve into pure deposit banks on the English model; it is just their mixed character which ensures them a position that cannot be threatened by their competitors.

CHAPTER IX

CONCLUSION

IN their earlier years the creditbanks (or *Effektenbanken*, as they were then called), were commonly regarded with disfavour as stock-jobbing concerns of questionable character. This attitude is expressed in the writings of several of the leading German economists of the last century. Thus Knies,[1] in 1879, considered their business essentially unsound: ' Since the activity and interest of the crédit mobilier banks centres not in the conduct and maintenance of joint stock undertakings but in their promotion, hence in making as many promotions as possible, a force comes into play here which creates large scale undertakings in joint stock form with excessive fertility, but encounters increasing difficulty in the realization of their purpose and financial success.' Adolf Wagner, writing a little later, develops the criticism more fully. ' In the quest of easy profits from share appreciation, the banks have encouraged speculation at times when the money market is buoyant and finally allowed it to develop into over-speculation. They have been responsible for a crowd of more or less unsound promotions and the distribution of untrustworthy obligations. In other ways, also, they have favoured and taken part in the most questionable bourse speculation. They have endangered both their own property and that entrusted to them by others. Accordingly the verdict must go

---

[1] *Der Credit*, ii. pp. 396 *et seq.* quoted Sattler, *Effektenbanken*, p. 108.

against these transactions and the banks which perform them.'[1] It is true, as Sattler has pointed out, that in a later edition of the article from which the foregoing quotation is taken, a concession is made to the banks —' But, on the other hand, the crédit mobilier business is to a certain extent necessary to an economic system organized on the basis of private capital and particularly to the tendency in industry towards large scale undertakings. . . . That which is undesirable in their business also is a symptom of our whole capitalistic economic development, although, as is usually the case, there are mutual interactions.'[2] Nevertheless Wagner is still severely critical of the banks in his Introduction to Sattler's book. 'When one sees that the same stock exchange speculation, the same fever to promote new companies and convert private undertakings into companies, have shown themselves possible under the new Company Law as under that of 1870 in 71-73; when one sees the most barefaced swindlery again gaining ground, and observes the fatal part of the banks in this development; then one cannot deny that the expectations that the Company Amendment Act of 1884 would put a check to this activity have been disappointed. Those who, like the writer, represented this view at the time have therefore proved to be right. Should there come soon, as must be expected, another general reaction, should it be found then that a large number of capitalists of small and moderate means have suffered heavy losses through the depreciation of shares in their hands, such people themselves will not be absolved from blame. For they have simply indulged their greed of gain and " sought to earn without working." But at the same time just complaints will not be lacking against company promoters and

[1] Article in Schönberg's *Handbuch*, 2nd edition, 1885, i. p. 440, quoted Sattler, *op. cit.* p. 104.

[2] Schönberg's *Handbuch*, 3rd edition, 1890, i. 423.

their fellows, wildcat speculators, etc.   And as in the years following 1855 and 1871, the Effektenbanken will not be exonerated from part of the blame.   The fat dividends and fat directors' fees may in individual cases have been earned by these banks in sound and solid ways—for the most part their size is due to the exploitation of the " carelessness, inexperience, and lust for gain " of those taking part in bourse speculation.'[1]

In the present century, however, the creditbanks have been regarded more sympathetically.   Looking back, it has been possible to see that the successive periods of boom produced real and enduring expansion as well as a certain amount of waste;   and the banks have had to be given credit for the former as well as blame for the latter.   In fact it has been generally recognized that the part played by the banks was one of the most important factors in Germany's industrial advance: to quote the *Deutsch-Oekonomist*—' Anyone who observes impartially the development of the German banking system and the policy of the guiding minds must see that, without the vigorous and, in some ways, daring initiative of the banks, the present proud edifice of the German national economy could not have been erected in so relatively short a time.'[2]   On their part the banks themselves have modified their policy, influenced to some extent by the changed conditions in which they found themselves once German industry was well established.   Not least, the true nature of the business of the creditbanks has come to be much better understood, as a result of the publication of a number of careful studies, beginning with the works of Riesser and Adolf Weber.   The banks have still been subject, of course, to a good deal of criticism.   In the years before the War they were often accused of favouring

---

[1] Sattler, *op. cit.* vii-viii.

[2] *Die deutschen Banken im Jahre 1911*, p. 2.

the annihilation of small businesses in the interest of the great monopolies, and were criticized for the smallness of their cash reserves; since the War there have been complaints about the terms they impose on their customers, their neglect of the smaller concerns, and —in contrast to the earlier charges—their too conservative credit policy. But in its essential features the modern creditbank has been accepted by German opinion as a legitimate type of financial institution and even upheld as superior to the types of bank found in other countries.

The distinctive characteristic of joint stock banking in Germany is the integration of branches of finance which elsewhere are often separated. The combination of diverse functions in one and the same institution has in general both advantages and disadvantages in comparison with a system of specialization. On the one hand, the connexion between the institution and its customers is closer, new connexions have to be established less frequently, and knowledge gained in one branch of business can be used in another. On the other hand, disadvantages are to be found in the absence of the checks which one type of specialized institution can impose on another, and in the danger that interests in one type of transaction will predominate unduly, or influence improperly the conduct of other types of transaction. Here these points require to be considered more fully in their application to the union of short term banking with the provision of long term capital.

It has been shown how the current or short term business of the creditbanks has assisted them in carrying out promotion and issue transactions. In most cases they have been able to approach the latter with a full knowledge of the undertakings concerned, or of similar undertakings, based on continuous business relations. They have been at hand to advise their customers as to the prospects for placing an issue in the capital market, and when the outlook has been temporarily unfavourable they have been able to make advances in anticipation of the success of a later issue. Finally, their wide connexions amongst the investing public, for whom they act as brokers, have assisted them in placing securities. In all these respects they have enjoyed advantages which would have been lacking in the case of specialized issuing houses.

The first question for the critic is whether this system does not give the banks too much influence over the direction to be taken by investment. Could not they use their position as brokers to push unduly the securities in which they are interested as promoters or issuers? Again, could not syndicates of the banks, such as are usually formed for the larger transactions, manipulate the security market and even the money market to ensure the success of a particular issue, leaving the public to suffer by the inevitable reaction?

The existence of these possibilities can hardly be denied. It can probably be said with safety that in their modern period the great creditbanks have valued their own reputation too highly to attempt any deliberate deception of the investing public. They recognize their responsibilities for the securities which they have placed on the market and generally endeavour to maintain their value, if necessary by re-purchase. But without intention to deceive they may easily be over-sanguine as to the prospects of ventures in which they are interested and thus mislead their clients. It is here that the check of another independent set of intermediaries would be useful. On behalf of the German system it is to be said that since the turn of the century there has not been much complaint against the banks on this score, and further that the latter tend to keep less responsible financiers out of the field.

This is perhaps as much as can be said on the possibility of misdirecting investment as between one avenue and another. But it has also to be considered whether the German system may not tend to produce over-investment in general, in the sense of excessive permanent investment at the expense of liquid resources. The creditbanks very largely control the supply of funds for all purposes and may be tempted to favour capital developments unduly, for the sake of the profits on the issuing transactions and also in the desire to extend their future business. As pointed out in Chapter IV, the question raised here is bound up with the further question as to whether the German system tends to engender temporary trade booms and so accentuate industrial fluctuations. On this point the historical evidence is inconclusive. On the one hand the ups and downs in trade between 1870 and 1914 were rather more marked in Germany than in England or France; but on the other hand they were at least as marked in the United States, with an entirely different banking system. So far as they go, these facts suggest that the rate of industrial progress had more to do with the degree of fluctuation than the type of financial organization. Probably it would be true to say of the past that the German banks were largely responsible both for Germany's rapid advance in industry and for the amplitude of her trade movements, and that they could hardly have induced the one without the other. In the future the tasks to be accomplished may be different, and it is difficult to foresee the adaptations they may evoke in banking policy. The suggestion may be thrown out, however, that, if steady rather than rapid progress comes to be the general aim, the German system may prove to have certain advantages. Just because it integrates the various banking functions in the same institutions (and in a few of these) it may make it easier to maintain a proper balance between the various uses for the available resources.

There remains the question of how far the active participation of the creditbanks in industrial finance has prejudiced their own soundness and stability. Although discussed last, this question is by no means least in importance: for many English critics, who recognize the great services which the German banks have rendered in the development of the nation's industry, still hold their policy to be unsound, on the ground that it involves them in risks which ought not to be combined with the receipt of deposits from the general public. And the unfortunate experiences of certain other continental banks (certain Austrian banks, for example) give this view some support. How are these misgivings to be judged in the light of the foregoing study?

In this matter, fortunately, a definite answer seems possible. The policy of the German banks has certainly involved them in losses from time to time, but not on such a scale as to threaten their safety. Their history shows that it is possible for banks to play a considerable part in promoting industrial developments without locking up their own resources; and when the latter has been unavoidable, the risks have been mitigated, firstly by diversifying their interests, and secondly by maintaining secret reserves. In certain cases where the risks of immobilizing capital have appeared too great, the banks have abstained from their usual part in financing developments, and have helped to form special financial companies, either in collaboration with German industrialists, as in the case of the electrical industry before the War, or, more recently, in conjunction with foreign capitalists. In these cases, as also in the case of overseas banking developments, experience has shown the necessity for some departure from the strictest form of integration.

These exceptions are themselves of interest as examples of a compromise between the principles of specialisation and integration. The same kind of compromise might be resorted to more extensively, and appears indeed to be finding favour as a solution of the whole problem of the relations between long term and short term financing in certain other countries, e.g. France and Italy. This should remind us that the practical choice in this matter need not be one between complete union or complete specialisation; the device of the associated or subsidiary company provides an intermediate possibility. The further examination of this possibility does not come, however, within the scope of this work.

APPENDIX I

A NOTE ON FORMS OF COMPANY ORGANIZATION IN GERMANY

THE following are the leading forms of company or business association (*Handelsgesellschaft*) recognized in German law:

(1) *Offenes Handelsgesellschaft.*
(2) *Kommanditgesellschaft.*
(3) *Aktiengesellschaft.*
(4) *Kommanditgesellschaft auf Aktien.*
(5) *Gesellschaft mit beschränkter Haftung.* (G.m.b.H.)

Special kinds of company are also recognized for mining and colonial undertakings (*Gewerkschaften, Kolonialgesellschaften*); and in addition, there are various kinds of non-profit making associations, such as co-operative societies, which may have economic functions.

The first type in the above enumeration—the *Offenes Handelsgesellschaft*—is an ordinary partnership, with unlimited liability for all the partners. The third type—the *Aktiengesellschaft*—is an ordinary joint-stock company, corresponding broadly with the English public limited liability company. Certain of the more distinctive features of German company law relating to *Aktiengesellschaften* have been noticed in Chapter II. No further account of these two types of organization seems necessary here.

A *Kommanditgesellschaft* ((2) above) is a partnership in which, in addition to the partners with unlimited liability, there are other partners whose liability is limited to the payment of their capital share. The latter are excluded from participation in the management of the firm, so that there is a division into managing partners and limited partners. This type of association was peculiar to the Continent until the present century, but we now have something very similar in our limited partnerships.

The *Kommanditgesellschaft auf Aktien* (4) is a hybrid form which combines features of the *Kommanditgesellschaft* with features of the *Aktiengesellschaft*.   Instead of an executive (*Vorstand*) elected by the shareholders, a company of this type has managing partners with unlimited liability (*Geschäftsinhaber*). On the other hand it has a General Meeting (*Generalversammlung*) and a Board of Supervisors (*Aufsichtrat*), and is subject to the same obligations as an *Aktiengesellschaft* with respect to publicity.   In addition to being irremovable, the managing partners are in law altogether more independent of their shareholders than are the directors of an *Aktiengesellschaft*; for in principle the shareholders of a *Kommanditgesellschaft auf Aktien* are in the position of the limited partners of a *Kommanditgesellschaft*, although their precise powers depend upon the terms of Articles of Association.   Before the War the distinction between the *Aktiengesellschaft* and the *Kommanditgesellschaft auf Aktien* tended to lose importance, because the larger powers which the shareholders of the former enjoyed in theory were seldom exercised in practice.   During the inflation period, however, the independent position of the managing partners of the *Kommanditgesellschaft auf Aktien* came to be regarded as a safeguard against the encroachments of ' inflation kings,' such as Stinnes, and of foreign investors, who could buy up shares cheaply owing to the depreciation of the mark.

The *Gesellschaft mit beschränkter Haftung* (5) may best be described as a private limited company.   In a comparison with the *Aktiengesellschaft*, the main differences are: the G.m.b.H. may have a smaller capital and fewer promoters, the provisions both as to promotion and subsequent constitution are more elastic (it need not have either a General Meeting or a Board of Supervisors), it need not publish a balance sheet (unless it engages in banking),[1] and (as the price of this freedom) the transference of its shares must be transacted in the presence of a notary.   Peculiar features of the G.m.b.H. are : each shareholder is liable not only for the capital subscribed by himself, but also for deficiencies on the part of his fellow shareholders in paying up their capital subscriptions ; membership of the company may be based not exclusively on capital contributions, but also on the contribution of services; the articles may give the company the right to make calls on the members beyond the

---

[1] Certain private bankers have turned their firms into companies of this type, e.g. Hardy & Co.

amount of their subscription—if they are unable to meet these calls they have to sell their shares. The *G.m.b.H.* form of organization is unsuitable for any large undertaking which depends on public confidence; the adoption of this form would arouse the suspicion that publicity was feared. It is very popular for small family undertakings, however, and is apt to be preferred in these cases to the *Kommanditgesellschaft*, just as in England the private limited company is more popular than the limited partnership. Moreover, it is commonly used by banks and other financiers, when developing an undertaking experimentally, or to provide a link in a concatenation of companies.

APPENDIX II

NOTE ON GERMAN METHODS OF ECONOMIZING THE USE OF CASH IN PAYMENTS

(*Bargeldlose Zahlungsverkehr*)

BEFORE giving a brief account of the organization existing in Germany for effecting payments otherwise than by the transference of actual cash, a distinction in the methods by which this can be accomplished must be explained. In all cases the use of cash is avoided by substituting the transference of a claim to cash; and in the cheque system with which we are familiar this is done by the payer giving the payee a document (cheque) assigning to the latter part of the former's claim on a bank. The transaction is then completed when the document has been brought to the payer's bank and the transference of the claim duly made. The same result could be achieved, however, by the payer directly addressing an order to his bank to transfer part of his claim to the credit of the payee. This is the method of the German *Giro* systems.

Both the cheque and the transfer order (*Giro-überweisung*) are used in Germany, but opinion generally regards the latter with more favour, and it is systems employing the latter which have been most actively developed in recent years. The *Giro* method of payment has, indeed, a decided advantage over the use of the cheque in payments between different places, particularly places far apart. This is because it effects a saving in the time required to complete the payment: only a single postal journey between the two places is necessary, from payer's bank to that of the payee (we assume the banks or offices concerned stand in such relations that the payee can be credited with the sum coming to him as soon as instructions have been received from the payer's bank), whereas a cheque is sent from payer to payee, back from payee's bank to that of payer's bank, and then has to be acknowledged as in order in a third communication.

But the advantages are not all on the side of the *Giro* method.

Its use presupposes that the payer knows the name or other description of his payee's banking connexion; and it does not provide something equivalent to money which can be actually handed over to the payee, where personal contact exists, like the cheque. For these and other reasons the cheque is unlikely to be supplanted entirely.

The centre of all the German systems for saving the use of cash is the Reichsbank with its *Giro-verkehr*. This system was established by the Bank in its earliest years and has been largely responsible for the extension of the network of Reichsbank offices.

The basis of the system is the *Giro* account, which does not carry interest and which must be maintained at a certain minimum figure—fixed in each case on the basis of the turnover and the amount of credit business done with the Bank. The profit which the Bank derives from the use of these balances meets a considerable part of the cost of operating the system, and until 1921 transfers were made from one member's account to another's, free of charge; but a fee has since been levied for transfers from one Reichsbank office to another. To make a payment from one account to another the payer makes out a so-called 'red cheque' stating the amount and the name of the payee, and gives it to his Reichsbank office (a 'cheque' may be made out for the total of a number of payments, which will then be particularized on another sheet); the Reichsbank office then makes the transfer in its own books or, if necessary, instructs another office to credit the payee. The payee is only informed by the Reichsbank of the sums put to his credit when he is given a periodic statement of his account: therefore, it is usually necessary for the payer to send him directly a notification of the payment. To withdraw cash from a *Giro* account or to enable the payee to do so, a 'white cheque' is used: this is a true cheque. The Reichsbank *Giro* system can be used for payments between a person having a *Giro* account and another without an account and vice versa—even between two persons, neither having an account, but in such cases it is usually cheaper to use the Postal system (described below).

Each of the creditbanks also provides a 'giro-organization,' it being possible for a customer to make a payment to any other customer, whether in the same town or not, by ordering the bank to transfer the sum from the credit of one to the credit of the other.   The organization embraces in each case, in addition to all the offices of the bank, also the offices of its associated banks, i.e. the banks in the same group or *Konzern*.   But the making of a payment by ' giro-transfer ' from an account in one creditbank to an account in another (not associated) creditbank is more difficult and involves the mediation of the Reichsbank *Giro* system.   The procedure is :   a customer of (say) the Deutsche Bank in Cologne orders his bank to transfer a sum to a customer of the Discontogesellschaft in Munich: the Deutsche Bank, Cologne, then orders the Reichsbank to transfer this sum from its account at Cologne to that of the Discontogesellschaft at Munich on behalf of the payee.   This takes a good deal of time and trouble.   In local payments between the big banks in Berlin some time is saved by what is known as the *Eilavisverfahren* or ' express notification procedure.'   By this arrangement representatives of the banks meet daily to exchange notifications of transfers being made between one another through the Reichsbank, thus enabling the payee customers to be credited earlier than would otherwise be the case.

It is only in Hamburg, however, that a real clearing-house for transfer (*Giro*) orders has been developed.   The system used there is sufficiently interesting to be given a brief description. Seven banks (including the Reichsbank) participate in the scheme —also for some purposes the Post Office.   Each of the participant banks is assigned a colour, and the customers of each bank are provided with transfer forms in all the colours.   A customer of one bank wishing to make a payment to an account with another bank must write his order on a form of the *colour of this latter bank*, although he will address the order to his own bank. Each bank will receive then a number of orders to pay to other banks, which it can easily sort out by the colour of the forms. Finally the forms are exchanged by the banks in a room provided by the Reichsbank, and each bank settles with the Reichsbank for what it has to pay or receive on the balance—as in a cheque clearing.   This system is only applied, it should be said, to local payments.

The creditbanks also give their customers facilities for using cheques.   There are now clearing-houses, maintained by the Reichsbank, through which cheques can be exchanged between banks in fifty-four towns,[1] but apparently it is only in Berlin—where the *Scheckaustauschstelle* (established 1914) serves as a 'country clearing'—that there is a clearing for cheques drawn on other towns.   The cheques of the big banks, such as the Deutsche Bank, are said to be payable at a large number of places—wherever the bank has offices or correspondents—but they are only payable at offices other than that at which the drawer's account is kept after verification, and can only be put through the local clearing in the drawer's town.

In addition to the Reichsbank and the ordinary joint stock banks, the Post Office and the municipal banking system have developed important organizations for the effecting of payments by book transfers.

The Post has long provided a means of remittance in the form of postal orders, but its so-called *Postscheck* system, based on the holding of balances, to and from which payments are made, was introduced at the beginning of 1908.   In all essentials the system is a *Giro* system, although the holder of an account may have payments made to another person in cash.   All the offices of the Reichspost can be used for cash payments in connexion with the *Postscheck* accounts, but the accounts are kept at special offices (*Postscheckämter*), of which there are about twenty, spread about the country.   Orders for transfers have to be sent to the *Postscheckamt* at which the payer's account is kept, and are either finally dealt with there or passed on to another *Postscheckamt*, as circumstances require.   The concentration of the booking of transactions in these offices simplifies business, but may involve a certain delay in carrying them through.   The following points may also be noticed as distinguishing the Postal system from that of the Reichsbank: the minimum balance is very low and is the same for all accounts; accounts are numbered and the numbers only are used in booking transactions; ingenious forms have been devised, each divided by perforation into several parts on which the essentials of the transaction are repeated, one part being returned to the payer as a receipt and one forwarded to the payee, who need not, therefore, be otherwise notified; the fees charged (if any) are relatively low.   It is difficult to give particulars in the last respect, as terms have changed several times in recent years.   But it can be said that transfers between one account and another (i.e. without cash

---

[1] There is also a clearing house in Berlin (in addition to that of the Reichsbank) maintained by the *Bank des Berliner Kassenvereins*.

payment) are made gratuitously, even when the accounts are kept at different *Postscheckämter*, and that no charge is made for postal communications in connexion with the system.   Against the latter advantage must be set the fact that a charge is now made for the forms used.   Judged by its growth, the *Postscheck* system has been a great success; it is used extensively, not only by private persons but also by commercial firms—many of which keep both a *Postscheck* account and an ordinary bank account.

The development of the municipal (or communal) *Giro* system, which also dates from the years immediately preceding the War, has been referred to in the text.   Here the holding of the individual accounts is decentralized, being left to the local savings banks, but the latter keeps accounts with the federal organizations, the *Giro-Zentralen*, through which the interlocal transfers are made.   (In cases of urgency, transfers can be made directly between one savings bank and another, but settlement is effected subsequently through the *Giro Zentrale*.)   The system again provides very cheap services, and most of the savings banks pay interest on *Giro* balances.   (In this they resemble the ordinary banks but differ from the Post and the Reichsbank.)

Finally, the co-operative credit societies undertake to make payments for their members.   Some of the rural societies have their own central banking organization, others use the *Preussische Zentral-Genossenschaftskasse* in this capacity; the urban societies are served by the co-operative department of the Dresdner Bank. The co-operative societies are also commonly linked up with the postal *Giro* system.   From the nature of their membership, however, these societies cannot play a large part in the system of payments as a whole.

It will thus be seen that the organization now existing in Germany for economizing the use of cash is very elaborate. Indeed the criticism readily suggests itself that there are too many different systems in operation.   It is true that there are bridges between one system and another—usually by way of the Reichsbank or Post Office systems—but the route thus provided is often round about, involving costs in time and trouble. Further, whilst to some extent each system caters for a different class of customer, there is also a good deal of overlapping.   This seems to be particularly true of the Post Office system, which has developed largely at the expense of the ordinary banks, to some extent also at the expense of the municipal system.   It may be surmised, however, that this system has come to stay.   It is very popular, and has a big advantage in the free use of the ordinary postal services.

Given that a number of different systems are to exist—and for this purpose each creditbank and its connexions may be regarded as a separate system—the problem is to improve the facilities for making payments from one to another.   It is recognized that a greater measure of uniformity in the forms used would help in this matter.   But here the issue of cheque versus transfer (*Giro*) order must again be considered.   The simplest arrangement for effecting payments between different institutions is the clearing procedure, but it is difficult to apply this procedure unless the documents handled show at a glance the institution *to which they are to be presented.*   Cheque forms fulfil this condition, transfer forms as a rule do not.   It is true that this difficulty has been overcome in the case of the Hamburg *Giro* system, with its forms of different colours, all available to every bank customer.   But this method can only be resorted to when the number of institutions using the clearing (therefore of different forms to be distributed) is small.   This suggests that the preference given to the ' giro-order ' as against the cheque may be mistaken, and that it would have been better to have restricted it to inter-local payments of an urgent character.

	Cash.	Bills.	Balances with Cor-respondents.	Bourse Loans	Advances against Com-modities.	Own Securities.
Dec. 31st						Million
1912 -	124·7	646·9	72·7	240·2	232·3	113·4
1913 -	127·4	639·4	61·7	233·2	216·8	161·2
1914 -	283·4	674·6	73·7	254·4	101·1	172·9
1915 -	302·0	1,018·6	105·6	329·8	166·3	168·0
1916 -	299·8	1,661·2	198·4	522·8	207·8	165·2
1917 -	496·6	3,053·2	509·6	600·0	120·5	253·8
1918 -	468·4	4,616·9	282·7	624·1	56·0	242·4
1919 -	749·7	9,733·6	1,189·5	273·5	214·9	175·8
1920 -	1,183·4	16,025·8	1,185·1	217·4	535·7	154·9
1921 -	1,478·7	24,244·4	3,868·4	301·8	1,022·2	124·3
1922 -	33,321·6	155,840·3	179,097·4	1,242·7	25,246·7	435·7
						Billion
1923 -	36,314,786	11,506,349	128,805,264	—	20,304,032	2,579,434
Jan. 1st						M llion Reich-
1924 -	36·3	11·5	157·3	7·2	23·3	15·0
Dec. 31st						
1924 -	67·5	229·3	226·5	10·2	72·2	15·0
1925 -	83·5	344·0	203·4	15·3	109·1	15·0
1926 -	58·6	405·7	174·6	174·9	124·6	30·0
1927 -	87·5	431·7	237·1	132·9	177·9	32·0
1928 -	95·8	672·4	241·2	157·5	317·3	35·0
1929[1] -	193·0	1250·0	431·9	152·4	700·0	78·7

[1] Deutsche Bank und

III

OF BERLIN BANKS

1929

BANK

Syndicate Participations.	Bank Participations.	Advances.	Capital and Reserves.	Deposits and Current Account Balances.	Acceptances.
Marks					
49·4	78·6	670·3	311·6	1,573·5	327·3
53·5	82·5	638·5	312·5	1,580·0	300·7
54·9	58·4	972·0	428·5	2,042·1	162·6
49·6	63·8	910·7	428·5	2,541·6	122·8
41·2	61·5	878·9	430·0	3,503·4	69·6
28·4	40·7	1,162·9	500·0	5,669·3	65·5
23·9	39·7	1,006·7	505·0	6,740·2	71·4
23·8	53·6	2,120·2	505·0	13,822·0	138·1
38·4	76·7	3,286·0	778·1	21,580·0	154·1
59·6	159·8	8,679·6	850·0	38,617·4	218·5
538·8	491·8	121,593·2	3,050·0	607,143·3	1,403·5
Marks			C. 1·5 Md.		
756,445	1,096,789	147,855,625	R. 600 Bill.	349,287,795	550,007
marks					
10·0	25·0	183·3	200·0	349·3	0·5
10·0	23·3	389·2	200·0	864·3	5·8
15·0	22·7	682·3	205·0	1,239·6	73·6
15·0	22·3	798·2	220·3	1,509·0	93·2
35·0	26·0	1,114·7	225·0	1,977·3	90·2
38·0	25·8	1,290·0	227·5	2,453·9	104·8
73·6	35·0	2507·4	445·0	4728·6	213·2

Discontogesellschaft.

DISCONTO-

	Cash.	Bills.	Balances with Correspondents.	Bourse Loans.	Advances against Commodities	Own Securities.
Dec. 31st						Million
1912 -	44·9	232·4	52·1	110·4	118·7	37·2
1913 -	49·8	257·5	71·2	105·0	133·8	30·1
1914 -	52·7	361·6	89·8	109·0	9·1	39·0
1915 -	133·8	629·0	91·1	119·2	18·5	44·0
1916 -	171·5	831·4	113·1	131·3	14·2	60·1
1917 -	218·4	1,618·2	231·4	289·1	29·7	77·4
1918 -	205·0	1,975·1	407·1	299·3	18·0	96·4
1919 -	718·9	4,236·0	874·6	99·0	85·7	85·7
1920 -	1,098·8	6,229·6	1,177·1	95·7	120·8	88·3
1921 -	2,531·5	8,878·0	3,339·6	139·4	639·6	79·4
1922 -	12,679·1	41,254·3	122,619·3	141·1	6,108·2	258·0
						Billion
1923 -	10,551,161	7,495,617	58,322,486	—	6,807,490	10 Mill.
Jan. 1st						Million Reich-
1924 -	10·6	7·5	74·3	—	6·8	4·8
Dec. 31st						
1924 -	15·8	124·4	100·2	0·8	41·8	5·7
1925 -	31·5	187·4	106·6	6·8	78·2	3·7
1926 -	49·6	223·4	106·0	88·9	59·7	6·7
1927 -	63·8	321·8	155·8	69·1	131·6	9·6
1928 -	77·0	437·0	139·5	102·8	228·3	12·8

[1] Including

GESELLSCHAFT

Syndicate Participations.	Bank Participations.	Advances.	Capital and Reserves.	Deposits and Current Account Balances.	Acceptances.
Marks					
46·6	106·7	385·9	285·1[1]	604·5	238·8
60·7	114·7	391·3	281·3	674·0	250·9
60·8	221·7	427·9	419·0	805·7	152·7
52·1	218·4	477·3	419·0	1,262·8	100·8
44·5	216·7	533·5	420·0	1,644·6	44·8
45·5	214·2	665·3	444·0	2,870·2	68·4
48·0	221·7	886·9	444·0	3,649·3	68·3
39·3	214·4	2,425·8	440·0	8,191·4	127·8
77·5	220·4	3,576·8	500·0	12,015·6	96·6
134·0	234·8	7,089·5	759·4	22,050·7	215·1
683·4	347·2	101,542·8	3,607·9	278,736·6	787·9
Marks					
10 Mill.	170 Mill.	57,182,218	C. 0·9 Md. R. 31,350 Bill.	140,078,681	250,388
marks					
20·5	59·8	74·5	134·0	163·4	0·25
22·7	61·8	280·4	134·0	534·5	5·8
19·7	66·0	384·0	135·0	726·3	44·1
18·3	69·9	462·5	183·0	864·2	54·9
24·3	70·7	527·8	186·0	1,139·4	68·3
32·8	71·3	564·2	187·0	1,437·0	62·2

Taxation Reserve.

	Cash.	Bills.	Balances with Correspondents.	Bourse Loans.	Advances against Commodities.	Own Securities.
Dec. 31st						Million
1912 -	58·8	285·6	41·2	148·1	106·9	61·1
1913 -	68·6	375·9	61·4	119·1	116·6	42·6
1914 -	98·9	330·0	62·4	95·5	22·7	52·7
1915 -	139·9	353·1	65·9	149·5	7·9	65·0
1916 -	206·6	708·0	86·6	176·5	8·3	55·4
1917 -	302·1	1,200·1	230·1	211·8	16·2	81·2
1918 -	391·6	2,371·8	104·4	320·2	13·4	148·7
1919 -	560·1	4,390·9	778·8	538·7	381·7	122·0
1920 -	665·0	6,767·9	894·6	235·1	456·8	175·0
1921 -	833·8	8,479·6	2,733·7	480·5	1,558·1	124·0
1922 -	16,353·2	46,414·2	144,342·7	4,222·5	45,898·7	111·8
						Billion
1923 -	20,985,134	6,762,398	76,069,980	701,513	19,576,112	1
Jan. 1st						Million Reich-
1924 -	20·9	6·5	81·9	0·7	23·3	6·4
Dec. 31st						
1924 -	32·4	153·1	136·9	3·8	77·5	11·2
1925 -	42·4	252·8	152·9	34·2	138·8	13·8
1926 -	39·2	377·7	198·7	145·6	128·8	25·7
1927 -	46·1	411·0	226·8	86·1	211·1	25·5
1928 -	62·7	507·3	310·3	114·3	379·4	28·9
1929 -	60·3	562·9	299·8	57·3	397·4	40·5

[1] Includin

BANK

Syndicate Participations.	Bank Participations.	Advances.	Capital and Reserves.	Deposits and Current Account Balances.	Accept-ances.
Marks					
50·2	36·8	623·8	261·6 [1]	887·0	267·8
55·3	36·8	624·9	261·0	958·4	287·3
63·6	37·9	574·1	261·0	948·5	146·6
59·6	38·5	648·7	261·8	1,192·8	92·3
54·6	36·8	736·0	262·0	1,759·8	68·9
55·0	63·8	1,176·3	340·0	2,947·7	75·5
56·5	67·4	1,048·1	340·7	4,150·8	63·7
53·4	53·7	1,868·9	340·9	8,126·2	297·9
71·6	77·2	2,741·2	341·4	11,582·0	108·9
51·6	118·1	6,002·9	920·5	19,293·8	160·2
—	149·4	73,938·5	970·5	326,795·7	1,480·8
Marks					
1	1	77,597,423	47 Md.	193,793,996	131,205
marks					
14·8	23·2	83·0	100·0	189·4	0·13
12·8	22·4	312·5	100·0	684·8	0·4
11·1	23·3	460·8	101·4	1,003·7	47·7
11·0	26·1	581·8	128·8	1,352·7	72·2
13·6	27·8	803·9	130·4	1,640·1	99·1
11·3	31·2	868·7	132·0	2,112·5	86·4
22·2	35·1	1003·6	134·0	2275·8	88·7

Taxation Reserve.

DARMSTÄDTER BANK. From 1921

	Cash.	Bills.	Balances with Correspondents.	Bourse Loans.	Advances against Commodities.	Own Securities
Dec. 31st						Million
1912 -	46·6	120·9	56·8	124·7	9·0	47·2
1913 -	48·4	185·0	52·2	110·5	17·2	54·4
1914 -	63·5	174·4	53·2	97·0	18·5	59·7
1915 -	92·2	191·9	81·3	119·3	8·5	57·2
1916 -	103·5	210·6	132·6	258·8	22·7	50·6
1917 -	124·8	379·8	184·2	360·8	41·6	56·4
1918 -	209·1	847·9	132·7	372·1	21·2	83·5
1919 -	272.2	2,140·3	311·9	297·1	119·3	70·1
1920 -	436·3	2,996·8	422·8	162·4	247·9	73·9
1921 -	417·2	4,871·2	3,192·6	2,860·3	1,348·0	115·3
1922 -	21,320·2	51,202·1	114,366·7	4,201·7	5,121·0	—
						Billion
1923 -	20,333,304	5,691,129	77,577,236	4,861,131	16,995,699	1
Jan. 1st						Million Reich-
1924 -	20·3	5·7	77·6	4·9	17·0	23·6
Dec.31st						
1924 -	49·3	195·8	118·5	9·9	41·9	17·9
1925 -	53·6	246·9	114·1	19·3	66·7	19·2
1926 -	76·4	331·4	200·4	159·1	84·1	18·1
1927 -	65·2	427·7	217·6	109·6	130·7	23·2
1928 -	92·4	556·8	270·1	138·7	266·4	20·5
1929 -	79·6	605·3	257·7	161·0	377·6	38·0

NATIONALBANK

	Cash.	Bills.	Balances with Correspondents.	Bourse Loans.	Advances against Commodities.	Own Securities.
Dec. 31st						Million
1912 -	17·7	78·2	22·2	76·9	—	26·6
1913 -	14·6	88·1	14·9	49·7	—	29·3
1914 -	20·5	65·0	14·9	40·8	4·9	27·0
1915 -	19·2	71·0	13·6	44·5	2·9	17·9
1916 -	29·0	98·9	12·7	68·1	3·6	17·8
1917 -	53·8	158·3	15·6	120·0	4·0	19·0
1918 -	50·1	237·1	17·9	152·2	3·8	27·7
1919 -	55·3	262·2	175·7	176·8	16·3	27·0
1920 -	335·3	603·0	213·4	373·7	134·0	39·5

[1] Including

DARMSTÄDTER UND NATIONALBANK

Syndicate Participations.	Bank Participations.	Advances.	Capital and Reserves.	Deposits and Current Account Balances.	Acceptances.
Marks					
45·4	19·1	409·0	193·6[1]	547·6	140·5
44·6	8·0	439·4	192·0	607·7	166·3
40·6	9·4	455·2	192·0	592·2	198·9
40·5	9·5	420·0	192·0	750·5	89·4
37·8	8·5	388·6	192·0	969·8	60·7
32·7	9·1	489·4	192·0	1,435·9	51·8
32·4	10·3	532·8	192·0	2,000·0	47·9
31·7	8·6	1,081·1	192·0	3,980·5	115·9
35·7	30·3	2,003·4	267·0	5,943·4	127·0
82·2	102·3	7,240·7	980·0	19,642·5	351·5
—	—	56,366·3	1,053·5	246,119·6	1,355·9
Marks					
1	1	96,249,905	2·6 Md.	207,515,480	255,002
marks					
15·5	12·8	96·3	100·0	194·9	0·25
14·0	20·8	291·5	100·0	669·1	5·3
16·1	21·4	429·3	100·0	859·1	36·2
15·7	20·6	580·1	100·0	1,326·5	57·9
23·9	21·5	727·4	110·0	1,563·9	72·5
25·0	25·0	889·3	115·0	2,082·6	80·4
37·0	24·0	1016·8	120·0	2,383·6	90·2

FÜR DEUTSCHLAND

Syndicate Participations.	Bank Participations.	Advances.	Capital and Reserves.	Deposits and Current Account Balances.	Acceptances.
Marks					
38·8	6·3	184·6	106·3[1]	270·3	69·4
39·4	5·0	180·0	106·0	240·7	69·6
33·0	4·9	180·6	98·0	210·2	85·9
28·5	4·9	159·2	98·0	212·0	50·6
22·4	3·3	164·1	99·0	283·0	36·5
22·4	3·3	187·5	100·0	453·5	27·5
21·7	6·3	210·1	100·0	606·1	18·6
20·3	6·4	338·8	100·0	911·2	56·5
38·1	12·8	1,070·3	180·0	2,519·1	91·6

[1] Taxation Reserve.

COMMERZ- U. DISCONTOBANK

	Cash.	Bills.	Balances with Cor-respondents.	Bourse Loans.	Advances against Com-modities.	Own Securities.
Dec. 31st						Million
1912 -	21·7	52·8	15·6	84·6	26·1	33·9
1913 -	17·3	75·7	40·1	86·1	21·6	28·1
1914 -	22·4	57·0	31·6	66·1	14·9	34·5
1915 -	16·4	86·6	36·4	108·4	2·5	41·0
1916 -	18·5	269·0	51·8	126·5	4·2	27·2
1917 -	23·8	453·9	81·2	185·1	2·9	25·6
1918 -	26·7	742·3	63·6	160·4	2·7	74·3
1919 -	62·7	1,288·7	151·0	180·8	31·9	31·2
1920 -	222·4	2,405·8	393·9	386·9	201·4	77·9
1921 -	45·4	3,011·9	578·3	1,913·8	362·5	199·2
1922 -	8,438·3	42,013·0	10,314·5	6,074·5	1,864·4	809·4
						Billion-
1923 -	13,592,975	5,623,866	58,735,256	4,156,048	3,985,308	10
Jan. 1st						Million Reich
1924 -	13·6	5·6	58·7	4·2	4·0	11·0
Dec. 31st						
1924 -	19·0	133·8	36·6	14·3	27·1	10·8
1925 -	20·2	188·6	54·6	42·6	47·3	10·7
1926 -	22·4	194·4	82·4	128·9	57·9	13·8
1927 -	48·8	235·6	152·0	116·4	120·7	17·4
1928 -	41·8	308·9	164·4	128·4	205·4	22·0
1929 -	49·1	390·4	181·3	124·8	252·8	30·1

[1] Including

From 1920 COMMERZ- U. PRIVATBANK

Syndicate Participations.	Bank Participations.	Advances.	Capital and Reserves.	Deposits and Current Account Balances.	Accept-ances.
Marks					
16·4	10·9	194·2	98·8[1]	281·6	77·4
18·8	12·3	197·8	99·0	316·0	83·5
22·5	12·3	214·4	99·5	299·1	77·8
17·2	12·3	222·2	100·0	406·1	36·3
16·4	12·3	221·1	100·1	616·9	27·6
15·0	12·3	296·1	100·6	945·6	45·1
20·8	12·3	366·7	102·0	1,317·9	50·6
18·9	12·3	594·3	102·7	2,128·5	135·3
48·0	39·5	1,684·6	251·0	5,057·9	175·4
139·5	119·3	3,399·4	672·1	9,255·6	345·0
155·5	29·4	27,379·0	3,199·7	100,570·8	2,694·9
Marks					
10	10	70,414,913	C. 0·8 Md. R. 3,252 Mill.	153,190,784	479,004
marks					
7·5	3·5	70·4	63·0	144·4	0·5
7·7	4·0	170·0	63·0	378·0	3·0
6·4	4·0	294·0	64·0	600·4	25·2
6·7	3·8	365·7	64·0	789·1	41·1
12·4	6·4	531·6	94·1	1,107·7	55·3
15·9	9·1	675·4	95·6	1,357·8	69·8
20·2	10·9	783·7	115·5	1,585·6	80·5

Taxation Reserve.

MITTELDEUTSCHE

	Cash.	Bills.	Balances with Cor-respondents.	Bourse Loans.	Advances against Com-modities.	Own Securities.
Dec. 31st						Million
1912 -	7·8	28·0	4·6	17·8	3·7	12·3
1913 -	9·0	40·8	6·6	24·8	3·5	13·5
1914 -	24·6	47·8	11·5	16·4	4·2	14·3
1915 -	22·3	42·5	15·8	6·8	3·2	14·7
1916 -	19·3	76·9	39·6	43·2	1·2	14·8
1917 -	31·5	148·9	93·8	55·9	0·1	9·9
1918 -	53·8	338·6	64·2	53·8	0·4	19·1
1919 -	106·0	507·4	92·2	28·6	1·3	12·2
1920 -	167·4	846·1	179·8	20·5	0·5	14·3
1921 -	526·3	1,032·9	114·1	173·2	3·1	19·3
1922 -	4,160·5	8,354·0	14,683·4	606·1	—	27·4
						Billion
1923 -	4,080,216	364,376	8,941,815	288,712	30,841	1
						Million Reich-
Jan. 1st						
1924 -	4·1	0·4	8·9	0·3	0·03	1·0
Dec. 31st						
1924 -	10·7	18·9	10·3	2·8	0·3	1·2
1925 -	17·3	29·1	10·8	3·2	3·1	0·7
1926 -	15·3	22·9	24·2	20·5	2·0	2·5
1927 -	15·3	29·7	44·3	16·1	3·5	1·8

[1] Including

CREDITBANK

Syndicate Participations.	Bank Participations.	Advances.	Capital and Reserves.	Deposit and Current Account Balances.	Acceptances.
Marks					
10·4	2·2	128·4	69·1 [1]	99·4	50·4
11·3	2·5	137·6	69·2	130·8	54·0
7·7	1·9	169·6	69·2	160·7	73·1
8·0	2·9	197·7	69·2	208·1	41·4
6·9	2·9	153·1	69·3	269·5	22·4
6·4	1·8	181·0	69·3	448·9	16·1
10·3	1·8	194·9	69·3	662·1	9·5
11·9	1·9	348·8	69·3	1,019·1	27·5
18·2	1·9	414·6	103·8	1,515·5	37·3
12·0	7·6	886·7	279·5	2,413·8	71·5
40·9	14·7	4,721·8	300·0	31,265·3	659·1
Marks					
1	1	8,902,100	C. 1·1 Md. R. 13,268 Bill.	20,367,567	12,104
marks					
4·4	0·3	10·2	24·2	16·3	0·01
—	—	34·0	24·3	61·9	1·1
1·9	0·3	50·3	24·3	90·2	9·4
—	—	60·2	24·3	127·8	4·3
—	—	90·2	24·3	179·3	8·7

Taxation Reserve.

BERLINER HANDELS-

	Cash.	Bills.	Balances with Cor-respondents.	Bourse Loans.	Advances against Com-modities.	Own Securities.
Dec. 31st						Million
1912 -	26·5	105·5	10·6	77·4	—	41·9
1913 -	20·2	103·9	10·9	66·1	—	42·9
1914 -	11·1	98·5	12·8	62·0	—	46·7
1915 -	10·2	100·3	13·4	16·2	—	35·0
1916 -	15·1	105·2	24·8	7·1	—	50·3
1917 -	14·2	139·7	16·4	5·5	—	55·1
1918 -	18·8	152·1	23·5	3·8	—	98·5
1919 -	15·1	538·6	37·6	—	—	62·9
1920 -	188·0	1,347·8	161·4	4·4	—	103·6
1921 -	299·3	2,619·5	48·8	54·2	—	85·5
1922 -	5,410·0	8,923·6	3,083·0	576·5	—	176·4
						Billion
1923 -	1,134,957	1,589,320	18,440,331	—	—	—
Jan. 1st						Million Reich-
1924 -	1·1	2·6	19·8	—	—	4·1
Dec. 31st						
1924 -	6·5	35·2	41·3	—	—	2·7
1925 -	7·5	74·4	35·2	3·7	28·2	3·2
1926 -	8·0	71·3	51·0	65·1	32·5	11·3
1927 -	7·8	66·0	54·5	43·3	62·3	20·2
1928 -	11·4	63·9	59·8	40·4	95·2	18·0
1929 -	8·3	79·1	59·7	32·5	114·4	14·9

[1] Including

GESELLSCHAFT

Syndicate Participations.	Bank Participations.	Advances.	Capital and Reserves.	Deposits and Current Account Balances.	Accept-ances.
Marks					
51·9	11·1	238·0	145·5 [1]	318·7	97·4
52·4	10·0	233·5	144·5	296·8	96·8
53·8	10·0	212·7	144·5	263·0	118·5
52·6	9·9	264·2	144·5	282·1	78·4
43·1	9·1	295·4	144·5	348·8	54·9
32·8	8·7	361·4	144·5	439·1	47·3
32·7	8·7	423·8	144·5	569·7	42·8
43·4	8·6	458·3	144·5	961·6	59·2
43·2	16·7	787·4	144·5	2,354·5	127·7
60·1	27·3	1,713·7	160·0	4,294·1	402·8
106·7	60·5	10,188·2	200·0	27,598·8	56·0
Marks					
—	591	4,429,617	600 Mill.	24,561,503	—
marks					
9·4	—	15·5	27·0	31·7	—
9·4	—	57·4	27·0	131·3	—
9·9	—	75·3	27·0	210·9	4·1
6·3	—	125·0	27·0	349·4	5·2
—	—	136·3	27·0	343·1	13·1
—	5·5	158·8	43·0	399·4	15·1
8·8	5·5	172·5	43·0	436·6	19·5

Taxation Reserve.

APPENDIX IV

RESOURCES OF RETURNING CREDITBANKS ON
FEBRUARY 28th, 1930

	Capital.	Reserves.	Deposits.[1]
	Million Reichsmarks.		
Deutsche Bank und Disconto-Gesellschaft -	285·0	160·0	4,826·2
Dresdner Bank - - - - -	100·0	34·0	2,282·4
Darmstädter und Nationalbank - - -	60·0	60·0	2,369·1
Commerz- und Privat-Bank - - -	75·0	40·5	1,524·9
Reichs-Kredit-Gesellschaft - - -	40·0	20·0	619·4
Berliner Handels-Gesellschaft - - -	28·0	15·0	412·4
	588·0	329·5	12,034·5
Bayerische Hypotheken- u. Wechselbank -	45·0	20·2	271·2
Allgemeine Deutsche Credit-Anstalt - -	40·0	11·0	363·6
Barmer Bankverein - - - -	36·0	18·0	366·0
Bayerische Vereinsbank - - -	31·1	13·8	200·9
Vereinsbank, Hamburg - - -	15·0	5·0	85·8
Deutsche Effecten- und Wechselbank - -	15·0	4·0	68·0
Bank für auswärtigen Handel - -	11·0	1·5	103·4
Deutsche Unionbank - - - -	10·0	3·1	63·4
90 Creditbanks - - - - -	980·3	449·4	14,504·7

[1] Deposits and Current Account Balances (*Kreditoren*) including credits obtained on behalf of customers.

354

APPENDIX V

BIBLIOGRAPHY

(a) WORKS DEALING WITH THE CREDITBANKS IN GENERAL

SATTLER, HEINRICH, *Die Effektenbanken.* 1890.

MODEL, PAUL, AND LOEB, ERNST, *Die grossen Berliner Effektenbanken.* 1896.

RIESSER, J., *Die deutschen Grossbanken und ihre Konzentration.* Editions 1905, 1906, 1910, and 1912. Also translated in series of U.S. National Monetary Commission as *German Great Banks.*

RIESSER, J., *Von 1848 bis Heute.* 1912.

WEBER, ADOLF, *Depositenbanken und Spekulationsbanken.* Editions 1902, 1915, and 1922.

BOSENICK, ALFRED, *Neudeutsche gemischte Bankwirtschaft.* 1912.

SCHULZE-GAEVERNITZ, G. V., *Die deutsche Kreditbank.* (Grundriss der Sozialoekonomik.) 1915. Later edition 1922.

HUTH, W., *Die Entwicklung der deutschen und französischen Grossbanken.* 1918.

SCHACHT, H., *Einrichtung, Betrieb und volkswirtschaftliche Bedeutung der Grossbanken.* 1912.

PRION, W., *Die deutschen Kreditbanken im Kriege und nachher.* 1917.

NEISSER, FRITZ, *Das deutsche Bankgewerbe und seine Bedeutung für den Wiederaufbau der Wirtschaft.* 1924.

U.S. NATIONAL MONETARY COMMISSION PUBLICATIONS:
Miscellaneous Articles on German Banking.
Interviews on Banking and Currency Systems.
See also sub Riesser.

DEUTSCH-OEKONOMIST, Annual Reviews of Banking, 1883 to 1913, 1918, 1919, 1920 and 1924.

STATISTISCHES REICHSAMT, *Die deutschen Banken*, 1924-26 (includes pre-war statistics). (Einzelschriften zur Statistik des Deutschen Reichs, No. 3.) 1927.

WILLIS, H. PARKER, AND BECKHART, B. H., *Foreign Banking Systems.* 1929. Article by Paul Quittner, *The Banking System of Germany.*

(*b*) DEVELOPMENT OF BANKING ORGANIZATION IN GERMANY (CONCENTRATION)

WALLICH, P., *Die Konzentration im deutschen Bankwesen.* 1905. (Münchener Volkswirtschaftliche Studien.)

DEPITRE, E., *Le Mouvement de Concentration dans les Banques Allemandes.* 1905.

SCHUHMACHER, H., *Ursachen und Wirkungen der Konzentration im deutschen Bankwesen*, in *Weltwirtschaftliche Studien.* 1911.

STRAUSS, W., *Die Konzentrationsbewegung im deutschen Bankgewerbe.* 1928.

FENDLER, A., *Zur Kapitalkonzentration der Berliner Grossbanken von 1914-1923.* 1926.

(*c*) THE TECHNIQUE OF BANKING IN GERMANY

BUCHWALD, B., *Technik des Bankbetriebes.* 1910, 1912.

OBST, G., *Das Bankgeschäft.* 8th edition 1924, 9th edition 1929.

OBST, G., *Geld-, Bank- und Börsenwesen.* 1919.

LEITNER, F., *Bankbetrieb und Bankgeschäfte.* 6th edition 1923.

LOEHR, J., *Das deutsche Bankwesen.* 1921.

KALVERAM, W., *Bankbilanzen.* (Gloeckners Handelsbücherei, Bd. 71.) 1922.

KALVERAM, W., *Bankbuchhaltung.* (Gloeckners Handelsbücherei, Bd. 117-118.) 1926.

BROSIUS, H., *Lehrbuch der Bankbuchhaltung.* 6th edition, 1922.

SCHMIDT, F., *Die Effektenbörse und ihre Geschäfte.* (Gloeckners Handelsbücherei, Bd. 70.)

(*d*) THE CREDITBANKS IN RELATION TO INDUSTRY

JEIDELS, O., *Das Verhältnis der deutschen Grossbanken zur Industrie, mit besonderer Berücksichtung der Eisenindustrie.* 1905. (Schmollers Forschungen, XXIV, Heft II.)

LIEFMANN, R., *Beteiligungs- und Finanzierungsgesellschaften.*
Editions 1909, 1913, 1921, 1923.

WOLFF, S., *Das Gründungsgeschäft im deutschen Bankgewerbe.*
1915.

FOXWELL, H. S., *The Finance of Industry and Trade.* Economic
Journal, December, 1917; also reprinted in *Papers on
Current Finance.* 1919.

U.S. FEDERAL TRADE COMMISSION, *Report on Co-operation in
the American Export Trade.* 1916.

RIPLEY, *Trusts, Pools and Corporations.* 1916. Article by
E. Schuster, *Corporate Promotion and Finance in Germany.*

(*e*) FOREIGN TRADE FINANCE AND FOREIGN
BANKING ORGANIZATION

ROSENDORFF, *Die deutschen Banken in ueberseeischen Verkehr.*
(Schmollers Jahrbuch, N.F. Bd. 28.) 1904.

ROSENDORFF, *Zur neuesten Entwicklung des Auslandbankwesens.*
(Schmollers Jahrbuch, N.F. Bd. 30.) 1906.

HAUSER, R., *Die deutschen Ueberseebanken.* 1906.

DIOURITCH, *L'Expansion des Banques Allemandes à l'Étranger.*
1909.

WOLFE, A. J., *Foreign Credits.* U.S. Department of Commerce, Bureau of Foreign and Domestic Commerce.
Special Agents Series, No. 62. 1913.

HAUSER, HENRI, *Les Méthodes Allemandes d'Expansion
Économique.* 1916. Also translated as *Germany's Commercial Grip on the World.* 1917.

STRASSER, K., *Die deutschen Banken im Ausland.* 1924.

BENFEY, F., *Die neuere Entwicklung des deutschen Auslandsbankwesens, 1914-1925.* 1925.

LANGE, F., *Expansion und volkswirtschaftliche Bedeutung
deutscher Ueberseebanken.* 1926.

LENZ, F., *Wesen und Struktur des deutschen Kapitalexports vor
1914.* Weltwirtschaftliches Archiv, 18 Bd., Heft I,
1922.

(*f*) THE MONEY MARKET AND THE CONTROL OF
CREDIT AND CURRENCY

PRION, W., *Das Wechseldiskontgeschäft.* (Schmollers Forschungen, Heft 127.) 1907.

HEILIGENSTADT, K., *Die deutsche Geldmarkt.* (Schmollers Jahrbuch, Bd. 31.) 1907.

LANSBURGH, A., *Die Massnahmen der Reichsbank zur Erhöhung der Liquidität der deutschen Kreditwirtschaft.* 1914.

LANSBURGH, A., *Die deutschen Banken von 1907-8 bis 1912-13.* 1913.

FRANKFÜRTER ZEITUNG, *Englands finanzielle Vormacht.* 1915. Translated as *England's Financial Supremacy.* 1917.

U.S. NATIONAL MONETARY COMMISSION, *German Bank Inquiry.* (Stenographic report.)
The Reichsbank, 1876-1900.
The Renewal of the Reichsbank Charter.

ESSLEN, J., *Konjunktur und Geldmarkt, 1902-1908.* 1909.

NEUBURGER, F., *Die Kriegsbereitschaft des deutschen Geld- und Kapitalmarktes.* 1913.

RIST, C., *Les Finances de Guerre d'Allemagne.* 1921.

LANSBURGH, A., *Die Politik der Reichsbank und die Reichs-schatzanweisungen nach dem Kriege.* 1924.

HIRSCH, J., *Die deutsche Währungsfrage.* 1924.

D'ABERNON, VISCOUNT, *German Currency : its Collapse and Recovery, 1920-6.* Journal of Royal Statistical Society. 1927.

SCHACHT, H., *Die Stabilisierung der Mark.* 1927. Translated as *The Stabilisation of the Mark.* 1927.

SCHOENTHAL, J., *Deutsche Währungs- und Kreditpolitik seit Währungsbefestigung.* 1926.

DERNIS G., *La Renaissance du Crédit en Allemagne.* 1927.

DALBERG, R., *Deutsche Währungs und Kreditpolitik, 1923-1926.* 1926.

PRION, W., *Kreditpolitik.* 1926.

HAHN, L. A., *Aufgaben und Grenzen der Währungspolitik.* 1928.

AGENT-GENERAL FOR REPARATIONS PAYMENTS. Half-yearly Reports. 1924-28.

COMMISSIONER FOR THE REICHSBANK. Half-yearly Reports. 1924-1928.

REICHSBANK, *Annual Reports* (published in English);
also, *Die Reichsbank, 1876-1900.*
and, *Die Reichsbank, 1900-1925.*

ENQUÊTE-AUSSCHUSS (Ausschuss zur Untersuchung der Er-zeugungs- und Absatzbedingungen der deutschen Wirtschaft). *Die Reichsbank*. 1929. (Verhandlungen und Berichte des Unterausschusses für Geld-, Kredit-, und Finanzwesen.)

WHALE, P. BARRETT, *A Note on the Amendment of the German Bank Act*. Economica, No. 18. November, 1926.

(*g*) ORGANIZATION FOR ECONOMIZING THE USE OF CASH

SCHMIDT, F., *Der nationale Zahlungsverkehr*. 2nd edition 1920.

SCHIPPEL AND SCHOELE, *Die Organisation des bargeldlosen Zahlungsverkehrs in Deutschland*. 1921. (Gloeckners Handelsbücherei, Bd. 32.)

MUSS, M., *Der bankmässige Zahlungsausgleich in Deutschland*. 1922.

(*h*) COMMUNAL BANKING (SAVINGS BANKS)

WEGNER, C., *Entwicklung und Organisation der deutschen Sparkassen und des kommunalen Giroverkehrs*. 1925.

HOFFMANN, E., *Das Anlagegeschäft der preussischen Sparkassen in seiner neueren Entwicklung*. 1926.

HARTMANN, G., *Die Entwicklung und Organisation des kommunalen Bankwesens in Deutschland*. 1926.

NISSEN, F., *Die bankmässige Betätigung der Sparkassen*. 1926.

(*i*) MISCELLANEOUS

SCHULZE, A., *Die Bankkatastrophen in Sachsen im Jahre 1901*. 1903. (Zeitschrift fur die gesamte Staatswissenschaft, Ergänzungsheft IX.)

WIEWIOROWSKI, ST., *Einfluss der deutschen Bankenkonzentration auf Krisenerscheinungen*. 1912.

HELFFERICH, K., *Deutschlands Volkswohlstand, 1888-1913*. 1913.

PILSTER, R., *Die Kartellierung der Geschäfts-Bedingungen im deutschen Bankwesen*. 1922. (In private circulation only.)

KLEBBA, W., *Börse und Effektenhandel im Kriege*. 1920.

BRINCKMEYER, H., *Hugo Stinnes*. 1921.

UFERMANN AND HUEGLIN, *Stinnes und seine Konzerne*. 1924.

PINNER, F., *Deutsche Wirtschaftführer*. 1925.

STATISTISCHES REICHSAMT, *Konzerne, Interessengemeinschaften, und aehnliche Zusammenschlüsse im Deutschen Reich.* (Einzelschriften zur Statistik des Deutschen Reichs. No. 1.) 1927.

KUCZYNSKI, R., *American Loans to Germany.* 1927.

PRÖHL, H., *Die Deutsche Rentenbank-Kreditanstalt.* 1926.

LEWINSOHN, R., *Histoire de l'Inflation.* 1926.

SOMARY, F., *Bankpolitik.* 1915.

CLAPHAM, J. H., *Economic Development of France and Germany, 1815-1914.* 1921.

BROCKHAGE, *Zur Entwicklung des preuss-deutschen Kapitalexports.* (Schmollers Forschungen, Heft 148.)

METZLER, L., *Studien zur Geschichte des deutschen Effekten-Bankwesens.* 1911.

PRION, W., *Die Preisbildung an der Wertpapierbörse.* 1910. 1929.

(*j*) PERIODICALS

Die Bank. Monthly. (Edited by A. Lansburgh.)

Bank-Archiv. Twice monthly. (The official organ of the Zentralverband des deutschen Bank- und Bankiergewerbes.)

Frankfürter Zeitung Wirtschaftskurven. Quarterly. (Particularly useful for statistics and studies of industrial groups.)

Magazin der Wirtschaft.
Der Deutsche Volkswirt. ⎱Weeklies.
Hamburger Wirtschaftdienst.⎰

Salings Börsenpapiere is very useful for information about German companies; also *Das Addressbuch der Direktoren,* and Wengel's *Deutscher Wirtschaftsführer.*

INDEX